RIGHTLY DIVIDING
THE WORD

By

CLARENCE LARKIN

Author of the Great Book on

"DISPENSATIONAL TRUTH"

And Other Biblical Works

A Digireads.com Book
Digireads.com Publishing
16212 Riggs Rd
Stilwell, KS, 66085

Rightly Dividing the Word
By Clarence Larkin
ISBN: 1-4209-2879-1

Please visit *www.digireads.com*

THE LIGHT OF PROPHECY

THIS BOOK IS

DEDICATED

TO THE

"DIVINE INTERPRETER"

THE HOLY SPIRIT

WHO THROUGH THE YEARS HAS BEEN
MY TEACHER AND HELPER

IN

"RIGHTLY DIVIDING THE WORD"

FOREWORD

The Author started to prepare an "A B C" book to introduce his larger Work on

"DISPENSATIONAL TRUTH,"

but after writing and condensing several times he felt led to abandon that idea and to prepare a book on "Rightly Dividing the Word," in which the "Fundamental Doctrines" should be "Rightly Divided" in a series of contrasts. The "Fundamental Doctrines" of the Christian Faith are clearly outlined in numerous books on Theology, but they are not available to the average reader and were mainly written for students. The Author has made it the work of his ministry to preach the "Fundamental Doctrines." To this end he has aimed to express them in the simplest and clearest manner possible. This book contains the cream and meat of his sermons for over thirty-five years, condensed and arranged in a form that will grip and interest the reader, because of the manner of their presentation. The Charts are clear and simple and add much to the value of the book, and will be suggestive to Preachers and Bible Teachers in presenting the "Fundamentals."

The book does not contain the opinions of the Author, nor quotations from other writers, but is based solely on the Scriptures, chapter and verse being given for every statement. The book is "Timely" in these days of Apostasy and denial of THE FAITH. The purpose of the book is to confirm in the Faith those who are wavering, and to instruct those who have not been clearly taught the great cardinal Doctrines of the Christian Faith.

THE AUTHOR.

"SUNNYSIDE,"

December, 1920.

TABLE OF CONTENTS

CHAPTERS

CHARTS

CONTENTS

I

Rightly Dividing the Word

"Study to show thyself approved unto God, a workman that needeth not to be ashamed, **RIGHTLY DIVIDING THE WORD OF TRUTH.**" 2 Tim. 2:15.

The Holy Scriptures are not a systematic treatise on Theology, History, Science or any other topic. They are a **REVELATION** from God of His Plan and Purpose in the Ages as to the earth and the human race. They were given to us piecemeal "at sundry times and in divers manners." Heb. 1:1. Holy men of God spake as they were moved by the Holy Spirit during a period of 1600 years, extending from B. C. 1492 to A. D. 100. The Bible consists of 66 separate books; 39 in the Old Testament, and 27 in the New. These books were written by about 40 different authors. By kings, such as David and Solomon; statesmen, as Daniel and Nehemiah; priests, as Ezra; men learned in the wisdom of Egypt as Moses; men learned in Jewish law, as Paul. By a herdsman, Amos; a tax-gatherer, Matthew; fishermen, as Peter, James and John, who were "unlearned and ignorant" men; a physician, Luke; and such mighty "seers" as Isaiah, Ezekiel and Zechariah.

It is not an Asiatic book though it was written in that part of the world. Its pages were penned in the Wilderness of Sinai, the cliffs of Arabia, the hills and towns of Palestine, the courts of the Temple, the schools of the prophets at Bethel and Jericho, in the palace of Shushan in Persia, on the banks of the river Chebar in Babylonia, in the dungeons of Rome, and on the lonely Isle of Patmos in the Aegean Sea.

While the Bible has been compiled in the manner described, it is not a "heterogeneous jumble" of ancient history, myths, legends, religious speculations and apocalyptic literature. There is a progress of revelation and doctrine in it. The Judges knew more than the Patriarchs, the Prophets than the Judges, the Apostles than

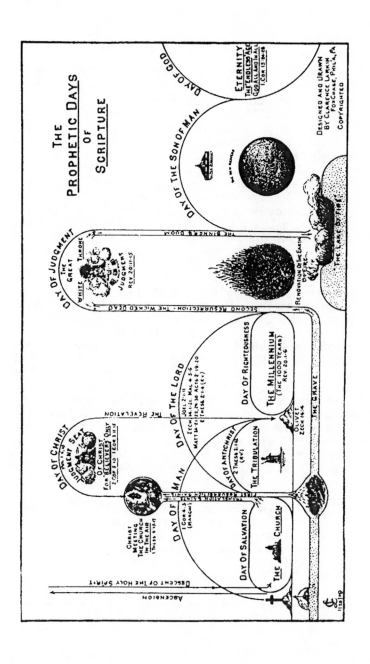

THE
PROPHETIC DAYS
OF
SCRIPTURE

Designed and Drawn
by Clarence Larkin
Fox Chase, Phila., Pa.
Copyrighted

the Prophets. The Old and New Testaments cannot be separated. You cannot understand Leviticus without Hebrews, or Daniel without Revelation.

While the Bible is a "Revelation from GOD" it is not written in a superhuman or celestial language. If it were we could not understand it. Its supernatural origin is seen in the fact that it can be translated into any language. The language of the Scriptures is of three kinds. Figurative, Symbolical and Literal. The Figurative is explained by the context, the Symbolical either in the context or somewhere else in the Scriptures, and the rest should be taken literally. That is, we are to read the Bible as we would read any other book, letting it say what it wants to say, without allegorizing or spiritualizing its meaning.

While the Bible was written FOR all classes of people, and FOR our learning, it is not addressed to all people in general. Part of it is addressed to the JEWS, part to the GENTILES, and part to the CHURCH. These three constitute the "Three Classes" into which humanity is divided. 1 Cor. 10:32. It follows therefore that while the whole Bible was written for the instruction of the Church, it is not all written about the Church. The Church is not mentioned in the Old Testament. The Old Testament is mostly taken up with the history of one nation, that of Israel. When we take the Old Testament promises and apply them to the Church we rob the Jew of that which is exclusively his. For illustration, the prophecy of Isaiah in the chapter headings is largely applied to the Church, whereas the very first verse declares that it is—"concerning JUDAH and JERUSALEM." Isa. 1:1. In the New Testament the Epistles of Hebrews and James are Jewish. The Epistle of James is addressed, not to the Church, but to the "TWELVE TRIBES scattered abroad." James 1:1. In the Epistle to the Hebrews many Christians stumble at the words "fall away" (Heb. 6:4-6), and "if we sin wilfully," Heb. 10:26. But these words do not apply to Christians. They were spoken to apostate Jewish professors of Christianity who had never been born again, and who, if they did not accept Jesus as their Messiah, practically cruci-

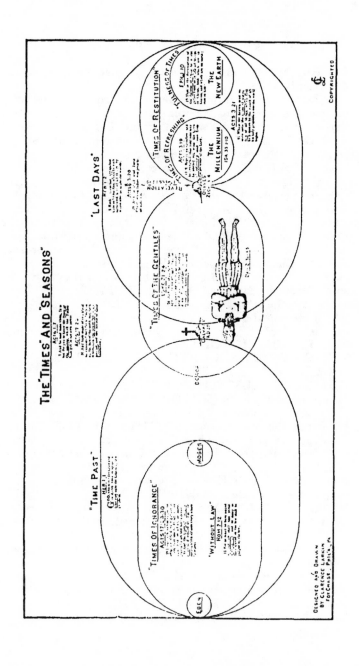

fied Him again, and were as bad as their brethren who did crucify Him.

ALL Scripture is profitable for doctrine, for reproof, for correction, for instruction, (2 Tim. 3:16), and what happened to Israel was written for our ENSAMPLE and ADMONITION, (1 Cor. 10:11), but we must not apply to the Church what does not belong to it. To do so is to misapply Scripture and lead to confusion.

In "Rightly Dividing" the Word we must also distinguish between the work or offices of Christ as Prophet, Priest and King. A careful study of the Chart, "The Threefold Work of Christ," page 250, will show that these offices are not held at the same time. We must also distinguish between the "Prophetic Days" of Scripture. See the Chart on "The Prophetic Days of Scripture," page 2. We must also distinguish between the "Times" and "Seasons." Between the "TIMES PAST" when He spoke by the Prophets, and these "LAST DAYS" in which He has spoken to us by His Son. Heb. 1:1-2. As to the "TIMES" we have them designated as the "TIMES OF IGNORANCE," (Acts 17:30); the "TIMES OF THE GENTILES," (Luke 21:24); the "TIMES OF REFRESHING," (Acts 3:19); the "TIMES OF RESTITUTION," (Acts 3:21); and the "Dispensation of the FULNESS OF TIMES." Eph. 1:10. See the Chart of "The Times and Seasons," page 4. From the statement the "TIMES OF THE GENTILES," we see that when the "Gentiles" are in power the "Jews" are not. And as the "Times of the Gentiles" is still running, the Church cannot be in this Dispensation a governing or Kingdom power. We must also not forget the "DIVINE CONJUNCTIONS" and the "DIVINE DISJUNCTIONS" of the Word of God. We must not separate what God has joined, as the "Word of God" and the "Spirit of God," nor join what He has separated as Baptism and Regeneration, Law and Grace, the Church and the Kingdom.

But it is not enough to classify the Scriptures in the manner already mentioned, we must learn to separate the Scriptures as to "TIME" and "ETERNITY," and the different "AGES" and "DISPENSATIONS" of "Time."

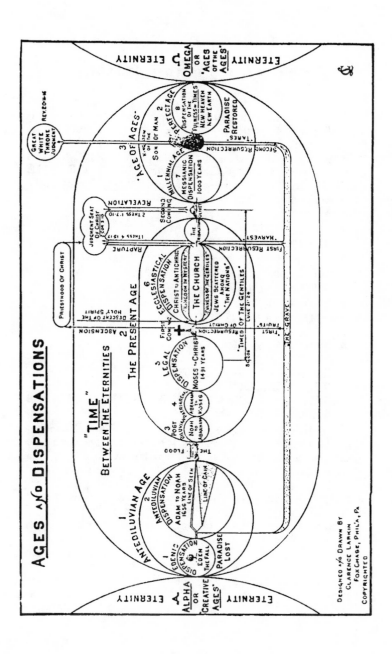

AGES AND DISPENSATIONS

"TIME" BETWEEN THE ETERNITIES

Designed and Drawn By
Clarence Larkin
Fox Chase, Phila., Pa.
Copyrighted

II

Ages and Dispensations

Reference to the Chart, "The Ages and Dispensations," page 6, will reveal the fact that outside of "Time" the Scriptures mention "Two Ages." Before "Time" the "ALPHA" or "CREATIVE AGES," and after "Time" the "OMEGA," or "AGES OF THE AGES." In "Time" there are three "Ages" and eight "Dispensations." The "Ages" are—

1. THE ANTE-DILUVIAN AGE.
2. THE PRESENT AGE.
3. THE AGE OF AGES.

The "Third Age" is a "Dual Age," composed of the "Millennial Age" and the "Perfect Age."

The "Dispensations" are—

1. THE EDENIC.
2. THE ANTE-DILUVIAN.
3. THE POST-DILUVIAN.
4. THE PATRIARCHAL.
5. THE LEGAL.
6. THE ECCLESIASTICAL.
7. THE MESSIANIC.
8. THE DISPENSATION OF THE "FULNESS OF TIMES."

The difference between an "Age" and a "Dispensation" is, that an "Age" stands for a period between two great physical changes in the earth's surface, while a "Dispensation" stands for a "moral" or "probationary" period in the world's history. For illustration, the "Present Age" began with "The Flood," and ends with the return of Christ to the Mount of Olives. "The Flood" caused such physical and climatic changes that the length of human life was reduced from 900 to 100 years; all this will be reversed when Christ comes back, when the whole contour of the Land of Palestine will be changed (Zech. 14:4-10. Ez. 47:1-12), and men shall live again for upwards of 1000 years. Isa. 65:20. While the Dispensations are probationary periods, the form of "Administra-

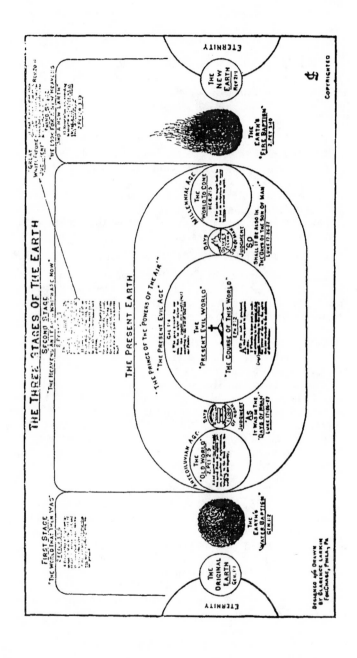

THE THREE STAGES OF THE EARTH

Designed and Drawn
By Clarence Larkin
Fox Chase, Phila., Pa.

COPYRIGHTED

tion" is different and progressive in each "Dispensation." For illustration, the Administration of the "Legal Dispensation" was that of **"LAW,"** of the "Present Dispensation" is **"GRACE,"** and of the one to follow is **"RIGHTEOUSNESS."**

I. THE CREATIVE AGES

The Scriptures begin with the sublime declaration—"In the beginning God **'CREATED'** the heaven and the earth." Gen. 1:1.

As the word "heaven" is in the singular it will clarify matters to limit this creative act to our own planet, and the solar system to which it belongs, rather than to the whole of the starry spaces or universe.

1. THE ORIGINAL OR PRE-ADAMITE EARTH

This creation was in the dateless past. The six days' work as described in Gen. 1:3-31 was the **restoration of the earth** to its original condition before it was made "formless and void" and submerged in water and darkness.

Peter speaks of it as the "World that **then was,** that being **overflowed with water,** perished." 2 Pet. 3:5-7. See Chart, "The Three Stages of the Earth," page 8.

The manner of the creation of the "Pre-Adamite Earth" is not revealed in the Scriptures. They simply declare that—"In the **beginning** God **CREATED** the heaven and the earth." And in that statement we have all the Millenniums of time that science may require for the formation of the earth as a planet. See the Chart on "The Prophetic Earth," page 10.

2. THE CHAOTIC EARTH

The "Original Earth" was doubtless a most beautiful earth, covered with vegetation and inhabited with fish, fowl and animal life, and probably with human life. How long it continued in this condition we are not told, but an awful catastrophe befell it, it became **"FORMLESS AND VOID,"** and submerged in water and darkness. Gen. 1:2. That it was not originally so we know from Isa. 45:18 (R. V.). "Thus saith the Lord that created the heavens; he is God; that formed the earth and made it;

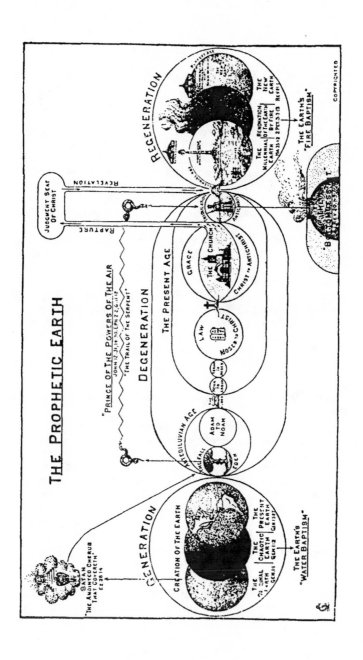

He established it. He created it **NOT A WASTE, He** formed it **to be inhabited.**" What caused the earth to become a "Waste" after its original creation is not clearly revealed. It is clear from the account of the Fall of Adam and Eve that sin existed before man was created. The inference is that Satan and his angels were in charge of the Pre-Adamite Earth, that they rebelled, and by rebellion brought destruction on the Pre-Adamite Earth and its inhabitants, and for their sin were excluded from Heaven, and now occupy the "Heavenlies," and that they are the "Principalities and Powers" over which Satan rules and of whom we are warned in Eph. 6:12.

The manner in which the Pre-Adamite Earth was made "formless and void," and this refers only to the exterior surface, the habitableness of the earth, is clearly revealed by Peter, where he says—

"For this they willingly are ignorant of, that by the word of God the heavens were of old, and the earth standing out of the water and in the water; whereby the world that then was, BE-ING OVERFLOWED WITH WATER, perished." 2 Pet. 3:5-6.

It is clear that Peter does not refer here to Noah's Flood, for the world of Noah's day did not perish, and Peter goes on to add that—

"The heavens and the earth which are now (that is, have been in existence since the restoration of the earth of Gen. 1:3-31), by the same word are kept in store, reserved unto fire against the day of judgment and perdition of ungodly men" (Great White Throne Judgment, Rev. 20:11-15.) 2 Pet. 3:7.

The manner then in which the Pre-Adamite Earth was made "formless and void" was by **WATER.** Violent convulsions must have wrecked the Pre-Adamite Earth and covered its surface with the waters of its oceans. Not a living creature remained alive upon it, and its atmosphere of murky darkness hid the light of the sun, moon and stars. To all intents and purposes it was a dead planet, though the seeds of its vegetable life remained entombed in its bosom ready to spring into resurrection life. The absence of the warm rays of the sun caused the earth to pass through the "Winter" of its life, and the submerging waters were congealed into ice that preserved in "COLD STORAGE" the remains of immense quadrupeds and winged creatures, that we might know the kind of animal life that inhabited the Pre-Adamite Earth. This was probably the Glacial Period of Geologic Times. The Prophet Jeremiah records a vision of the time:

> "I beheld the earth, and, lo, it was WITHOUT FORM AND VOID; and the heavens, and they had NO LIGHT. I beheld the mountains, and, lo, they TREMBLED, and all the hills MOVED LIGHTLY. I beheld, and, lo, there was NO MAN, and all the BIRDS OF THE HEAVENS WERE FLED. I beheld, and, lo, the fruitful place was a WILDERNESS, and all the CITIES thereof were broken down at the presence of the Lord, and by His fierce anger." Jer. 4:23-26.

If this was, as it appears, an account of the destruction of the Pre-Adamite Earth, then the Pre-Adamite Earth was inhabited, and its inhabitants dwelt in cities, and God's purpose in destroying the Pre-Adamite Earth was to efface all historic monuments and evidences of the sinfulness of its occupants.

How long a period elapsed between the creation of the earth and its becoming "formless and void" we do not know; neither do we know how long it continued in that condition, but when the time came in the purpose of God to restore the earth to its habitable state, and make it fit for the abode of man, He did it in six periods of longer or shorter duration. The Hebrew word translated "day" may mean either a day of 24 hours or a longer period of time. The probability is that the time was short.

3. THE PRESENT EARTH

The six days' work as described in Gen. 1:3-31 is not a description of how God made the "Original Earth," but how He restored it from its "formless and void" condi-

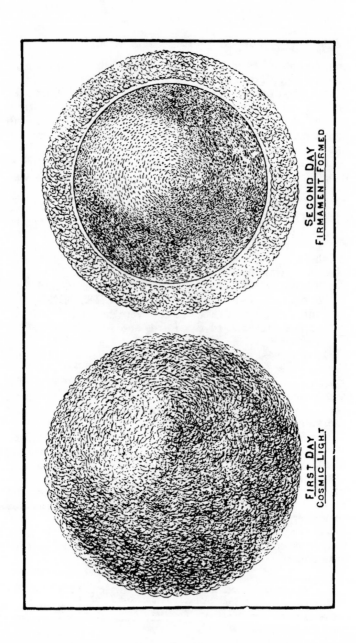

FIRST DAY
COSMIC LIGHT

SECOND DAY
FIRMAMENT FORMED

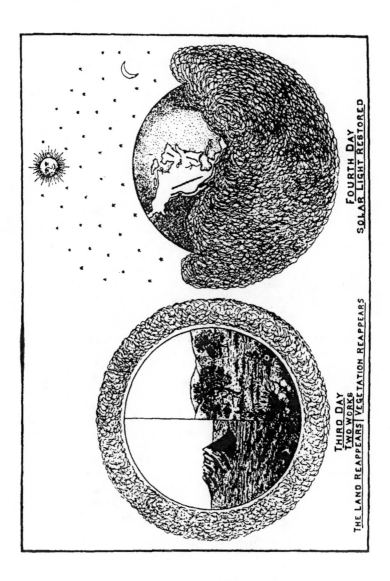

THIRD DAY
TWO WORKS
THE LAND REAPPEARS | VEGETATION REAPPEARS

FOURTH DAY
SOLAR LIGHT RESTORED

tion to its present state. He began by reversing the process He took to make it uninhabitable. He said "Let there be Light," Gen. 1:2-5. The light was not sunlight, that did not appear until the "Fourth Day." It was doubtless "Electric Light," the incandescence of which dispelled the gloom and generated enough heat to melt the icy covering of the earth and form water. Thus the earth passed out of the "Night" of its history into the morning of its "Resurrection Day."

The "Second Day's" work was the Readjustment of the "Atmosphere" to the needs of the present earth. Gen. 1:6-8. It is worthy of note that God does not say of this Day's work that it was **GOOD**, as He did of the work of the other days. This may not be without significance, for we read in Eph. 2:2 of the "Powers of the **AIR**" over whom Satan is the Prince, and it may have been that as soon as the atmosphere of the earth again became habitable the "Powers of Evil" swarmed into it. Eph. 6:12.

The work of the "Third Day" was twofold, the emergence of the land from the sea, and the reappearance of vegetable life. Gen. 1:9-13. This was not a new creation, but a **RESURRECTION**. The earth rises up from its "Watery Grave," and seeds, and the roots of plants and herbs and trees that were in the earth sprang into life as they do in the spring of the year after the winter is over. This reveals the fact that the Pre-Adamite Earth was clothed with verdure, and covered with plants and trees like those of the Present Earth.

The work of the "Fourth Day" was the re-appearance of the Sun, Moon, and Stars. Gen. 1:14-19. They were not created on the "Fourth Day." They had shone on the Pre-Adamite Earth, but the cloudy atmosphere of the restored earth hid them from view until the "Fourth Day," when the clouds broke away and permitted them to shine on the earth, and from that time they were appointed to mark the days, months, and years, of the Present Earth.

The work of the "Fifth Day" was the **CREATION** of fish and fowl. Gen. 1:20-23. Here is the first time we come across the word **"CREATE"** since we read of the

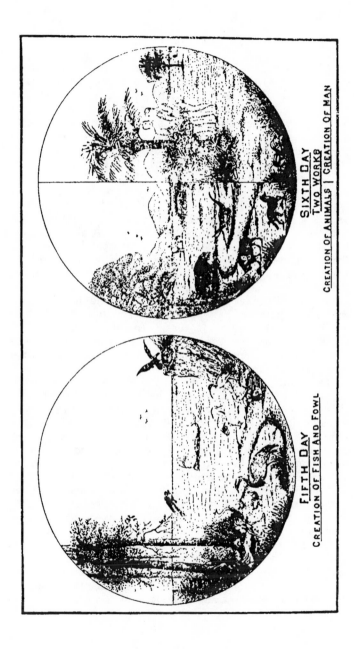

FIFTH DAY

CREATION OF FISH AND FOWL

SIXTH DAY

TWO WORKS

CREATION OF ANIMALS | CREATION OF MAN

original creation of the earth in verse one. This shows that all animal life was destroyed in the catastrophe that overtook the Pre-Adamite Earth. The fish and fowl that were created on the "Fifth Day" were the same that we have today. The fossil remains of huge marine animals and gigantic birds belong to the Pre-Adamite Earth.

The creative work of the "Sixth Day" was twofold, that of land animals and of man. Gen. 1: 24-28.

These land animals were doubtless the same kind as we have today. The fact that they were created,

"AFTER THEIR KIND,"

which is 5 times repeated, shows that they were not **"evolved" from one common species.** That all the different species of animals were created **"separately"** is proven from the fact that when species are crossed their offspring are sterile. The crossing of the jackass and a mare is the mule, and a mule is a hybrid and is sterile. If the "Evolutionary Theory" of the development of animal and vegetable life was true, we should expect to find evidence to that effect in fossil remains of the intermediate links, and we should also see "evolutionary processes" at work now whereby higher orders of animal and plant life are coming into being. But we see nothing of the kind. Animal and plant life exists today in the same form that it has existed in the knowledge of man. The birds build their nests and raise their young as they always did. The beaver builds his dam, and the bee constructs his honeycomb as they have always done. Man alone has the faculty of improving his mode of construction. This is seen in the development of farming instruments from the crude plow and winnowing fan to the complex plow and cultivator, and the combined reaper, binder, and thresher. But here we can trace the various steps by the obsolete specimens of farming implements. This is not true in the animal and vegetable kingdoms for there we find no intermediary links. If the Evolutionary Theory is correct, it should apply to man as well as animals, and we should see by the crossing of the best specimens of the human race the evolution of a **SUPERMAN**, but the history of the race disproves this.

That man was **CREATED** (Bara) **A MAN** shows that he has not descended from an "ape." Man was made in the "**IMAGE OF GOD**," not in the image of an ape, and was not formed from a brute but of the "Dust of the Earth." While Adam and Eve were not both fashioned in the same way, Eve being "builded" from a rib taken out of Adam (Gen. 2:21-23), they were not evolved from some lower creature, but were both direct creations of God, "**male** and **female CREATED** He them." Gen. 1:27.

On the "Seventh Day" of the "Restoration Week" God rested. Gen. 2:2-3. He rested because His work was finished. That is the only justifiable reason for resting. He rested because His work was not only finished but was **GOOD**. There could be no reflection on it. But when God's perfect work was marred by sin, by the "Fall of Man," His "Sabbath Rest" was broken, and He had to resume work for the purpose of the redemption of man that he might become a "**NEW CREATION**" in Christ Jesus. 2 Cor. 5:17.

II. THE ANTE-DILUVIAN AGE

This extends from the restoration of the earth from its "chaotic" condition to the Flood. It is divided into two "Dispensations."

1. The Edenic Dispensation

This Dispensation extends from the creation of Adam to the Expulsion from the Garden. As to its duration we know nothing. It was probably very short, and was the "Dispensation of **INNOCENCE**." For an account of "The Fall" see the chapter on "The Two Adams."

2. The Ante-Diluvian Dispensation

This extends from the "**Fall**" to the "**Flood**." It was the "Dispensation of **CONSCIENCE**," and shows what man will do when guided only by his conscience. Adam and Eve had no conscience before the "Fall." Conscience is a knowledge of "Good" and "Evil," and this Adam and Eve did not have until they had their eyes opened by eating of the "**Fruit**" of the "Tree of the Knowledge of Good and Evil." Gen. 2:17. Conscience may produce fear and remorse, but it will not keep men from doing wrong, for conscience imparts no **"POWER."**

Adam and Eve had no children before the "Fall." That they were created for that purpose is clear from the words God spake to them after their creation, when He said—"Be fruitful and multiply and **REPLENISH THE EARTH."** Gen. 1:28. In the words "Replenish the Earth" we have unmistakable evidence that the earth had been peopled before it was thrown into a chaotic condition.

How soon after the "Expulsion" from the Garden the first child was born to Adam and Eve we are not told. It probably was not very long. The first child was a son, Cain. It does not follow that Abel was the second child. There may have been a number of children, both sons and daughters, born between Cain and Abel. Cain and Abel are **"Representative Men,"** one of the wicked line, and the other of the righteous line from Adam. There is an intimation in the curse imposed on Eve— "I will greatly multiply thy conception" (Gen. 3:16), that births were not only frequent, but that several children were born at a time. In no other way could the human race multiply as it did in those early days, and for some time after the Flood. Intermarriages among the children of the same family were not forbidden until after the Flood.

Cain and Abel were not children when Cain killed Abel. They were probably over 100 years of age. Abel was a **"keeper of sheep,"** not his father's but his own. Cain was an agriculturist and the possessor of large estates. We read that Adam was 130 years old when he begat Seth. Gen. 5:3. Seth was probably born soon after the death of Abel. Gen. 4:25. This would make Abel over 100 years of age at his death.

The death of Abel was probably due to a religious dispute between Cain and Abel as to the character of religious offerings. Abel claimed that a **"Bloody Sacrifice"** was necessary, Cain claimed that an offering of **"Works"** taken from the soil which God had cursed was sufficient. They put the matter to a test. God accepted Abel's offering and rejected Cain's, probably answering as on Mount Carmel by **fire.** This angered Cain. He did not kill Abel that day. The Lord remonstrated with Cain and reminded him that there was still time to bring a "**SIN** (blood) **OFFERING.**" The expression "**sin lieth at the door**" (Gen. 4:7), may be translated a "**sin offering lieth at the door.**" But Cain would not listen and nursed his anger, possibly for a long time. One day while alone in the field with Abel, Cain brought the subject up again, for we read that Cain "talked with Abel" about the matter (Gen. 4:8), and Cain's anger became uncontrollable and he arose from the ground where he was sitting and killed his brother. The whole thing was a scheme of Satan to destroy Abel, through whom the "**Promised Seed**" was to come. Satan was not only the instigator of Abel's murder, he was the author of "**Cain's Religion,**" spoken of by Jude as "**THE WAY OF CAIN**" (Jude 11). Here we have the origin of all religions that ignore the **BLOOD** and magnify **WORKS.**

Cain fled to the land of Nod and built a city. Here we have the beginning of the city with all its attendant evils. Among the descendants of Cain was Jubal, the inventor of musical instruments, and Tubal-Cain, an instructor of workers in brass and iron. Men in those days used their brains to improve and upbuild a "**Godless Civilization,**" and when we recall that in that Age men were not cut off at threescore and ten, but lived on for nearly a 1000 years, their immense accumulation of knowledge, experience, and skill, must have advanced the Arts and Sciences and resulted in the invention and manufacture of all the appliances of a luxurious civilization, with a rapidity to us almost inconceivable. The building of such a ship as the Ark constructed by Noah is an illustration. We have the echo of that skilled civilization in the construction, after the Flood, of the Tower of Babel, and later of the Great Pyramid, which involved, in its construction, such a knowledge of mathematics and astronomy as the world has never as yet surpassed.*

The outcome of that brilliant but godless civilization was to promote the rapid increase of population. "Then

*For a description of the Great Pyramid with its Dispensational teaching see my larger work on "Dispensational Truth."

men began to 'multiply' on the face of the earth." Gen. 6:1. In the midst of this "Godless Civilization" a startling event occurred. "The 'Sons of GOD' saw the 'Daughters of MEN' that they were fair; and they took them WIVES of all which they chose." Gen. 6:2.

This polygamous relation was not between the "Sons of SETH," and the "Daughters of CAIN," a union of the godly and wicked people of that day, as some suppose, but it has a far deeper meaning. The expression "Daughters of MEN" includes the daughters of Seth as well as the daughters of Cain, hence the expression "Sons of GOD" must mean beings different from the HUMAN RACE.

The title "Sons of God" has not the same meaning in the Old Testament that it has in the New. In the New Testament it applies to those who have become the "Sons of God" by the New Birth. John 1:12; Rom. 8:14-16; Gal. 4:6; 1 John 3:1-2. In the Old Testament it applies to the angels, and is so used five times. Twice in Genesis (Gen. 6:2-4) and three times in Job. Job 1:6, 2:1, 38:7. A "Son of God" denotes a being brought into existence by a creative act of God. Such were the angels, and such was Adam, and he is so called in Luke 3:38. But Adam's natural descendants are not the special creation of God. Adam was created in the "likeness of God" (Gen. 5:1), but his descendants were born in his likeness, for we read in Gen. 5:3, that Adam "BEGAT a son in his own likeness, after his image." Therefore all men born of Adam and his descendants by natural generation are the "SONS OF MEN," and it is only by being "BORN AGAIN" (John 3:3-7), which is a "NEW CREATION," that they can become the "SONS OF GOD" in the New Testament sense.

From this we see that the "Sons of GOD" of Gen. 6:2-4 could not be the "Sons of Seth," for they were only unregenerate MEN, while the "Sons of GOD" were of a superior race, in other words ANGELS. To this, however, objection is made that the Angels do not marry nor are given in marriage (Luke 20:27-36), therefore they must be "sexless" and could not cohabit with either themselves or human beings. But this does not necessarily follow. The Angels are created beings and do not die, therefore there is no need for marriage to prevent their extermination, but this does not imply that they are "sexless" and do not have the power of procreation. We must not forget that Angels can assume the **form of MEN** and eat and drink (Gen. 18:1-8), and the whole difficulty vanishes when we see that it was **AS MEN** that the "Sons of God" (Angels) married the "Daughters of Men."

We have only to turn to the Epistles of Peter and Jude for confirmation of this. In 2 Pet. 2:4-9 we are told of the "Angels that **SINNED**," and in Jude (6-7) of the Angels that **"KEPT NOT THEIR FIRST ESTATE,"** but **"LEFT THEIR OWN HABITATION,"** and are now **"RESERVED IN EVERLASTING CHAINS UNDER DARKNESS"** unto the "Judgment of the Great Day," the "Great White Throne Judgment." These Angels are not Satan's Angels, for his angels are free. They must therefore be a **"special class"** of angels who have been imprisoned for some particular sin, and we are told what that sin was, it was **"FORNICATION"** and **"going after STRANGE FLESH."** Jude 7. And the time of the commission of the sin is given as just **BEFORE THE FLOOD.** 2 Pet. 2:4-5. This proves beyond the shadow of a doubt that the "Sons of God" of Gen. 6:2-4 were **Angels**.

As further confirmation of this view we have the fact that the "offspring" of the union of the "Sons of God" and the "Daughters of Men," were a race of **"GIANTS," "MIGHTY MEN," "MEN OF RENOWN."** Gen. 6:4. Now the **godly** descendants of men have married **ungodly women**, but their offspring have never been such **"MONSTROSITIES"** as the offspring of the "Sons of God" and the "Daughters of Men" of Noah's day, therefore that union must have been of an **unnatural** character as is evidenced by the term **"Strange Flesh."** God could not permit such an abnormal race as the "progeny" of the union of angels and human beings to exist on the earth, so the outcome of this "Invasion" of the earth by the **"Denizens of the Air"** was the Flood, by which the contour and elevation of the Ante-diluvian Earth were changed, thus wiping out the "Garden of Eden," and diminishing the length of human life on the earth.

In the Ante-diluvian Dispensation mankind was treated as a whole. There were no nations. That Dispensation is called in Acts 17 : 30, the "TIMES OF IGNORANCE," and is contrasted with the "Times that are NOW," and we are told that in that Dispensation God "WINKED AT" what He could not "OVER-LOOK" in the Legal Dispensation. See the Chart on "The Times and Seasons." Page 4.

III. THE PRESENT AGE

This "Age" extends from the Flood to the second stage of Christ's Second Coming, called the "Revelation." It covers four Dispensations.

1. The Post-Diluvian Dispensation

This was the "Dispensation of HUMAN GOVERN-MENT." If ever the human race had an opportunity to work out the theory of "Human Government" it was right after the Flood. Noah was an old man over 600 years of age, full of wisdom and experience, and his family, all of whom had reached maturity — for the youngest, Shem, was 98 years old — were qualified for self-government. Behind them was the Flood with all its warnings, and in addition the accumulated knowledge from Adam down to their day. The fact that Noah set up an altar and offered sacrifice implies that he and his family were godly. And when God commanded Noah and his sons to be fruitful and multiply and replenish the earth His purpose doubtless was to repeople the earth with a godly race. But 325 years after the Flood the "Tower of Babel" was built, revealing the proud and rebellious spirit of the people, and God came down and confused the language of the people and scattered them abroad over the face of the earth. Gen. 11 : 1-9. Here we have the origin of nations and the different languages of the earth. So this Dispensation was a failure like its predecessors.

2. The Patriarchal Dispensation

This Dispensation extended from the "Call of Abra-ham" to the "Exodus," a period of 430 years, and is known as the "Dispensation of **THE FAMILY.**" It ended with all of Abraham's descendants working as abject slaves in the brickyards of Egypt.

3. The Legal Dispensation

This Dispensation extended from the "Exodus" to the "Birth of Christ," and is known as the "Dispensation of **LAW.**" Heretofore God had allowed man to govern himself, now He purposed to organize a Commonwealth with laws and regulations and a "visible" system of worship with a local habitation or place of worship. The government was "Theocratic." That is, God ruled through representative men that He appointed, as Moses, Joshua, and the Judges. But the people grew tired of such a mode of government and demanded a king which eventually led to their undoing. God's dealing with the people was based on a **"WRITTEN LAW"** given at Mt. Sinai. This "Civil" and "Ceremonial" Law was given to Israel only, and not to any other nation. Its observance ceased at the destruction of Jerusalem in A. D. 70. The wonderful feature of this Dispensation was that it was filled with the "Miraculous Interposition" of God in behalf of His chosen people. For them He opened the Red Sea, fed them in the Wilderness in a miraculous manner for 40 years, walled back the waters of the Jordan that they might cross over in safety into the Promised Land, and helped them to conquer it. For centuries God watched over and protected them, but they repaid His love and kindness by rejecting His Son, and this Dispensation ended, like its predecessors, in revealing the ungrateful and disobedient nature of fallen man.

4. The Ecclesiastical Dispensation

This is the "Dispensation of **GRACE,**" and extends from the "Cross" to the "Crown" for Christ, and from "Pentecost" to the "Rapture of the Church" for the Believer. This is a

PARENTHETICAL DISPENSATION

thrown in between the **"Dispersion"** of Israel, and their **"Restoration"** to their own land. The purpose of this Dispensation is to gather out a "People for His Name," called **THE CHURCH.** In this Dispensation we are under the "Davidic Covenant," the sign of which is a **"SON"** (Jesus), and neither Jews nor Gentiles are dealt with as such. The characteristic of this Dispensation is, that "Blindness **IN PART** is happened to Israel until the **'Fulness of the Gentiles'** be come in." Rom. 11:25. The "Fulness of the Gentiles," with some Jews, make up a "New Body," the **CHURCH.** This "New Body" is not under **LAW** but **GRACE.** Rom. 6:14. When Christ took His seat upon the "Father's Throne" He changed it from a "Throne of **JUSTICE**" to a "Throne of **GRACE,**" and God's attitude in this Dispensation is one of favor and "longsuffering" toward wicked men and nations. 2 Pet. 3:9. This Dispensation we are foretold will end in **APOSTASY,** for Christ Himself said that when He came back He would not find **FAITH** (the Faith) on the earth. Luke 18:8.

Between the "Ecclesiastical" and "Millennial" Dispensations there is another **"Parenthetical Dispensation"** the
"DISPENSATION OF JUDGMENT,"
during which the Jews, the Gentiles, and the Church are to be judged. The Church is to be "caught out" at the **beginning** of the Dispensation and judged at the "Judgment Seat of Christ." 2 Cor. 5:10. The Jews are to be judged **during** the Tribulation under Antichrist on the earth. Their Judgment is known as the "Time of Jacob's Trouble." Jer. 30:4-7. Dan. 12:1. The Gentiles (the Nations) are to be judged at the **close** of the Tribulation, when the Lord Jesus Christ shall descend from Heaven and sit on the "Throne of His Glory," and all nations shall be gathered in their representatives before Him, and the **"SHEEP** Nations" shall be rewarded by entrance into the "Millennial Kingdom," and the **"GOAT** Nations," as **NATIONS,** shall be destroyed. Matt. 25:31-46. The Judgment of the Church is as **individuals,** while that of the Jews and Gentiles is **national.**

IV. THE AGE OF AGES
This is a "Dual Age," and includes the "Millennial Age" and the "Perfect Age," between which the earth is "Renovated by Fire." It will be ushered in at the "Second Stage" of Christ's Second Coming.

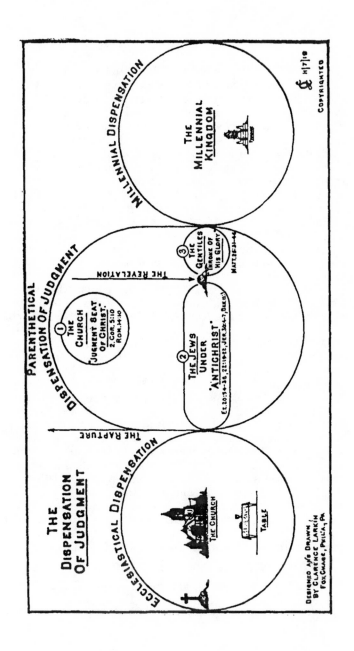

THE
DISPENSATION OF JUDGMENT

ECCLESIASTICAL DISPENSATION

THE RAPTURE

PARENTHETICAL
DISPENSATION OF JUDGMENT

① THE CHURCH
"JUDGMENT SEAT OF CHRIST."
2. COR. 5:10
ROM. 14:10

② THE JEWS UNDER "ANTICHRIST"
EZ. 20:33-38, 22:19-22, JER. 30:4-7, DAN. 9:1

THE REVELATION

③ THE GENTILES
THRONE OF HIS GLORY
MATT. 25:31-46

MILLENNIAL DISPENSATION

THE MILLENNIAL KINGDOM

THE CHURCH

TABLE

DESIGNED A/ø DRAWN
BY CLARENCE LARKIN
FOX CHASE, PHILA., PA.

COPYRIGHTED

1. The Millennial Age

This is not only an "Age," it is also a "Dispensation," the "Messianic Dispensation" or rule of Christ as King. Writers and poets have written and sung of a "Golden Age," an Age of universal righteousness and peace; and the Jews believe that the "Seventh Thousand" of years from the Creation is to be a "Sabbath of Rest," and that a description of that Age is given to us in the Old Testament. That there is to be a period of 1000 years during which Satan shall be bound and Christ shall reign over the earth is clearly revealed in the New Testament. This period is mentioned six times in the Book of Revelation. Rev. 20:1-7.

In the Millennial Age God will again deal with mankind as a whole, but as made up of nations. The Church will not be on the earth, only as it is represented by those who will assist Christ, **THE KING,** in His Administration of the Millennial Kingdom. The Jews, as a nation, will then be the **"HEAD OF THE NATIONS."** Deu. 28:13. While they will in part observe the "Ceremonial Law," they will be under a **"NEW COVENANT."** Jer. 31:31-37. Heb. 8:7-13. The principle under which God will deal with men in those days will not be Law, Grace, or Judgment, but **RIGHTEOUSNESS.** It will be an "Autocratic Government," for Christ will rule with a **"ROD OF IRON"** (Isa. 11:1, 4; Rev. 2:27, 19:15; Psa. 2:9), but that rule will be based on **LOVE.** As Satan will be bound at that time, the character of the "Messianic Dispensation" will be entirely different from all preceding Dispensations, and cannot be classed with them. But we shall see, as we study the outcome of the "Millennial Age" in the Chapter on "The Kingdom," that when Satan is loosed at the end of the Millennium man will reveal the fact that he is still a rebellious creature, with an evil heart of unbelief, for that Dispensation, like all that preceded it, will end in **APOSTASY.** Rev. 20:7-10.

RENOVATION OF THE EARTH BY FIRE

Between the "Millennial Age" and the "Perfect Age" the earth is to be "Renovated by Fire." See the Chart on "The Three Stages of the Earth," page 8. This

"Renovation" is described in 2 Pet. 3:7-13. The earth as a "planet" is not to be destroyed, only the exterior surface is to be burned over for the purpose of destroying all poisonous and obnoxious plant growths, and the diseases and pests that prey on vegetable life that sin has produced, and the heavens (the earth's atmosphere) "shall pass away with a great noise," like an explosion of gas, and a new atmosphere (a new Heaven) shall take its place, which shall be free from all disease germs and "evil spirits" and destructive agencies.

2. The Perfect Age

It is this "Perfect Age," or "Kingdom of the New Heaven and Earth" that Christ surrenders to the Father (1 Cor. 15:28), for the "Millennial Kingdom" is not perfect, there is sin in it, and it ends in Apostasy. As there is no room for this "Perfect Kingdom" before the "Renovation of the Earth by Fire" it must come after it. This "Perfect Kingdom" is also a "Dispensation," the "Dispensation of the FULNESS OF TIMES." Eph. 1:10. The "Millennial Kingdom" and the "Perfect Kingdom" make up the "Kingdom of the SON OF MAN."

V. THE AGES OF THE AGES

As the "Creative Ages" were the "Alpha" Ages, these will be the "Omega" Ages. With the surrender of the "Perfect Kingdom" to the Father, what we speak of as "Time" ceases, and the "Eternal Ages," called the "Ages of the Ages" begin. They correspond to what the Apostle Paul in his Letter to the Ephesians calls the "Ages to Come." Eph. 2:7. And John in the Book of Revelation says that the "Devil" and the "Beast" and the "False Prophet" shall be tormented day and night forever and ever, or for the "Aions of the Aions," the "Ages of the Ages," Rev. 20:10, and that the "Servants of God" shall reign for the same period. Rev. 22:5.

What those "Ages of Ages" shall reveal of the Plan and Purpose of God we do not know, but if we are His we shall live to know, and possibly take part in their development. What we do know is that we are but in the beginning of things, and as concerning the "Ages," Eternity is still young.

III

Jew and Gentile

The Scriptures treat of "Three Classes" of Persons. The "Jews," the "Gentiles," and the "Church of God." The Jews and the Gentiles are distinct from each other, while the Church of God is composed of both Jews and Gentiles, but not as Jews or Gentiles but as a "New Body." All the human race that are not Jews are Gentiles. The Jews date back to Abraham, and became a distinct and separate nation at the Exodus. The most of the Old Testament is taken up with their history. They are an **earthly** people, while the "Church of God" are a **heavenly** people. Like the Jews the "Church of God" had a beginning. It began at the "Day of Pentecost" and will end chronologically at the Second Coming of Christ. At the present time the Jews are, as a nation, "sidetracked." When the "Church of God" is taken out of the world, the Jews will again be restored to their own land and become the "Head of the Nations." Nationally the Gentiles now govern the earth. This is what the Scriptures speak of as the "Times of the Gentiles." Luke 21:24.

I. THE JEWS

As has been said the Jews had their origin in the morning time of history when God called Abraham, a Shemite, to be the father of a new nation. Gen. 12:1-3. God appeared to Abraham 10 times. These appearances were called "Theophanies," and were progressive and unconditional in their promises, and the promises were unconditionally confirmed to Abraham's son Isaac (Gen. 26:1-4), and to his grandson Jacob. Gen. 28:10-15.

The history of the Jewish race is without a parallel in human history. Though oppressed, downtrodden, carried captive to other lands and scattered through the nations, the Jew has outlived all his conquerors and walks unscathed amid the nations. Any other race would have been swallowed up and its identity and national characteristics lost. The preservation of the Jewish race is

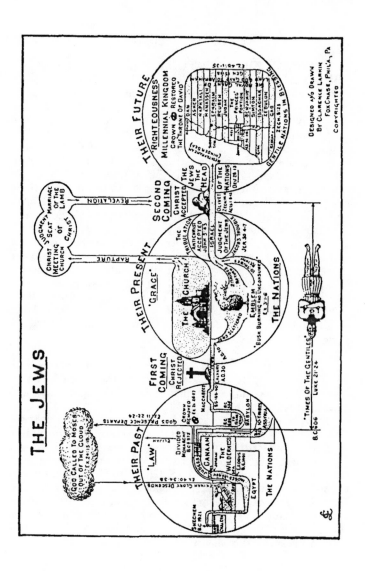

THE JEWS

THEIR PAST · THEIR PRESENT · THEIR FUTURE

"LAW" · FIRST COMING · "GRACE" · SECOND COMING · RIGHTEOUSNESS

Designed and Drawn By Clarence Larkin Fox Chase, Phila., Pa. Copyrighted

the "MIRACLE OF HISTORY." Their "Emblem" is a "BUSH BURNING AND UNCONSUMED."

No nation has ever had such manifest and visible tokens of the "Divine Presence." For them the Red Sea was driven back and the Jordan parted. They were miraculously fed in the Wilderness and Divinely sheltered and guided by the "Pillar of Cloud and Fire." At the blowing of "ram's horns" the walls of a besieged city fell (Joshua 6:1-27), and the Sun and Moon stayed in their courses that they might have time to slay their enemies. Joshua 10:12-14. The "Angel of the Lord" encamped about them, and one angel slew 185,000 of the army of Assyria for their deliverance. 2 Kings 19:35. No nation has given to the world such a number of great men. Such a man of faith as Abraham; such a great leader and lawgiver as Moses; such statesmen as Joseph in Egypt and Daniel in Babylon; such a king as David, and wise man as Solomon. No nation has produced such "seers" as the Hebrew Prophets, Isaiah, Jeremiah, Ezekiel and Daniel, and no such man as that man above all men, the

"MAN OF GALILEE."

In the first Christian century there is no name that shines more resplendent than that of the Apostle Paul. And in modern days the men who have made and are making history are **JEWS.**

How are we to account for the wonderful preservation of the Jewish Race? Only on the supposition that God had, and still has, some great work for them to do. In the first place they were raised up to reaffirm and teach that there was but **ONE** God. In the second place to be the **Writers, Preservers** and **Transmitters of the Holy Scriptures.** To them were committed the **"ORACLES of God."** Rom. 3:1-2. Every page and book in the Bible was written by Jews. The Jews took especial care to preserve the Scriptures and keep them from being tampered with. In the third place they were raised up that God through them might give the world a **SAVIOUR.** Who was Jesus? A **JEW.** In the fourth place they were raised up that they might save the world from **moral putrefaction.** When Jesus said, **"Salvation** is of the Jews" (John 4:22), did He simply mean that from them should come the Saviour—Jesus? or did He mean, as when He said—"YE Are the 'SALT OF THE EARTH,'" that the Jewish Race were to be the means of preventing the "Moral Putrefaction" of the world, and that if they became extinct as a nation the world would be ripe for judgment? The writer thinks he meant the latter, and that the salvation of the Nations, morally and physically, and the preservation of the human race on the earth depends on the preservation and continuance of the Jews as a RACE.

The present degenerate condition of the world is owing to the fact that the Jews have lost their savor, as the salt its saltness, and until they recover it degeneration will continue to develop until the time comes that the smell of the decomposition of the decaying nationalities of the earth shall call for Divine interposition and the Jewish SALT be resavored by the conversion of the Jews, and their becoming the leading nation of the world.

For the Jews today there is no "Pillar of Cloud" by day, nor "Shechinah Flame" by night. They have no altars, no sacrifices, no priesthood as in former days. They observe the "Passover," but no paschal lamb is slain. They keep the "Great Day of Atonement," but no blood is shed to make reconciliation for sin. All sacrifices and oblations have ceased. They have no King, no Judges, no Prophets, no inspired writers. The "Urim" and "Thummin" give no Divine token. The word of God is precious, but there is no "open vision." Their last Great Prophet was the "Man of Galilee," but Him they rejected. Like their forefathers, who took Joseph, after they had rejected him, and sold him for 20 pieces of silver, and he was hidden from their view in Egypt on the Throne of Pharaoh, so the Jews took Jesus, their Joseph, and having rejected Him, sold Him for 30 pieces of silver, and He is now hidden from them on His Father's Throne.

Why Is This? Have they been supplanted as a "Nation" by the Gentiles, and as "God's People" by the Church? Are they never again to have a land of their own, and a King, and a Capital City, and a National Existence?

Is not their condition today the fulfillment of the prophecy of Hosea 3:4?

"The Children of Israel shall abide **MANY DAYS** without a King, and without a Prince, and without a Sacrifice, and without an Image, and without an Ephod, and without Teraphim?"

Is it not that Jerusalem must be—

"Trodden down of the Gentiles **until the 'Times of the Gentiles' be fulfilled?"** Luke 21:24.

What does Paul say—

"Blindness **in part** is happened to Israel **until the 'Fulness of the Gentiles' be come in.** And so **All Israel Shall Be Saved."** Rom. 11:25, 26.

From these scriptures we see that the Jews have not been supplanted by either the Gentiles or the Church, and when the time comes they will again become a nation.

We indulge in no idle and profitless speculations when we attempt to forecast the future of the Jewish People. All we have to do is to gather together and place in their logical order what the Holy Spirit through the Prophets, has foretold. The method is as simple as the result is sure.

THE RESTORATION OF THE JEWS

1. **As to the FACT.**

"And I will bring again the captivity of my people 'Israel' and they shall build the waste cities, and inhabit them; and they shall plant vineyards and drink the wine thereof; they shall also make gardens, and eat the fruit of them. And I will plant them upon their land, and they shall **no more be pulled up out of their land."** Amos. 9:14, 15.

But you say this prophecy was fulfilled in the restoration from the "Babylonian Captivity." Not so, for they were driven out of the land after that, and this promise is, that they shall **no more be pulled up out of their land,** and must refer to some future restoration. The return from the "Babylonian Captivity" was the **First** restoration, and the Scriptures speak of a **Second.**

> "And it shall come to pass in **"That Day"** (Millennial Day) that the Lord shall set his hand again the **SECOND TIME** to recover the remnant of His People, which shall be left, from Assyria, and from Egypt, and from Pathros, and from Cush, and from Elam, and from Shinar, and from Hamath, and from the islands of the Sea." Isa. 11:11.

The Jews have never been **restored** but **ONCE,** and that was from Babylon. The march from Egypt to Canaan was not a restoration. You cannot have anything restored to you unless it **has been in your possession** before, and Palestine was never in possession of the Children of Israel until **after** its conquest by Joshua.

Again the Jews are to come this time, not from the **"East,"** as when they returned from the "Babylonish Captivity," but from the **"North,"** and from **"All Countries."**

> "Therefore, behold, the days come, saith the Lord, that it shall no more be said, The Lord liveth, that brought up the Children of Israel out of the Land of Egypt; but the Lord liveth that brought up the Children of Israel **from the land of the NORTH and from ALL THE LANDS** whither He had driven them; and I will bring them again into their land that I gave unto their fathers." Jer. 16:14, 15. Also Isa. 43:5-7.

2. **As to the TIME.**

When the "TIMES OF THE GENTILES" Have Been Fulfilled.

> "And they shall fall by the edge of the sword, and shall be led away captive into all nations; and Jerusalem shall be trodden down of the Gentiles, **UNTIL** the 'Times of the Gentiles' be fulfilled." Luke 21:24.

3. As to the MANNER.

a. Gathered Back UNCONVERTED.

"I will take you from among the heathen, and gather you out of all countries, and will bring you into your own land. THEN will I sprinkle clean water upon you, and ye shall be clean; from all your filthiness, and from all your idols will I cleanse you. A New Heart also will I give you, and a New Spirit will I put within you; and I will give you an Heart of Flesh. And I will put My Spirit within you, and cause you to walk in my statutes; and ye shall keep my judgments, and do them." Ezek. 36: 24-27.

b. Before Conversion They Are To Be JUDGED.

"I will bring you out from the people, and will gather you out of the countries wherein ye are scattered, with a mighty hand, and with a stretched out arm, and with fury poured out. And I will bring you into the wilderness of the people, and there will I plead with you face to face. . . . And I will cause you to

'Pass Under The Rod,'

and I will bring you into the bond of the Covenant; and I will purge out from among you the rebels, and them that transgress against Me: I will bring them forth out of the country where they sojourn, and they shall not enter into the Land of Israel." Ezek. 20: 34-38.

Then God will cast them into His
"Melting Pot."

"Therefore thus saith the Lord God; Because ye are all become dross, behold, therefore I will gather you into the midst of Jerusalem. As they gather silver, and brass, and iron, and lead, and tin, into the midst of the furnace, to blow the fire upon it, to melt it; so will I gather you in Mine anger and in My fury and I will leave you there, and MELT YOU. Yea I will gather you, and blow upon you in the fire of My wrath, and ye shall be **melted in the midst thereof**. As silver is melted in the midst of the furnace, **so shall ye be melted in the midst thereof**; and ye shall know that I the Lord have poured out My fury upon you." Ezk. 22:19-22.

"Behold, I will send My messenger (Elijah—Malachi 4:5, 6), and he shall prepare the way before Me, and the Lord, whom ye seek, shall **suddenly come to His Temple**, even the Messenger of the Covenant, whom ye delight in: behold, He shall come, saith the Lord of hosts. But who may abide the day of His coming? and who shall stand when He appeareth? for He is like a **Refiner's Fire**, and like **Fuller's Soap**: and He shall sit as a **Refiner and Purifier of Silver**: and He shall **Purify the Sons of Levi**, and purge them as gold and silver, that they may offer unto the Lord an offering in righteousness." Malachi 3:1-3.

And I will bring the **third part through the fire**, and will **refine them as silver is refined**, and will try them as gold is tried: they shall call on My name and I will hear them: I will say, it is My people; and they shall say, the Lord is my God." Zech. 13:9.

The Jews have never as yet had such an experience as this. It is spoken of in Jer. 30:4-7, and Dan. 12:1, as the **"Time of 'Jacob's Trouble,'"** and Christ called it **"THE GREAT TRIBULATION,"** and He and Zechariah the Prophet associate it with the **Return of the Lord**. Matt. 24:21-31. Zech. 14:1-11.

The result of these terrible judgments will be that the Jews will call in their misery upon the Lord.

"And I will pour upon the 'House of David' and upon the inhabitants of Jerusalem **The Spirit of Grace and of Supplications**." Zech. 12:10. Then Christ will come back to Jerusalem—

"And **His feet shall stand in that day upon the Mount of Olives which is before** Jerusalem **on the east**." Zech. 14:4.

"And they shall look upon **ME Whom They Have Pierced.**" Zech. 12:10.

And a nation, the **Jewish Nation,** shall be **born** (converted) **IN A DAY.**

"Who hath heard such a thing? who hath seen such things? Shall the earth be made to bring forth in one day? or shall a **Nation Be Born at Once?** for as soon as **Zion Travailed, She Brought Forth Her Children.**" Isa. 66:8.

As the Children of Israel when they came out of Egypt took with them of the "Riches of the Egyptians," (Ex. 12:35, 36), so when they return to their own land they will take with them the "Riches of the Gentiles." Isa. 60:9; 61:6.

When they return to their own land it will be to possess and occupy all that was promised to Abraham.

"The Royal Grant"

given by the Almighty to Abraham extended from the "River of Egypt" unto the "Great River," the River Euphrates (Gen. 15:18); and according to Ezekiel (Ezek. 48:1-29), from Hamath, north-east of Damascus, to Kadesh on the south. The Temple will be rebuilt. The Glory of the Lord will return. Sacrifices will again be offered. The Government shall be reestablished, and the nations of the earth will be blessed through Israel. Zech. 8:20-23.*

II. THE GENTILES

The prominent Gentile nations of the world have been Egypt, Assyria, Babylon, Medo-Persia, Greece and Rome. When God's chosen people the Israelites fell into idolatry, and were carried into Captivity to Babylon, they were supplanted by the Gentiles. For a long time the nations of Egypt, Assyria and Babylon were anxious to fall upon Israel and conquer them, but God held them in an unseen leash until the iniquity of Israel was full, and then let them loose, and permitted the world power to pass into

---

*For a fuller account of the Jews see my book on "Dispensational Truth," the chapters on "The Jews," "The Tribulation" and "The Kingdom."

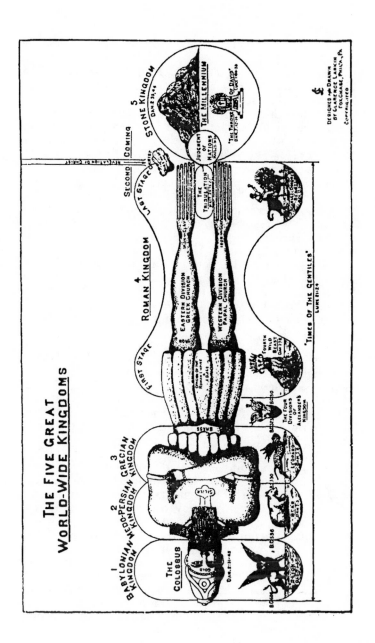

the hands of Nebuchadnezzar, King of Babylon. This happened in B. C. 606, and marked the beginning of the "Times of the Gentiles," spoken of by Christ in Luke 21:24, and which is a period that in the mind of God has certain chronological limits. It is not to be confounded with the "Fulness of the Gentiles" spoken of by Paul in Rom. 11:25. The "Fulness of the Gentiles" refers to the Gentiles that are "gathered out" to make up the Church, and "blindness in part" will continue among the Jews until the "Fulness" (the whole number of the elect) of the Gentiles be come in, then the Church is "caught out" and the Jews restored to their own land. The "Fulness of the Gentiles" began at Pentecost and ends at least seven years before the "Times of the Gentiles" end.

The "Times of the Gentiles" are fully outlined in the Book of Daniel. The Book of Daniel contains one "Dream" by Nebuchadnezzar, and four "Visions" of Daniel all relating to the "Times of the Gentiles." In the second year of Nebuchadnezzar's reign he had a dream. Dan. 2:31-45.

In his "Dream" he saw an immense "Image" or **"COLOSSUS."** This "Colossus" symbolized the "World Kingdoms" in their "Unity" and "Historical" Succession. Gentile dominion is represented by a huge **"METALLIC MAN."** See the Chart "The Five Great World-Wide Kingdoms," page 38. The degeneration of the "World Kingdoms" is seen in the diminishing value of the metals used. The weight of the Image also declines. The "Colossus" is "Top-Heavy." The four metals of which the "Colossus" was composed represent "Four World-wide Kingdoms" which were to arise in succession. Dan. 2:37-40. Four Great Kingdoms, and only four, are to succeed each other in the government of the world from Nebuchadnezzar to the "Second Coming" of Christ—the Babylonian, Medo-Persian, Grecian and Roman. These Kingdoms are not only made known as to number, but their names, in the order of their succession, are given. Dan. 2:38-40, 8:20-21, 9:26. The deterioration of the Colossus, as shown in the character of the metals composing it, is prophetic of the character of the governments as they were to succeed each other from an "Absolute

THE GENTILES

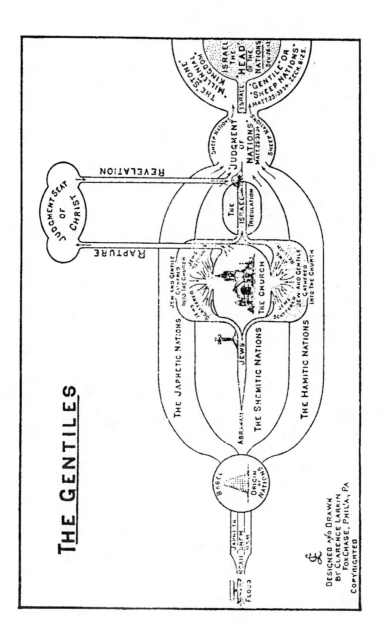

DESIGNED AND DRAWN
BY CLARENCE LARKIN
FOX CHASE, PHILA., PA
COPYRIGHTED

Monarchy," as seen in the rule of Nebuchadnezzar (Dan. 5:19), to an "Autocratic Democracy" as seen in the "Iron and Clay" of the feet of the Image. Dan. 2:41-43. Thus showing that Gentile Dominion passes gradually from the "**Head,**" or the organ which ought to direct the members, to the "**Feet,**" which are only made to carry the body whither the head directs.

The "Colossus" comes to an end by being smitten on the **FEET** by a "Stone Cut Out of a Mountain." The "Stone" does not fill the earth by degrees and thus crowd out the Colossus, it at **one blow DEMOLISHES IT.** The action of the "Stone" is **JUDGMENT,** not Grace. It therefore cannot mean Christianity, for it is a **process,** whereas the action of the "Stone" is **SUDDEN** and **CALAMITOUS.** Again the "Time" of the destruction is not until **after the formation of the "Toes,"** and we know that the "Two Limbs" of the Colossus did not appear until A. D. 364, and the "Ten Toes" have not yet developed. The "Time" when the "Stone" falls on the Colossus is distinctly stated in the interpretation as "**in the days of those kings,**" that is, in the days of the kings represented by the "Ten Toes" which is yet future. Dan. 7:23-24.

The "Stone" represents Christ. As the Four King-doms represented by the four metals are literal King-doms, it follows that the "Stone Kingdom" must be a literal Kingdom, for it takes the place of those Kingdoms and conquers the whole earth. The "Stone Kingdom" then is the "Millennial Kingdom" of Christ, and the "Colossus," or the "Times of the Gentiles" typified by it, cannot come to an end until the "Second Stage" (Revelation) of Christ's Second Coming.

Forty-eight years after Nebuchadnezzar had his dream of the "Colossus" Daniel had a "vision" of "Four Wild Beasts." Dan. 7:1-8, 15-27. In character they descended from the Lion, the "King of Beasts," to a non-descript monster with teeth of iron, and toe nails of brass, and "Ten Horns" on its head. Daniel saw that the "Beasts" corresponded with the metals of the Colossus and represented the same thing. But while Daniel con-sidered the "Beasts" he was surprised to see a "Little

Horn" spring up among the "Ten Horns" of the "'Fourth Wild Beast." Dan. 7:8. This mystified him, for he had seen no "Little Toe" spring up among the "Ten Toes" of the Colossus. He therefore concluded that it was an additional revelation that God had not seen fit to reveal to the Gentile king Nebuchadnezzar.

Daniel noticed that the "Little Horn," that rose among the "Ten Horns" of the "Fourth Wild Beast," "plucked up by the roots" three of the "Ten Horns," and that it had the "eyes" and the "mouth" of a **MAN**. Thus was revealed to Daniel not only the "Four World-wide Kingdoms" in the order of their succession, but a vision, in the "Little Horn," of the last Gentile King—the **ANTICHRIST**.

The reason why these Four Kingdoms are represented first as a "Golden-Headed Metallic Image," and then as a succession of "Wild Beasts," is to show the difference between man's view and God's view of the World Kingdoms. Man sees in them the concentration of wealth, majesty and power; God sees them as a succession of **rapacious wild beasts devouring one another.**

While these "Four World-wide Kingdoms" were to succeed each other in the order named, they were not to succeed each other without a break. This was revealed to Daniel in his vision of the "Ram and He Goat," (Dan. 8:1-27), and is shown on the Chart. By the death of Alexander the Great, the "Great Horn" of the "He Goat," the Grecian Kingdom was divided into four minor Kingdoms, Macedonia, Thrace, Syria and Egypt. They lasted from B. C. 323 to B. C. 30, when the Roman Empire became the Fourth World-wide Kingdom and continued as such until A. D. 364, when it was divided into its Eastern and Western Divisions. But while the Roman Empire as such disappeared in A. D. 364, it still in its laws and religious influence holds sway, and is to be revived and again become a "World Power" in a "Ten Kingdom" form, represented by the "Ten Toes" of the Colossus and the "Ten Horns" of Daniel's "Fourth Wild Beast."

As to the date when the "Times of the Gentiles" will end we have no knowledge. There are those who claim that the word **"Times"** is prophetic, and that a prophetic

"'Time" is a year of 360 days, each day standing for a YEAR, thus making a "Time" equal to 360 YEARS. They also claim that Moses in the Book of Leviticus (Lev. 26: 18-21, 24-28), foretold, and four times repeated it, that if the Children of Israel disobeyed God He would punish them "Seven Times," and that Jesus referred to these "Seven Times" when He spoke of the "TIMES" of the Gentiles. Therefore if a "Time" is 360 YEARS, "Seven Times" would be 2520 YEARS, and as the "Times of the Gentiles" began in B. C. 606, they should end in A. D. 1914. The fallacy of the argument is seen in the fact that that date is past and the "Times of the Gentiles" is not yet ended.

In Scripture a month is 30 days (Gen. 7: 11-24; 8: 3-4) and a year 360 days. But from B. C. 606, to A. D. 1914, there were 2520 "Julian Years" of 365¼ days each, which, when we reduce them to "Calendar Years" of 360 days each, make 2556¾ years, or 36¾ years more than 2520 years, so that the "Times of the Gentiles" should have ended in A. D. 1877.

The fact is the "Seven Times" of Leviticus are not "Prophetic Times." The Children of Israel have been punished, given over to "Servitude" and "Captivity," exactly SEVEN times. Their present "Dispersion" is neither a "Servitude" nor "Captivity" and does not count. All we can know then as to the "length" of the "Times of the Gentiles" is, that they began in B. C. 606, and will end when Christ comes back and sets up the "STONE" or "Millennial Kingdom."

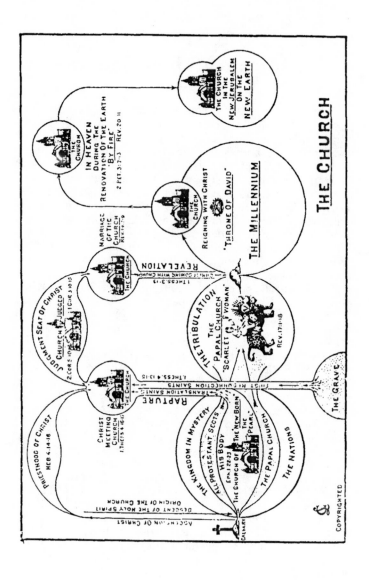

IV

Church and Kingdom

The Church is not a continuation of the "Jewish Dispensation" under another name, nor does the Church edifice take the place of the Synagogue. It is because some religious bodies believe that the Christian Church is but another phase of what they call the "Jewish Church," that they insist on a "Ceremonial Ritual" and retain the Priesthood with its altar, vestments, etc., and Temple-like buildings; and call the ordinances of the Christian Church "Sacrifices" and "Sacraments." They also go further and advocate a "State Church," with the Church as the head, and claim that all the Old Testament promises of riches and glory have been transferred from the Jew to the Church.

The Church is not to be confounded with "The Kingdom." The Church is compared to a "House" (1 Tim. 3:15), to a "Temple" (1 Cor. 3:16-17), to a "Body" (1 Cor. 12:27-31), but never to a "Kingdom." Christ is the **"HEAD"** of His Church (Eph. 1:22; 4:15; Col. 1:18), but He is never spoken of as its **KING**. The Church is a **"MYSTERY"** and was first revealed to Paul. Eph. 3: 1-11. The Kingdom was no Mystery. The Old Testament prophets describe it in glowing terms. What they could not understand was, what was to come in between the "Sufferings" and "Glory" of Christ. 1 Pet. 1:9-12. That is, between the **"CROSS"** and the **"CROWN."** That the Gentiles were to be saved was no Mystery. Rom. 9:24-30. The "Mystery" was, that God was going to form an entirely **"NEW THING"** composed of both **"JEW"** and **"GENTILE,"** to be called the **"CHURCH."** The purpose of this Dispensation is seen in the "Divine Program" outlined by the Apostle James in his address to the First Church Council held at Jerusalem (Acts 15:13-18), where he declares that God has visited the Gentiles to "take out of them 'A PEOPLE' for His Name." The purpose of this Dispensation then is not the bringing in of the Kingdom, or the conversion of the world, but the gathering out of an "elect body," the Church.

While Israel is a "called out body" it is a "National Body," composed exclusively of the descendants of Abraham, but the Church is not a "National Body," for it is not composed of the people of any one nation, but of individuals from every kindred, people, tribe and nation.

I. THE CHURCH

The Church is not only a "called out Body," it is the **"BODY OF CHRIST."** In Eph. 1:22-23, we read— "And hath put all things under His feet, and gave Him (Jesus) to be the 'Head' over all things to the Church which is His **BODY.**" The context shows (vs. 20) that this "Headship" was not possible until Jesus had been raised from the dead, and seated at the right hand of the Father. The Church then could not have been in existence before there was a "Head," for God does not make headless things. The Church then is the "Body" of which Christ is the "Head." In 1 Cor. 12:12-13 we are told how this "Body" is formed: "For as the body is one, and hath many members; and all the members of that one body being many, are one body; so also is Christ. For by one 'Spirit' (Holy Spirit) are we all baptized into **'ONE BODY,'** whether we be Jew or Gentile, whether we be bond or free." From this we see that it is the "Baptism of the Spirit" that incorporates us into the "Body of Christ." That is, there could be no Church until the "Day of Pentecost."

The fact that the Church is a "Body" made up of "living members" shows that it is not an "Organization" but an **"ORGANISM."** As the human body is for the manifestation of a Personality, so the Church, the "Body of Christ," is for the purpose of manifesting "His Personality." The only way then the world can see Christ is through His Body the Church.

But the Church is not only the "Body" of Christ, it is to be His **BRIDE.** At present it is but a virgin espoused. 2 Cor. 11:2. Some hold that the Church cannot be both the "Body" and "Bride" of Christ, and that the "Bride" must be Israel. But we must not forget that there are "Two Brides" mentioned in the Scriptures, one in the Old Testament, and the other in the New Testament. The one in the Old Testament is Israel, the Bride of Jehovah; the one in the New Testament is the Church, the Bride of Christ. Of Israel it is said—"Thy Maker is thine husband." Isa. 54:5-8. Because of her Whoredoms, Israel is a cast-off wife, but Jehovah, her husband, promises to take her back when she ceases from her adulteries. Jer. 3:1-18; Ez. 16:1-63; Hosea, 2:1-23, 3:1-5. She will not be taken back as a "Virgin," but as a "Wife." But it is a VIRGIN that the Lamb (Christ) is to marry. So the "Wife" of the Old Testament cannot be the "Bride" (Virgin) of the New Testament. Again the "Wife" (Israel) is to reside in the earthly Jerusalem during the Millennium, while the "Bride" (the Church) will reside in the New Jerusalem. These distinctions make it clear that Israel cannot be the "Bride" of Christ. As to the Church being both the "Body" and "Bride" of Christ, we have the type of Eve who was of the "body" of Adam before she became his "bride."

WHO BELONG TO THE CHURCH?

If the Church had its origin at Pentecost and ends at the "Rapture of the Saints" (1 Thess. 4:14-17), then only those who are saved between those two events belong to the Church. The Old Testament Saints are the "Friends of the Bridegroom," but they are not the "Bride." In Rev. 19:9 we read, "Blessed are they which are called unto the 'Marriage Supper' of the Lamb." The Bride is not "called" (invited) to her own wedding, she has a place there of her own right. The "called" are the "Guests." The Old Testament Saints will be "Guests," as will also the "Blood-washed Multitude" that come out of the Tribulation, for they are not saved until after the Rapture of the Church. Rev. 7:9-17.

Angels and Heavenly Beings will be spectators of the scene, but they cannot be "Guests," as that honor is reserved for those who have been redeemed by the "Blood of the Lamb."

THE MISSION OF THE CHURCH

As we have seen, the Church is not an "Organization" but an **"Organism."** Therefore it is not a "Social Club," organized and supported solely for the benefit of its members. Neither is it a "Place of Amusement" to pander to the carnal nature of man. Nor is it a "House of Merchandise" for the sale of "Indulgences," or other commodities, whereby the money of the ungodly can be secured to save the penurious church member a little self-sacrifice. Neither is it a "Reform Bureau" to save the "bodies" of men. The reformation of men is very commendable, as are all forms of "Social Service," but that is not the work or mission of the Church. The world was just as full, if not fuller, of the evils that afflict society today, in the days of Christ, but He never, nor did the Apostles, organize any reform agencies. All the great philanthropic and civilizing agencies of the world are "By-Products" of Christianity. We are told in Acts 5: 15, that the people laid their sick in the streets that the **"Shadow of Peter"** might fall upon them and heal them. But if Peter had spent his time **"casting shadows,"** and neglected his Apostolic work of trying to save the **"SOULS"** of men, his shadow would have lost its power. Jesus knew that the source of all the evils in the world is **SIN,** and that the only way to eradicate sin is to **Regenerate the Human Heart,** and so He gave the **GOS-PEL,** and the "Mission" of the Church is to carry this Gospel to the world. **"EVANGELISM,"** not "Social Service," is the "Mission" of the Church. Mark. 16: 15-16.

The great mistake the Church has made is in appropriating to herself in this Dispensation the promises of earthly conquest and glory which belong exclusively to Israel in the "Millennial Age." As soon as the Church enters into an "Alliance with the World," and seeks the help of Parliaments, Congresses, Legislatures, Federations and Reform Societies, largely made up of ungodly men and women, she loses her spiritual power and becomes helpless as a redeeming force.

When the Church is complete it is to be "caught out" at the First or "Rapture Stage" of Christ's Second Coming. 1 Thess. 4:13-17. After the Rapture the Church is to be judged. Not for sin, but for works. Then comes

THE MARRIAGE OF THE CHURCH.

The "Marriage" of the Church is prophetically referred to by Jesus in the Parable of the "Marriage of the King's Son" (Matt. 22:1-14), and is consummated in Rev. 19:7-9.

> "Let us be glad and rejoice and give honor to Him; for the
> ### 'Marriage of the Lamb'
> is come, and His **wife** hath made herself ready. And to **her** was granted that she should be arrayed in fine linen, clean and white; for the fine linen is the righteousness of Saints. And he saith unto me, write **Blessed are they which are called unto the MARRIAGE SUPPER OF THE LAMB.**"

Notice that it does not say the "Marriage of the Bride," but the "Marriage of the **LAMB.**" That grand event will be not so much the consummation of the hopes of the Bride, as it will be the consummation of the **plan of God for His Son,** arranged for **before the foundation of the World.** Eph. 1:4. The "Marriage of the Lamb" is the consummation of the joy of Christ as a **MAN.** It would not have been possible if Christ had not been born **in the flesh.** Otherwise it would have been the union of "dissimilar natures" for the "Bride" is of "human origin." This is why Jesus took His "human nature" back with Him to Heaven, and today we have in Heaven the **MAN** Christ Jesus. 1 Tim. 2:5.

While the "Bride" was chosen for Christ "before the foundation of the world," the "espousal" could not take place until Christ assumed humanity and ascended to Heaven as the **Man** Christ Jesus. There have been many long betrothals, but Christ's has been the longest on record. He has been waiting for His Bride nearly 1900 years, but He will not have to wait much longer. Soon Heaven shall resound with the cry—

> "Let us be glad and rejoice, and give honor

to Him, for the **Marriage of the Lamb is Come.**"
Rev. 19:7.

There have been many royal weddings of international interest, where the invited guests and spectators witnessed a spectacle magnificent in its appointments, and rejoiced in a union that bound together different nations. But the wedding of the Lamb and His Bride the Church will surpass them all, for it shall unite Heaven and Earth in a bond that shall never be broken, for what God (the Father) shall join together, no man shall ever put asunder, and that union no divorce shall ever break.

II. THE KINGDOM

It is clear from the Scriptures that God has been trying to set up a "visible" Kingdom on this earth ever since the creation of man, to whom He gave dominion. Gen. 1:26-28. But that dominion was lost by the "Fall," and Satan set himself up as the "Prince of this World." Matt. 4:8-10. John 14:30. In the "Call of Abraham" God took the first step toward the setting up of a visible Kingdom on this earth, which assumed an outward form in the "Jewish Commonwealth" under Moses, but the plan was blocked by the Jews losing their "National Existence" at the time of the Babylonian Captivity B. C. 606, and the beginning of the "Times of the Gentiles." But when 600 years of the "Times of the Gentiles" had run their course, God again made a move to set up the Kingdom, and the angel Gabriel announced to Mary the Birth of the King. Luke 1:26-33. Thirty years later the King's forerunner, John the Baptist, announced that the Kingdom was "at hand" (Matt. 3:1-2), and when the King manifested Himself to Israel He Himself made the same announcement (Matt. 4:17-23), and later He sent out the "Twelve" (Matt. 10:7), and the "Seventy" (Luke 10:1-9), to proclaim the same thing. But the King was rejected and crucified, and the setting up of the Kingdom postponed, and the Kingdom took on its "Mystery Form" under the name of the "Kingdom of Heaven."

There are some who object to what they call the "Postponement Theory," and claim that the Kingdom which was "At Hand" was not an outward visible Kingdom, but a **spiritual** Kingdom, and that it was not withdrawn but is seen today in "New Born" believers. They base their claim on the fact that the earthly visible Kingdom of Christ could not be set up until after He had suffered and died on the Cross as the Saviour of men, and had risen from the dead, and ascended to the Father and received the Kingdom, and that therefore the offer of an **outward visible and earthly** Kingdom at that time was not a "bona fide" offer, and that John the Baptist and Jesus must have meant by the "Kingdom of Heaven" something else than an outward visible and earthly Kingdom. What are the facts? First, that the Old Testament scriptures teach that there is to be an earthly and visible Kingdom over which the Son of Man is to rule (Dan. 7: 13-14, 2: 34-35, 44-45; Jer. 23: 5; Zech. 14: 9), and we know that at the time of Jesus' birth there was a widespread expectation of the coming of the Messiah, and that Simeon and Anna waited in the Temple for the "Consolation of Israel." Luke 2: 25-38. We are also told that "Wise Men" came from the East to Jerusalem inquiring "Where is He that is born **KING OF THE JEWS?**" and when they had found Jesus they worshipped Him as **KING.** Matt. 2: 1-11. There can be no question but that Jesus was born to be a **KING.** It was not until Jesus was 30 years old that John the Baptist appeared at the Jordan preaching—"Repent ye: for the Kingdom of Heaven is **AT HAND."** Matt. 3: 2. And we are told that his mission was to **"Prepare the Way of the Lord."** Matt. 3: 3. Isa. 40: 3. Prepare the way of the Lord for what? Not for the "Cross" but the "Kingdom." John's message had no meaning to those who heard him and were looking for the setting up of the "Messianic Kingdom," if he did not mean by the "Kingdom of Heaven" an outward and visible earthly Kingdom. That John himself so believed is evident from the question he sent his disciples while in prison to ask Jesus—"Art Thou He that should come or do we look for another?" Matt. 11: 3. The fact that Jesus answered John's question by a number of miracles of healing, which are the "signs" of the Messianic Kingdom (Isa. 35: 1-10), and were proofs of Christ's Messiahship, and told John's disciples to so report, is proof that both John and Jesus had in mind the earthly Messianic Kingdom when they proclaimed that the "Kingdom of Heaven was **AT HAND**." It was the "Kingdom of Heaven," not because it was a Heavenly or Spiritual Kingdom, but because it was not received from men, but was given from Heaven by God the Father.

While it is true that John the Baptist pointed out to two of his own disciples Jesus as the "Lamb of God" (John 1:29), this was after Jesus' return from the "Wilderness Temptation," and had been revealed to John at the Baptism of Jesus, and does not nullify or alter the character of his previous proclamation that the Kingdom of Heaven was at hand. We must not forget that as soon as Jesus was baptised He was **"immediately"** driven into the Wilderness to be tempted of the Devil (Matt. 4:1-11, Mark 1:11-13), and it was not until 40 days after His Baptism that John pointed out to his disciples Jesus as "the Lamb of God, which taketh away the sin of the world." The words "next day" (John 1:29) refer not to the day after Jesus' Baptism, but the next day after the Priests and Levites had inquired of John whether he was the Christ or Elias. John 1:19-28. In John 1:32-34, John the Baptist testifies that he knew not Jesus as the "Lamb of God" until His Baptism. Then he knew by the descent of the Holy Spirit in the form of a dove upon Christ that He was the **"SON OF GOD."** Therefore John the Baptist knew nothing about Christ's sacrificial work at the beginning of his ministry, and his proclamation that the Kingdom of Heaven was at hand could have had no reference to a Spiritual Kingdom.

When Nathanael exclaimed—"Rabbi, Thou art the Son of God; Thou art the **KING OF ISRAEL"** (John 1:49), Jesus did not disclaim the title. When Jesus entered on His own ministry His message was the same as John the Baptist's—"Repent, for the Kingdom of Heaven is **AT HAND**." Matt. 4:17. The repentance called for was a **"NATIONAL REPENTANCE."** The Old Testament scriptures clearly teach that the Messianic Kingdom cannot be set up until Israel as a nation **REPENTS**. In Matt. 4:23 we read—"And Jesus went about all Galilee, teaching in their synagogues and preaching the 'Gospel of The Kingdom.' " While this was attended with "signs of bodily healing" we are nowhere told that the "Gospel of the Kingdom" had anything to do with the **salvation of the soul,** and as it is to be preached again after the Rapture of the Church for a "witness" unto all nations, that the time has come for the setting up of the Kingdom (Matt. 24: 14) the inference is that the "Gospel of the Kingdom" has nothing to do with "salvation," but is simply an announcement that the "Messianic Kingdom" is **AT HAND.**

When Jesus sent forth the Twelve Disciples He commanded them, saying, "Go not into the way of the Gentiles, and into any city of the Samaritans enter ye not; but go rather to the 'lost sheep' of the **HOUSE OF ISRAEL, and as ye go, preach, saying—**'The **Kingdom of Heaven** is **AT HAND.**' Heal the sick, cleanse the lepers, raise the dead, cast out devils (demons)." Matt. 10: 5-8. Note again that the works they were to perform were "Kingdom **SIGNS,**" and had no reference to the **salvation of the soul.** They did not **preach the** "Gospel of Salvation," but the "Gospel of the Kingdom." And further the "Gospel of Salvation" is for the whole world, but the Disciples were forbidden to go to any but the **"House of Israel,"** thus showing that what they preached was exclusively for Israel. That the Disciples were expecting the setting up of a visible earthly Kingdom is evidenced by the request of James and John that they might sit, one on the right hand, and the other on the left hand of Jesus in His Kingdom. Mark 10: 35-41. If there was to be no earthly Kingdom Jesus would have disabused their minds of that idea, but He confirmed it by saying that the place of honor was not for Him to give, but would be bestowed by His Father. Matt. 20: 23.

The fact that after the miracle of the "Loaves and Fishes" the multitude was desirous to take Jesus by force and make Him a **KING** (John 6: 15), reveals what they understood by the preaching of the Kingdom of Heaven being **AT HAND.** That Jesus prevented their doing so by escaping to a mountain is no evidence that He repudiated the idea of Kingship over a visible earthly Kingdom, but that to have received the Kingdom from them

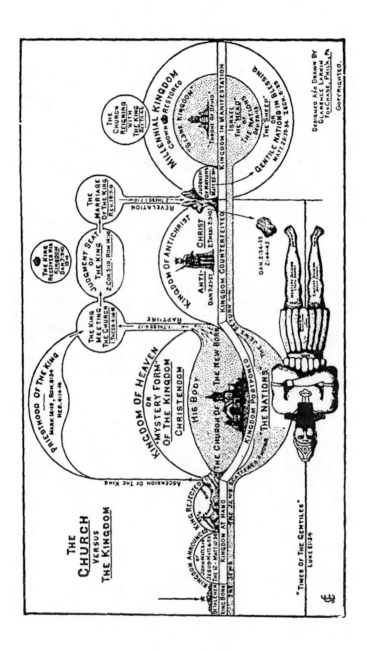

would have been wrong, for He is to receive the Kingdom from the **FATHER,** and not from men. Dan. 7:13-14. That Jesus did not deny His Kingship of an outward and visible earthly Kingdom is clear from the fact that He accepted the "Hosannahs" of the multitude when He rode into Jerusalem on Palm Sunday in fulfillment of the Messianic prophecy of Zech. 9:9. John 12:12-15. And it was as **"King OF THE JEWS"** He was crucified. Matt. 27:37. When Pilate asked Jesus—"Art Thou the King of the **JEWS?"** He evaded the question, but admitted that He was a **KING,** and to that end had been born, but that His Kingdom was **"not of this world,"** that is, it would be given to Him by God the Father, and therefore would be from Heaven. John 18:33-37.

But some one may ask, "What would have happened if the Jews, as a nation, had **repented,** and accepted Jesus as King, would the earthly Messianic Kingdom have been set up?" Certainly, but not necessarily immediately, for certain Old Testament prophecies as to Jesus' death and resurrection had to be fulfilled, for He had to die for the redemption of the race, before He could assume His office as King. But this could and would have been fulfilled by the Roman Government seizing Jesus and crucifying Him as a usurper, and with Jesus' Resurrection and Ascension, Daniel's 69th week would have terminated, and the 70th week begun without a break, and at its close Jesus would have descended and set up His earthly Kingdom.

But you ask, "What about the Church? If it was God's Eternal Purpose to form the Church (Eph. 1:4), how could it have been formed if there was no break or gap between Daniel's 69th and 70th week, and how therefore could there have been a 'bona fide' offer of an earthly Kingdom to Israel?" The question is hypothetical and based on the supposition that something might have happened that God foresaw would not happen. God's foreknowledge that the Jewish nation would not at that time heed the announcement that the Kingdom of Heaven was at hand and repent, does not militate against the sincerity of the announcement any more than the offer of spiritual salvation by a preacher of the Gospel to an audience of

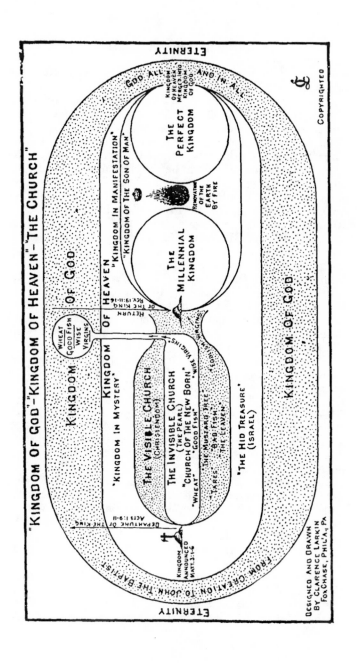

"KINGDOM OF GOD"–"KINGDOM OF HEAVEN"–"THE CHURCH"

FROM CREATION TO JOHN THE BAPTIST

ETERNITY

ETERNITY

KINGDOM OF GOD

KINGDOM OF GOD

KINGDOM OF GOD

KINGDOM OF HEAVEN

"Kingdom in Mystery"

"Kingdom in Manifestation"

"KINGDOM OF THE SON OF MAN"

GOD ALL AND IN ALL

THE PERFECT KINGDOM

KINGDOM OF HEAVEN MERGED INTO KINGDOM OF GOD

THE MILLENNIAL KINGDOM

RENOVATION OF THE EARTH BY FIRE

RETURN OF THE KING
REV. 19:11-16

THE VISIBLE CHURCH
(CHRISTENDOM)

THE INVISIBLE CHURCH
(THE PEARL)

"CHURCH OF THE NEW BORN"

"WHEAT"
"TARES"
"THE MUSTARD TREE"
"THE LEAVEN"
"GOOD FISH"
"BAD FISH"
"WISE VIRGINS"
"FOOLISH VIRGINS"

WHEAT
GOOD FISH
WISE VIRGINS

"THE HID TREASURE"
(ISRAEL)

DEPARTURE OF THE KING
ACTS 1:9-11

KINGDOM ANNOUNCED
MATT. 3:1-16

COPYRIGHTED

DESIGNED AND DRAWN
BY CLARENCE LARKIN
FOXCHASE, PHIL'A., PA.

sinners who he has every reason to believe will refuse his offer, is not a sincere and "bona fide" offer.

God's Plan and Purpose in the Ages is based upon His **FORE-KNOWLEDGE.** If God had not foreseen that the Jews would reject the King and therefore the Kingdom, He would have planned for the formation of the Church at some other time than this present Dispensation. As the Church was to be purchased by the precious blood of Christ (Acts 20:28, 1 Pet. 1:18-21), it was necessary that Jesus should be rejected and crucified, and that by His own nation, for the Prophet Zechariah (Zech. 12:10) foretold that the Jews should look upon Him whom they had **PIERCED.** But God's foreknowledge did not require or compel the Jewish nation to reject Jesus, any more than Jesus' foreknowledge that Judas would betray Him compelled Judas to so do. The possibility of the Church being crowded out by the repentance of the Jewish nation did not enter into the "Plan of God," who foresaw the refusal of Israel to accept Jesus as King, and that Israel would not nationally repent until after the Church had been formed and taken out of the world.

In expounding the Scriptures we are not to take something that belongs to a **"PAST"** and a **"FUTURE"** Dispensation and put it in the **"PRESENT"** Dispensation. For instance, **"THE KINGDOM."** The **"PAST"** and **"COMING"** Dispensations have to do with **"THE KINGDOM,"** but the "Present" has to do with the **CHURCH.** The **"Kingdom"** is an outward, visible and earthly **"POLITICAL ORGANIZATION,"** and is to be **"set up"** on the earth (Dan. 2:44); while the "Church" is an invisible and heavenly **"SPIRITUAL ORGANISM"** that is to be **"caught out."** 1 Thess. 4:16-17. The "Kingdom" was prepared **FROM** the "Foundation of the World." Matt. 25:34. The "Church" was chosen in Him **"BEFORE"** the "Foundation of the World." Eph. 1:4. The "Church" then is not the "Kingdom." See the Chart on "The Church versus The Kingdom." Page 54.

Here we must distinguish between the "Kingdom of God," the "Kingdom of Heaven," and the Church. See the Chart on the above, page 56. The "Kingdom of God" is the "Reign of God" in the Universe over all His created creatures, and includes time and eternity, heaven and earth. It is spiritual and "cometh not with observation." Luke 17:20, 21. It is entered by the "New Birth," (John 3:5); and is not "meat" and "drink," but "Righteousness and Peace, and Joy in the Holy Ghost." Rom. 14:17.

The "Kingdom of Heaven" is a New Testament term, and is found in Matthew's Gospel only, where it is mentioned 32 times. Its character is described in the 12 "Kingdom of Heaven Parables" given in **Matt. 13:1-50; 18:23-35; 20:1-16; 22:1-14; 25:1-30.** From these Parables we see that the "Kingdom of Heaven" is limited as to its Time and its Sphere. Its Time is from the First to the Second Coming of Christ, and its Sphere is over that part of the world that we call Christendom. In the "Kingdom of Heaven" there is a mixture of good and evil, of "Wheat" and "Tares," of "Good Fish" and "Bad Fish," of "Wise Virgins" and "Foolish Virgins."

After the Resurrection of Jesus the hope of an earthly visible Kingdom was revived, and just before His Ascension the Disciples asked Him—"Lord, wilt Thou **at this time** restore the Kingdom to Israel?" His reply was—"It is not for you to know the 'Times' and 'Seasons' which the Father hath put in His own power." Acts 1:6-7. Now Jesus did not deny that there was to be a "visible earthly Kingdom," He simply told the Disciples that it was not for them to **"know"** when it would be set up. If Jesus came simply to set up a "Spiritual" Kingdom in this Dispensation then common honesty demanded that He at that solemn moment when He was about to leave His Disciples and go back to the Father should have disabused His Disciples' minds of their false hope, and told them plainly that the Kingdom He came to set up was "Spiritual" and not earthly. But He did nothing of the kind. He left them with the belief that there was to be an "earthly and visible Kingdom" some day.

The King having been rejected it was impossible then to set up the Kingdom, so the Kingdom took on another aspect known as the "Kingdom in Mystery," described in the twelve "Kingdom of Heaven" parables of Matthew's Gospel. When the Disciples of Jesus said unto Him—

"Why speakest Thou unto them in 'Parables?'" He replied, "Because it is given unto you to know the 'MYSTERIES' of the Kingdom of Heaven." Matt. 13:10-11. In verse 35 He gives as His reason for speaking to them in Parables, that it might be fulfilled as spoken by the Prophet—"I will open my mouth in 'Parables'; I will utter things which have been kept 'SECRET' from the foundation of the world." The "Kingdom of Heaven Parables" therefore cannot describe the "Millennial Kingdom" for it was no "secret" to the Old Testament Prophets. Neither do they describe a "Spiritual Kingdom," for the figures they use are all of an "earthly" nature. They must then describe the character of the Present Dispensation in its earthly aspect during the absence of the King. For a full exposition of these Parables see my Larger Work on "Dispensational Truth."

THE KINGDOM IN MANIFESTATION

Jesus is the "Certain Nobleman" who went into a "Far Country" to receive for Himself a Kingdom, and to return. Luke 19:12. And when He comes back He will reward His servants, the Jews, and give them authority over as many cities as they deserve. Jesus has not yet received the Kingdom. He must finish His High Priestly and Mediatorial work first. Daniel describes the event in Dan. 7:13-14. The form of Government will be a "Theocracy." Christ will reign through a "King" or "Prince" called **DAVID** (Hosea 3:5; Jer. 30:9; Ez. 37:24; Ez. 34:24), whose Throne shall be at Jerusalem. The Temple will be rebuilt, and the "Aaronic Priesthood" re-established. Ez. 44:15-31. There will be a revival of the Land of Palestine (Joel 3:18), and the length of human life extended. Isa. 65:20-22. Zech. 8:4. For a full description of the Kingdom and the Millennium see my Larger Work on "Dispensational Truth."

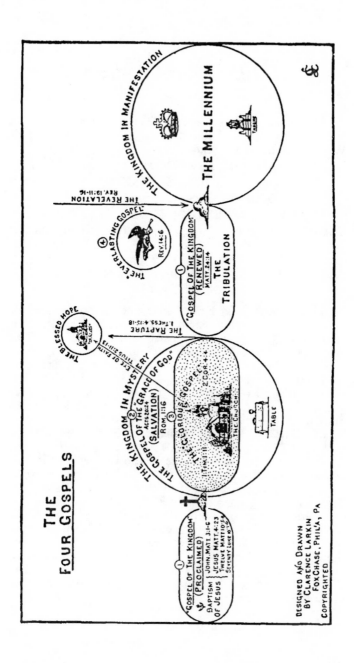

THE
FOUR GOSPELS

THE KINGDOM IN MANIFESTATION

THE MILLENNIUM

THE REVELATION
REV. 19:11-16

THE EVERLASTING GOSPEL
REV. 14:6

"GOSPEL OF THE KINGDOM"
(RENEWED)
MATT. 24:14
THE TRIBULATION

THE BLESSED HOPE
TITUS 2:11-13

THE RAPTURE
1.THESS. 4:13-18

THE KINGDOM IN MYSTERY

THE GOSPEL OF THE "GRACE OF GOD"

THE GOSPEL OF THE "GRACE OF GOD"
(SALVATION)
ROM. 1:16

"THE GLORIOUS GOSPEL"
2 COR. 4

1 TIM. 1:11

"EYE OF FAITH"

THE CHURCH

TABLE

"GOSPEL OF THE KINGDOM"
(PROCLAIMED)
BAPTISM { JOHN MATT. 3:1-6
OF JESUS { JESUS MATT. 4:23
          { TWELVE MATT. 10:5-8
          { SEVENTY LUKE 10:1-9

DESIGNED AND DRAWN
BY CLARENCE LARKIN
FOX CHASE, PHILA., PA
COPYRIGHTED

V
The Four Gospels

The word "Gospel" means "**Good News,**" and is so familiar that its application is supposed to be uniform. When, therefore, we read of

The Gospel of the **KINGDOM,**

The Gospel of the **GRACE OF GOD,**

The **GLORIOUS GOSPEL,** and

The **EVERLASTING GOSPEL**

it is taken for granted that they all refer to one and the same thing. But this is not true.

1.   THE GOSPEL OF THE "KINGDOM."
Matt. 24 : 14.

This is the "Good News" that God purposes to set up a Kingdom on this earth over which David's Son, JESUS, shall reign, as prophesied in Luke 1 : 32-33. Two preachings of this Gospel are mentioned, one past, beginning with the ministry of John the Baptist, and preached by Jesus and His Disciples, but it ended with the rejection of Jesus as King. This Gospel is to be preached again after the Church is taken out. It will be the fulfilment of Matt. 24 : 14, where it says: "This Gospel of '**THE KINGDOM**' shall be preached in all the world for a **WITNESS** unto all nations; and then shall the end come." This has no reference to the Gospel that is now being preached to the nations. It is the Gospel of **SALVATION,** but the "Gospel of the Kingdom" is not for "Salvation" but for a **WITNESS,** that is, it is the announcement that the time has come to SET UP THE KINGDOM. It will be preached by Elijah the forerunner (Mal. 4 : 5-6), and by others who shall be commissioned to bear the news to all nations as a proclamation of the coming of Christ as King to occupy the "Throne of David," and for the purpose of regathering Israel to the Promised Land.

2. THE GOSPEL OF "THE GRACE OF GOD."
Acts 20:24.

This is the "Good News" that Jesus Christ, the rejected King, died on the Cross for our **SALVATION.** This form of the Gospel is described in many ways. It is called the **"GOSPEL OF GOD"** (Rom. 1:1), because it has its source in the **LOVE OF GOD.** John 3:16. Its **Character** is **GRACE.** Acts 20:24. Its Subject is **CHRIST** (Rom. 1:16; 2 Cor. 10:14), and it is the **POWER OF GOD UNTO SALVATION.** And it is the **"GOSPEL OF PEACE,"** because it makes peace between the sinner and God, and brings peace to the soul. Eph. 6:15.

3. THE "GLORIOUS" GOSPEL.
2 Cor. 4:4; 1 Tim. 1:11.

The **"GLORIOUS GOSPEL"** is that phase of the Gospel of "The Grace of God" that speaks of Him who is in the **GLORY,** and has been **GLORIFIED,** and who is bringing many sons **TO GLORY.** Heb. 2:10. It has special reference to His Second Coming, and is especially comforting to those who are looking for His **GLORIOUS APPEARING** (Titus 2:13), and it is to this Gospel that Satan, the "God of this Age," is particularly anxious to "blind the minds" of those who believe not in the Pre-Millennial coming of the Lord. 2 Cor. 4:3-4.

4. THE "EVERLASTING" GOSPEL.
Rev. 14:6.

This Gospel will be proclaimed just before the "Vial Judgments," and by an angel. It is the only Gospel committed to an angel. It is neither the Gospel of the "Kingdom," nor of "Grace." Its burden is not **SALVATION** but **JUDGMENT**—"Fear God, and give glory to Him; for the **HOUR OF HIS JUDGMENT IS COME."**

It is "Good News" to Israel, and all who are passing through the "fires of Judgment," because it declares that their troubles will soon end in the Judgment and Destruction of Antichrist and his followers. It calls on men to

worship God as **"CREATOR,"** and not as "Saviour" and
so it is called in the Revised version—**"THE ETERNAL
GOSPEL,"** the Gospel that has been proclaimed from
Eden down by Patriarchs and Prophets, and not an
"Everlasting Gospel" in the sense that it saves men for
all eternity. Its burden is not "Repent," or "do this" or
"do that," but—**"FEAR GOD,** and give **GLORY TO
HIM;** for the **HOUR OF HIS JUDGMENT IS COME;**
and **WORSHIP HIM THAT MADE HEAVEN, AND
EARTH, AND THE SEA, AND THE FOUNTAINS
OF WATERS."** From this we see how important it is
to distinguish between the various Gospels, not only as to
their message, but the period to which they apply, otherwise there will be confusion and false teaching. See
Chart, "The Four Gospels." Page 60.

There is also **"ANOTHER GOSPEL"** (Gal. 1:6-12,
2 Cor. 11:4), which is not another, and which Paul repudiated. It is a perversion of the true Gospel and has
many seductive forms, and in the main teaches that
"FAITH" is **NOT SUFFICIENT** to Salvation, nor able
to keep and perfect, and so emphasizes **"GOOD
WORKS."** Col. 2:18-23, Heb. 6:1, 9:14. The Apostle
Paul pronounces a fearful "Anathema" upon its preachers
and teachers. Gal. 1:8-9.

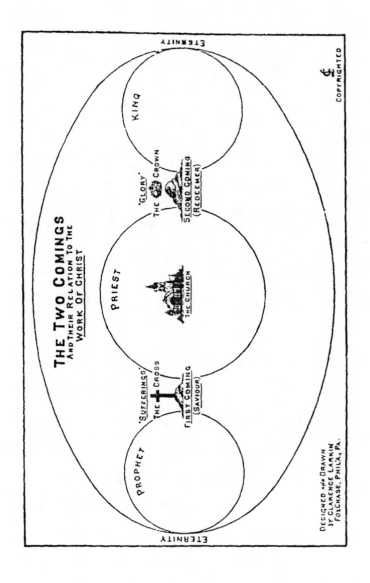

THE TWO COMINGS
AND THEIR RELATION TO THE
WORK OF CHRIST

ETERNITY

ETERNITY

PROPHET

PRIEST

KING

"SUFFERINGS"
THE CROSS
FIRST COMING
(SAVIOUR)

THE CHURCH

"GLORY"
THE CROWN
SECOND COMING
(REDEEMER)

DESIGNED AND DRAWN
BY CLARENCE LARKIN
FOXCHASE, PHILA., PA.

COPYRIGHTED

VI

The Two Advents

The careful reader of the Old Testament will perceive that there are two lines of prophecy in reference to the Messiah. The first speaks of Him as a

SUFFERING SAVIOUR

1. The **TIME** of His First Coming. Dan. 9:25.

2. The **PLACE** of His Birth. Micah 5:2 (Luke 2:4).

3. His **VIRGIN BIRTH.** Isa. 7:14 (Matt. 1:18).

4. His **ANOINTING BY THE HOLY SPIRIT.** Isa. 61:1 (John 1:32-34).

5. **DESPISED** and **REJECTED,** a **MAN OF SORROWS** and acquainted with **GRIEF.** Isa. 53:3. (Matt. 26:36-39).

6. **SOLD** for 30 pieces of silver. Zech. 11:12 (Matt. 26:15).

7. **BETRAYED** by a friend. Psa. 41:9 (Matt. 26:49-50).

8. **FORSAKEN** by His Disciples. Zech. 13:7 (Mark 14:27).

9. **ACCUSED** by "False Witnesses." Psa. 35:11 (Matt. 26:59-60).

10. **SPIT UPON** and **SCOURGED.** Isa. 50:6 (Mark 14:65).

11. **NAILED** to the Cross. Psa. 22:16 (Luke 23:33).

12. **MOCKED** on the Cross. Psa. 22:7-8. (Matt. 27:39-40).

13. **INTENSE SUFFERER.** Psa. 22:14. (Luke 22:44).

14. **CRUCIFIED** with thieves. Isa. 53:12 (Mark 15:27-28).

15. **BURIED** as a rich man. Isa. 53:9 (Matt. 27:57-60).

The second line of prophecy speaks of Messiah as a

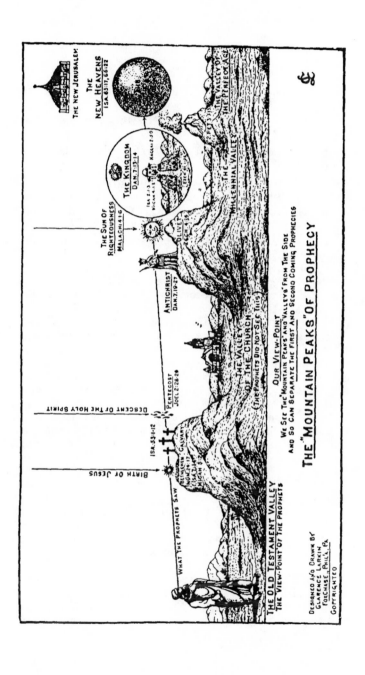

THE "MOUNTAIN PEAKS" OF PROPHECY

DESIGNED AND DRAWN BY
CLARENCE LARKIN
FOXCHASE, PHILA., PA.
COPYRIGHTED

GLORIOUS KING.

1. He was to be a "**RIGHTEOUS BRANCH.**" Jer. 23: 5-8.

2. He was to have a "**KINGDOM.**" Dan. 2: 44. Dan. 7: 13-14.

3. He was to reign on the "**THRONE OF DAVID.**" 1 Sam. 7: 16. Isa. 9: 6-7.

4. He was to rule the nations with a "**ROD OF IRON.**" Psa. 2: 6-9.

5. His reign was to be **GLORIOUS.** Psa. 72: 1-20. Isa. 2: 1-4. Isa. 32: 1-4, 15-20. Zech. 14: 16-21.

These are but a few of the many prophecies contained in the Old Testament as to the coming of the Messiah.

Peter tells us (1 Pet. 1: 10-11) that the Old Testament prophets did not perceive the difference between the "**Sufferings**" and "**Glory**" of Christ. That is, they did not see that there was a "**TIME SPACE,**" between the "**CROSS**" and the "**CROWN**" covering the "Present Dispensation," and that the "Cross" would precede the "Crown." It was because of this that the religious leaders of Christ's day rejected Him. But we have no such excuse. We live on this side of the "Cross," and we can readily pick out all the prophecies that were fulfilled at Christ's "First Coming" and apply the remainder to His "Second Coming." It is clear then that Christ's "First Coming," important as it was, is not the "doctrinal centre" of the Scriptures, that is, Christ's "First Coming" was not the centre of a circle that contains all doctrine, but was one of the foci of an ellipse of which the other is the "**SECOND COMING.**" See the Chart of "The Two Comings," page 64.

On this Chart the "First Coming" is indicated by the "**CROSS,**" and the "Second Coming" by the "**CROWN.**" Between the "Comings" we have the "**TABLE**" which points backward to the "Cross" and forward to the "Crown."

While the First and Second Comings of Christ are separated by this Dispensation they are nevertheless not complete in themselves, the Second necessitated the First, and the First demands the Second. They are both neces-

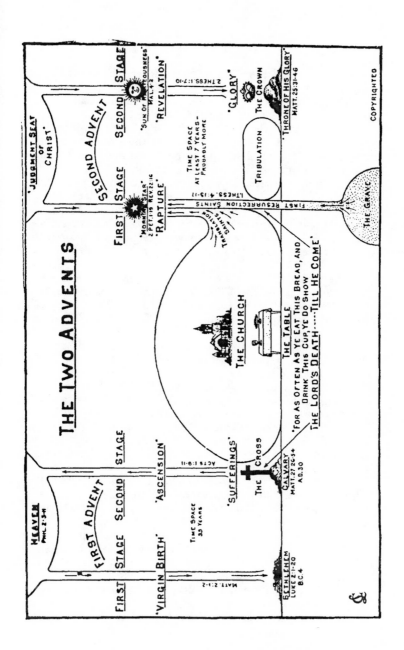

sary to complete the Plan of Salvation. The First Coming was for the salvation of my "SOUL"; the Second is for the salvation of my "BODY," for there can be no resurrection of the body until Christ comes back.

The Chart on the "Mountain Peaks of Prophecy," page 66, illustrates how it was that the Old Testament Prophets failed to distinguish between the "First" and "Second" Comings. From the Prophets' "viewpoint" they saw the Birth of Jesus, the Crucifixion, the Outpouring of the Holy Spirit, the Antichrist, Christ coming as the "Sun of Righteousness," the Kingdom, as peaks of one great mountain, they did not see what we standing off to the side now see, that those peaks belonged to two different mountains separated by the "Valley of the Church."

The Chart of "The Two Advents," page 68, will give us a clear idea of the "Two Advents." The "First Advent," like the "Second Advent" was in "Two Stages." In the "First Stage" Jesus came "SECRETLY" from Heaven and was born of a virgin as had been foretold by the Prophet Isaiah. Isa. 7:14. Matt. 1:18-23. In the "Second Stage" He came "PUBLICLY" and was proclaimed as King, as foretold by the Prophet Zechariah. Zech. 9:9. Luke 19:28-40. Matt. 21:4-5. Between the two stages of His First Coming there was a "Time Space" of 33 years, from B. C. 4 to A. D. 30.

At His "Second Coming" there will also be "Two Stages." At the "First Stage" He will come "SECRETLY" into the atmosphere of the earth, and the Church will be "caught out" to meet Him. 1 Thess. 4:16-17. This was not revealed to the Old Testament Prophets. This is known as the "Rapture." At the "Second Stage" He will come "PUBLICLY" all the way to the earth and stand again on the Mount of Olives from which He ascended, as foretold by the Prophet Zechariah (Zech. 14:1-4), and by the "Two MEN" (Moses and Elijah) who stood by when He ascended. Acts 1:9-11. This is spoken of as the "Revelation." 2 Thess. 1:7-10. The "Time Space" between the "Rapture" and the "Revelation" will be at least 7 years, unless it be shortened (Matt. 24:22), but probably it will be longer, as the "Rapture

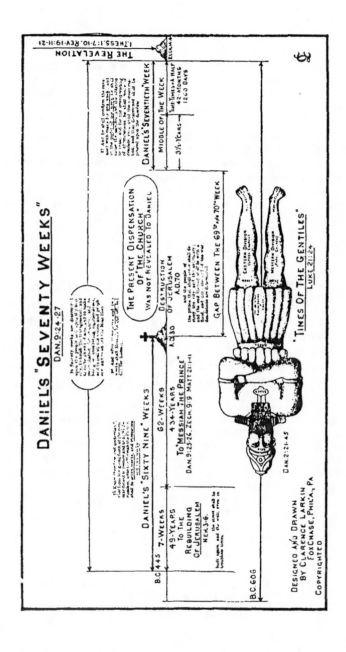

Daniel's "Seventy Weeks"
Dan.9:24-27

THE REVELATION
I.THESS.I:7-10, REV.19:11-21

Daniel's "Sixty Nine" Weeks

Daniel's Seventieth Week

7-Weeks
49-Years To The Rebuilding Of Jerusalem
Neh.3-6.

62-Weeks
434-Years To "Messiah The Prince"
Dan.9:25-26, Zech.9:9 Matt.21:1-11

Middle Of The Week
3½-Years

That Time + A Half
42 Months
1260 Days

B.C.445

B.C.606

Destruction Of Jerusalem A.D.70

The Present Dispensation Of "The Church" Was Not Revealed To Daniel

Gap Between The 69th And 70th Week

A.D.30

Eastern Division

Western Division

Dan.2:21-45

"Times Of The Gentiles"
Luke 21:24

Designed And Drawn By Clarence Larkin FoxChase, Phila., Pa
Copyrighted

of the Church" may take place some time before the commencement of the "Last Week" of Daniel's "Seventy Weeks." Dan. 9:27. See the Chart of "Daniel's Seventy Weeks," page 70. When Christ comes at the "Rapture" He will be the "Bright and Morning Star," 2 Pet. 1:19, Rev. 22:16. When He comes at the "Revelation" He will be the "Sun of Righteousness." Malachi 4:2.

As the prophecies in reference to Christ's First Advent were **literally** fulfilled, so must the prophecies of His Second Advent. We cannot **literalize** one and **spiritualize** the other. Let us see what the New Testament has to say about

THE SECOND ADVENT.

I. AS TO THE FACT

1. THE TESTIMONY OF JESUS HIMSELF.

John 14:2, 3. "In my Father's house are many mansions; if it were not so I would have told you. I go to prepare a place for you. And if I go and prepare a place for you I will **come again,** and receive you unto myself; that where I am, there ye may be also."

2. THE TESTIMONY OF HEAVENLY BEINGS.

Acts 1:10, 11. "And while they looked steadfastly toward heaven as he went up, behold, two **men** stood by them in white apparel; which also said, 'Ye men of Galilee, why stand ye gazing up into heaven? This **SAME JESUS,** which is taken up from you into heaven, shall so come **IN LIKE MANNER** as ye have seen him go into heaven.'"

This passage declares that the **SAME JESUS** shall return **IN LIKE MANNER** as He went, that is, that His return will be **visible** and **personal.** The two "men" that "stood by" were probably Moses and Elijah. They appeared with Jesus on the Mt. of Transfiguration, they were doubtless the **"two men"** who testified to the women at the tomb that Jesus had risen (Luke 24:4, 5), and they will be the **"Two Witnesses"** that shall testify during the Tribulation. Rev. 11:3-12.

3. THE TESTIMONY OF THE APOSTLES.

PAUL—"For our conversation is in heaven; from whence also we look for the Saviour, the Lord Jesus Christ, who shall change our vile body, that it may be fashioned like unto his glorious body, according to the working whereby he is able even to subdue all things unto himself." Phil. 3:20, 21.

JAMES—"Be patient therefore, brethren, unto the coming of the Lord." James 5:7.

PETER—"For we have not followed cunningly devised fables when we made known unto you the power and coming of our Lord Jesus Christ, but were eye-witnesses of his majesty." 2 Pet. 1:16.

Peter here refers to the Transfiguration of Christ on the mount (Matt. 17:1-5), which was a type of His Second Coming. Moses was a type of the "resurrection saints," and Elijah of those who shall be translated without dying.

JOHN—"And now, little children, abide in him; that, when he shall appear we may have confidence, and not be ashamed before him at his coming." 1 John 2:28.

"Behold, he cometh with clouds; and every eye shall see him, and they also which pierced him, and all kindreds of the earth shall wail because of him. Even so, Amen." Rev. 1:7.

4. THE TESTIMONY OF THE LORD'S SUPPER.

"For as often as ye eat this bread, and drink this cup, ye do show the Lord's death till he come." 1 Cor. 11:26.

The Lord's Supper is not a permanent ordinance. It will be discontinued when the Lord returns. It is a Memorial Feast. It looks back to the "Cross" and forward to the "Coming."

THE FIVE THEORIES

While the majority of professing Christians admit the fact of the Second Coming of Christ, they are not agreed as to the "manner" or "time." There are five theories as to the Second Coming.

1. **That His Coming Again Is "SPIRITUAL" and Was Fulfilled at Pentecost.**

It was not Christ but the Holy Spirit that came at Pentecost, and his coming was conditioned on Christ's absence, for Jesus said, "It is expedient for you that I go away; for if I go not away, the Comforter (H. S.) will not come unto you; but if I **DEPART**, I will **SEND HIM UNTO YOU.**" John 16:7. If the Holy Spirit is only another manifestation of Christ, then they are identical, and that **NULLIFIES THE TRINITY.** The fact is, the whole New Testament was written after Pentecost, and declares over 150 times that the Second Coming of Christ was still future. And more, none of the events predicted as accompanying the Second Coming occurred at Pentecost, such as the **Resurrection of the "Dead in Christ,"** the **Translation of the "Living Saints,"** the "Binding of Satan," etc.

2. **That the "CONVERSION OF THE SINNER" is the Coming of the Lord.**

This cannot be, for at conversion the sinner comes to Christ, not Christ to the sinner; and the sinner's conversion is the work of the Holy Spirit, and not the work of Christ. It is true that there is such a thing as the spiritual indwelling of Christ in the believer, but His Second Coming, like His First Coming is to be an outward, visible, personal coming.

3. **That "DEATH" is the Coming of the Lord.**

The text that is used more than any other for funeral sermons is—"Watch, therefore; for ye know neither the day nor the hour wherein the Son of Man cometh." Matt. 25:13. The context shows that this refers to a future coming of Christ. Christ could not come to the earth every time a person dies for two reasons—

(1) A soul passes into eternity every second, and this would necessitate Christ's remaining continuously on the earth.

(2) Christ is engaged in His High Priestly functions in the Heavenlies, and could not leave them to come to the earth for the souls of the dying.

The fact is, that at death the believer goes to Christ. Christ does not come for him. Death is always spoken of as a departure. "Absent from the body, **present** (at home) with the Lord." 2 Cor. 5:6-8.

If Jesus had meant by His Second Coming "**Death**," he would have said to His Disciples—"If I go and prepare a place for you, I will send 'Death' to bring you to myself," but He did not. He said—"**I will come again** and receive you unto myself." The last chapter of John's Gospel settles the matter. Peter said to Jesus—"Lord, and what shall this man (referring to John) do? Jesus saith unto him, If I will that he tarry **till I come**, what is that to thee? Follow thou me. Then went this saying abroad among the brethren, that that disciple (John) **should not DIE**." John 21:21-23. We see from this that the Disciples did not think that the "Coming of the Lord" meant "death." There was a great difference between these two things in their mind. Death is an enemy (1 Cor. 15:26, 55), it holds us in the grave, it robs the body of its attractiveness, it is the "Wages of Sin" (Rom. 6:23), and the result of God's wrath, while the Second Coming of Christ is a manifestation of His love. Christ is the "Prince of Life." There can be no death where He is. Death flees at His coming. When He was on earth nothing could remain dead in His presence. His Coming is not death but resurrection. He is the "**Resurrection**" and the "**Life**," and when He Comes, He will change our **vile body**, that it may be fashioned like unto His "Glorious Body." Phil. 3:20, 21.

4. That the "**DESTRUCTION OF JERUSALEM**" in A. D. 70 by the Romans Was the Second Coming of the Lord.

The Lord was not present at the destruction of Jerusalem. It was destroyed by Roman soldiers and none of the things that are to occur at the "Second Coming" occurred at the destruction of Jerusalem such as the resurrection of the dead, the translation of living saints, and the physical changes that are to occur at Jerusalem and in the land of Palestine at Christ's coming. Zech. 14:4-11. Ez. 47:1-12. Christ's purpose in coming back is not to destroy Jerusalem, but to **RESTORE** it. It must be trodden down of the Gentiles until the "Times of the Gentiles" are fulfilled, "then shall they see the Son of Man coming in a cloud with power and great glory." Luke 21 : 24-28. The Book of Revelation, written 26 years after the destruction of Jerusalem, speaks of the Second Coming of Christ as still future.

5. That the "DIFFUSION OF CHRISTIANITY" is the Second Coming of the Lord.

This cannot be true, for the "Diffusion of Christianity" is gradual, whereas the Scriptures declare that the "Return of the Lord" shall be SUDDEN and UNEXPECTED, as a "Thief in the Night." Matt. 24 : 27, 36, 42, 44. 1 Thess. 5 : 2. Rev. 3 : 3. Again the "Diffusion of Christianity" is a process, while the Scriptures invariably speak of the "Return of the Lord" as an EVENT. The diffusion of Christianity brings Salvation to the wicked, whereas the "Return of the Lord" is said to bring not salvation but SUDDEN DESTRUCTION. 1 Thess. 5 : 2, 3 ; 2 Thess. 1 : 7-10.

II. AS TO THE TIME

Of the exact time we cannot be certain. When Jesus was on the earth He said—"But of that day and that hour knoweth no man, no, not the angels which are in heaven, neither (not yet) the Son, but the Father." Mark 13 : 32. After His Resurrection and before His Ascension, He refused to satisfy the curiosity of His Disciples, saying to them—"It is not for you to know the 'times' or the 'seasons' which the Father hath put in his own power." Acts 1 : 7.

While we do not know the day or the hour of Christ's Coming we know that it will be

PRE-MILLENNIAL.

By Pre-Millennial we mean before the Millennium. That is, before the period of a "Thousand Years" spoken of in Rev. 20 : 1-6. This period is spoken of in other scriptures as "The Kingdom," and is described in glowing terms by the prophets as a time when the earth shall be blessed with a universal rule of righteousness. The passage in Rev. 20 : 1-6 simply tells us that the length of the period shall be 1000 years.

The very structure of the New Testament demands that Christ shall return **before** the Millennium. Here are a few reasons.

1.   When Christ comes He will **RAISE THE DEAD**, but the Righteous dead are to be raised **BEFORE** the Millennium, that they may reign with Christ during the 1000 years, hence there can be no Millennium before Christ comes. Rev. 20:5.

2.   When Christ comes He will **SEPARATE THE "TARES" FROM THE "WHEAT,"** but as the Millennium is a period of **UNIVERSAL RIGHTEOUSNESS** the separation of the "Tares" and "Wheat" must take place **BEFORE** the Millennium, therefore there can be no Millennium before Christ comes. Matt. 13:40-43.

3.   When Christ comes Satan **SHALL BE BOUND**, but as Satan is to be bound during the Millennium, there can be no Millennium until Christ comes. Rev. 20:1-3.

4.   When Christ comes Antichrist is to be **DE-STROYED**, but as Antichrist is to be destroyed **before** the Millennium there can be no Millennium until Christ comes. 2 Thess. 2:8; Rev. 19:20.

5.   When Christ comes the Jews are to be **RE-STORED TO THEIR OWN LAND**, but as they are to be restored to their own land **BEFORE** the Millennium, there can be no Millennium before Christ comes. Ez. 36:24-28; Rev. 1:7; Zech. 12:10.

6.   When Christ comes it will be **unexpectedly**, and we are commanded to watch lest He take us **unawares**. Now if He is not coming until **AFTER** the Millennium, and the Millennium is not yet here, why command us to watch for an event that is over 1000 years off?

III.   AS TO THE MANNER

He will return in the **SAME MANNER** as He went. Acts 1:11. He went up **BODILY** and **VISIBLY** and He shall come in like manner. He went in a cloud, and He will return in a cloud. "Behold, He cometh with the **clouds; and every eye shall see Him**, and they also which **pierced Him**; and all kindreds of the earth shall wail **because of Him**." Rev. 1:7. The only difference will be **that He went** up alone, He will return as a King (Luke

19:12), followed by a retinue of the angelic hosts. "For the Son of Man shall come in the glory of His Father with his angels; and then He shall reward every man according to his works." Matt. 16:27. His "Return" however will be in

TWO STAGES.

He will come first into the region of our atmosphere, and the "dead in Christ," and the "living saints" shall be "caught up" to meet Him "IN THE AIR." Then after the risen and translated saints have been judged and rewarded for their works, and they, as the Church, the Bride of Christ, have been married to Him, He will come with them to the earth and land on the Mount of Olives, the place from whence He ascended. Zech. 14:4.

The First Stage of His Return is called "THE RAPTURE"; the Second Stage—"THE REVELATION." The time between the two Stages is not less than seven years, and is occupied in the heavens by the "JUDGMENT OF BELIEVERS FOR WORKS," and on the earth by "THE GREAT TRIBULATION."

THE RAPTURE

The Rapture is described in 1 Thess. 4:15-17. "For this we say unto you by the word of the Lord, that we which are alive and remain unto the coming of the Lord shall not prevent them which are asleep. For the Lord HIMSELF shall descend from heaven with a shout, with the voice of the Archangel (Michael) and with the trump of God; and the DEAD IN CHRIST shall rise first; then we which are ALIVE AND REMAIN (saints only) shall be caught up together with them in the clouds, to meet the Lord IN THE AIR, and so shall we ever be with the Lord."

From this we see that "The Rapture" will be twofold.
1. The Resurrection of the "DEAD IN CHRIST."
2. The Translation of the "LIVING SAINTS."

This twofold character of "The Rapture" Jesus revealed to Martha when He was about to raise her brother Lazarus. He said to her:

"I am the 'Resurrection and the Life,' he that believeth in Me, though he were dead yet shall he LIVE (First

Resurrection Saints) ; and whosoever **LIVETH** (is alive when I come back) and believeth in Me shall **NEVER DIE.**" John 11:25, 26. This twofold character of The Rapture, Paul emphasizes in his immortal chapter on the Resurrection.

"Behold, I show you a **Mystery**, we shall not all **Sleep**, but we shall **All Be Changed**, in a moment, in the twinkling of an eye, at the last trump; for the trumpet shall sound, and the **dead** shall be **raised**, and **we** shall be **changed**. For this **Corruptible** (the dead in Christ) must put on **incorruption**, and this **mortal** (the living saints) must put on **immortality**. So when this **corruptible** shall have put on **incorruption**, and this **mortal** shall have put on **immortality**, then shall be brought to pass the saying that is written, **DEATH IS SWALLOWED UP IN VICTORY.**

   O DEATH, WHERE IS THY STING?
   O GRAVE, WHERE IS THY VICTORY?"
               1 Cor. 15:51-57.

The last two lines refer only to those who are "changed without dying," for it is only those who will not die who can shout—

   "O Death, Where Is Thy Sting?
   "O Grave, Where Is Thy Victory?"

In 2 Cor. 5:1-4, Paul expresses his longing, and the longing of the Saints, to be among those who should not be "unclothed" by Death, but who should be "clothed upon" by Immortality "without dying."

"For we know that if our earthly house of this tabernacle (the body), were **dissolved** (that is die), we have a building of God, an house not made with hands eternal in the heavens. For in this (body) we groan, earnestly desiring to be 'clothed upon' with our house which is from heaven; if so be that being 'clothed' we shall not be found naked. For we that are in this tabernacle (the body) do groan, being burdened; not for that we would be **'unclothed'** (by death), but **'clothed upon'** (by immortality), that 'mortality' might be swallowed up of life."

In his letter to the Philippians, while Paul hopes that—

"If by any means he may attain unto The (out from among the dead) **Resurrection,**" yet he pressed "toward the mark for the 'prize' of the **High** (out and up) **Calling of God** in Christ Jesus." Phil. 3:11-14.

That is, while Paul would esteem it a great thing to "rise from the dead" at the First Resurrection, and be "caught up" with those who should be "changed," yet he would esteem it a "prize" if he could be caught up "without dying," that is, live until Jesus came back.

THE RAPTURE WILL BE A "SURPRISE"

"Watch therefore; for ye know not what hour your Lord doth come. But know this, that if the goodman of the house had known in what watch the thief would come, he would have watched, and would not have suffered his house to be broken up. Therefore be ye also ready; for **in such an hour as ye think not the Son of Man COMETH.**" Matt. 24:42-44.

We see from this that when Christ comes back it will be when we are not expecting Him. He will come as a thief comes. A thief does not announce his coming. He comes for a certain purpose. He does not take everything there is in the house. He takes only the precious things. The jewels, the gold, the silver and fine wearing apparel. He does not come to stay. As soon as he secures what he is after he departs. So Jesus at the Rapture will come and take away the saints only. The thief leaves much more than he takes. He leaves the house and the furniture and the household utensils. So the Lord at the Rapture will leave the wicked and the great mass of the heathen behind, for those who will be taken will be comparatively few.

THE RAPTURE WILL BE "ELECTIVE"

It will not only separate the saints from unbelievers, but it will separate husbands from wives, brothers from sisters, friends from friends.

"I tell you, in that night there shall be two men in one bed; the one shall be taken, and the other shall be left. Two women shall be grinding together; the one shall be taken, and the other left. Two men shall be in

the field; the one shall be taken, and the other left."
Luke 17:34-36. The words "men" and "women" in this
passage are in italics. That means that they are not in
the original, and so the passage should read there shall be
"two in one bed," husband and wife, or two brothers, or
two sisters, or two friends. Two in "bed" indicates night;
two grinding at the mill, morning or evening; two in the
field mid-day. This shows that the Rapture will happen
all over the earth at the same time, or as the Apostle describes it, in a "moment," or the "twinkling of an eye."
"As the lightning cometh out of the east, and shineth even
unto the west; so shall also the coming of the Son of Man
Be" (Matt. 24:27) is the way Jesus puts it.

The "Rapture" will be the most startling "event" of
this Age and Dispensation. As it is to occur in the
"twinkling of an eye" and all over the earth at the same
time, that part of the world that is not asleep will witness
the event. As to the "Shout of the Lord," the "Voice of
the Archangel," and the "Trump of God" we do not know
whether their sound will be heard and distinguished by
others than the "dead in Christ" and the "living saints."
We know that one day the Father spoke to Christ in a
voice that He understood, but the people who stood by
mistook it for "thunder." John 12:28, 29. If the dead
slip out of their places of sepulchre without disturbing
them, the First Resurrection will be secret and probably
unknown to the world, but it will not be so with the "Living Saints" who are translated. If it is night on our side
of the globe when the Rapture occurs the community
will wake up in the morning to find all the real Christians
gone, disappeared in the night.

If it be day, the "EVENT" will be startling. If it be
at a pleasant time of the year, the boats, and cars, and
parks will be filled with pleasure seekers. If it be in the
midst of the week, and during the business hours of the
day, the shops and stores will be filled with shoppers
and the mills with toilers, and the streets of the cities
lined with men and women and children on pleasure and
business bent. Suddenly a noise from heaven will be
heard like a great peal of thunder. The people will rush
to doors and windows, and those on the streets and in the

fields will look up to see what has happened. To the vast majority it will be but a startling and alarming sound, but to many it will be the

"VOICE OF THE LORD."

But when the people recover from their surprised and affrighted condition they will discover that a great many people are missing, and that the missing were the best people in the community.

At first the whole thing will be a **Mystery,** until some one who had heard or read about the "Rapture of the Saints," realizing what has happened, will explain the situation.

But one of the surprises of that day will be that so many professing Christians, and among them many ministers and Christian workers, will be left behind, while some who were not known to be Christians will be missing. For a few days the excitement will be intense. Then the people will settle down to the inevitable. With the exception of a few who will repent and turn to God, the mass of the people will become more hardened and wicked than before, and some who lost loved ones will be embittered. As the Holy Spirit will have gone back with the "Raptured Ones," and the "Saints," the **SALT** of the earth, been taken out, there will be nothing to prevent the rapid degeneration and **"Moral Putrefaction"** of those who are "left," and sin and iniquity and all manner of crime and worldliness will increase and pave the way for the manifestation of Antichrist, under whose administration the world will rapidly ripen for judgment.

THE REVELATION

At the "Second Stage" of Christ's Second Coming, the "Revelation," we shall behold His **"Glory."** When Jesus came the first time He was disguised in the flesh. The "Incarnation" was the hiding of His Power, the veiling of His Deity. Now and then gleams of glory shot forth as on the Mt. of Transfiguration; but when He comes the Second Time we shall behold Him clothed with the glory He had with the Father before the world was. The "Revelation" will be as sudden and unexpected as was the "Rapture." The people will be buying and selling, building and planting, eating and drinking, marrying and giving in marriage. The statesmen will be revolving in their minds new plans for the world's betterment. The pleasure-loving will be seeking new sources of pleasure. The wicked will be plotting dark deeds; and the unbelieving will be proving to their own satisfaction that there is no God, no heaven, no hell, no coming judgment, when suddenly there will be a change. In the distant heaven there will appear a

"POINT OF LIGHT,"

outshining the sun. It will be seen descending toward the earth. As it descends it will assume the form of a bright cloud, out of which shall stream dazzling beams of light, and flashes of lightning. It will descend apace as if on the wings of the whirlwind, and when it reaches its destination over the brow of the Mt. of Olives it will stop and unfold itself to the terrified and awestricken beholders, and there will be revealed to them Jesus seated on a "White Horse" (Rev. 19:11-16) and accompanied with His Saints and the armies of Heaven. Then shall be fulfilled what Jesus foretold in His Olivet Discourse—"Then shall appear the sign (a cloud) of the Son of Man in heaven; and then shall all the tribes of the earth mourn, and they shall see the Son of Man coming in the **clouds of Heaven WITH POWER AND GREAT GLORY."** Matt. 24:30.

Following the "Revelation" will be the "Battle of Armageddon," and then Christ will sit upon the **"THRONE OF HIS GLORY"** and judge **"The Nations,"** (Matt. 25:31-46), after which He will set up His "Millennial Kingdom."*

---

*See my booklet on "The Second Coming," containing 46 pages and 8 Charts.

VII

The Spirit World

The Scriptures are full of the "Supernatural." The only cure for the "Materialism" of the present day is to discover what the Scriptures reveal as to the "Spirit-World." There is but a step from the "Natural" World to the "Spirit" World. The dividing veil is our "fleshy" bodies. The "Heavenlies" are peopled with **Spirit Beings.** They are of two classes, good and evil. They are classified as **"Seraphim," "Cherubim," "Angels"** (Good and Bad), **"Principalities," "Powers," "Age Rulers of Darkness,"** **"Wicked Spirits,"** (Eph. 6:12), **"Thrones," "Dominions,"** (Col. 1:16), **"Fallen Angels,"** (2 Pet. 2:4), **"Spirits in Prison,"** (1 Peter 3:18-20), **"Demons," "Seducing Spirits."** (1 Tim. 4:1.)

The Angels are "innumerable in number." Heb. 12:22. They are "mighty in power" but not almighty. 2 Thess. 1:7. They excel in strength. One angel destroyed 185,000 of the Assyrian army in a night. An angel rolled away the stone from the Tomb of Christ, and one angel shall bind Satan and cast him into the "Bottomless Pit." They are "Glorious" beings (Luke 9:26), and have "great knowledge," but are not Omniscient. The Angels are "Ministering Spirits" to them who are "heirs of salvation," (Heb. 1:13, 14), and "Executioners of God's Wrath" on the "wicked." 2 Thess. 1:7-8. They will gather the "elect of Israel" from the four corners of the earth, (Matt. 24:31), and are commissioned to supply the physical needs of God's people. Matt. 4:11; 1 Kings 19:4-8.

Among the "Principalities and Powers" of the Spirit World there are three great leaders:

1. Michael.

He is mentioned three times in Daniel (Dan. 10:13, 21; 12:1), where he is called a "Prince" who stands for Daniel's People—the Jews. He is called in Jude 9 the Archangel. In Rev. 12:7 he is seen in command of the

THE TABERNACLE

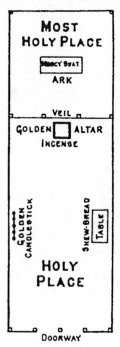

MOST HOLY PLACE

MERCY SEAT

ARK

VEIL

GOLDEN ALTAR INCENSE

GOLDEN CANDLESTICK

SHEW-BREAD TABLE

HOLY PLACE

DOORWAY

LAVER

BRAZEN ALTAR

OUTER COURT

Angelic "Army of Heaven."   His work seems to be to deliver God's people, particularly the Jews, from the power of Satan, and finally to oust him and his angels from the Heavenlies, and cast them down on to the earth. Rev. 12:7-9. He also has something to do with the resurrection of the dead, for he is associated with the "Resurrection" mentioned in Dan. 12:1, 2, and he contested with the Devil the resurrection of Moses (Jude 9), and the "voice" of the Archangel that will be heard when the "Dead in Christ" shall rise (1 Thess. 4:16), will be the "voice" of Michael, for he is the only Archangel mentioned in the Scriptures.

2. Gabriel.

He is mentioned by name four times. In Daniel twice, and in Luke twice. He seems to be associated with the redemptive work of God. He appeared to Daniel (Dan. 8:16; 9:21-27), to inform him as to the "time" of Christ's "First Coming," and when the "time had come" he announced to Zacharias the birth of Christ's "Forerunner"—John the Baptist, and later to Mary the birth of Jesus. Luke 1:19, 26, 27. His position in heaven is lofty, for he said of himself to Zacharias—"I am Gabriel that **Stand in the Presence of God.**"

3. Satan.

We speak of Satan last not because he is the least of the three, for in many ways he is the greatest, but because of his evil character. He is the source of all the anarchy and rebellion in the Universe. See the Chapter on Satan.

MAN'S RELATION TO THE "SPIRIT-WORLD"

Man in his physical and spiritual makeup, was made for two worlds, the Physical and the Spirit world. Writing to the Thessalonians Paul says,

"I pray God your whole 'Spirit' and 'Soul' and 'Body' be preserved blameless unto the coming of our Lord Jesus Christ." 1 Thess. 5:23. Writing to the Hebrews he says—

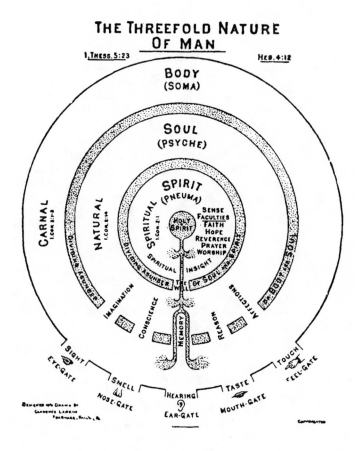

"The Word of God is quick (alive), and powerful, and sharper than any two-edged sword, piercing even to the **dividing asunder** of 'Soul' and 'Spirit,' and of the '**Joints and Marrow**' (body), and is a discerner of the thoughts and intents of the heart." Heb. 4:12.

From these references we see that man is a **Trinity**, and is composed of "Body," "Soul," and "Spirit." Man was made in the "Image of God" and God is a **Trinity**.

The Tabernacle was a tent surrounded by a court, which court was enclosed by a curtain fence. (See diagram of the Tabernacle.) The tent was divided into two parts, one twice the length of the other, by a "veil" or curtain. The larger part was entered from without by a curtained doorway, and contained the "Table of Shewbread," the "Altar of Incense," and the "Seven-Branched Candlestick." This part was called the "Holy Place." The smaller part was entered from the "Holy Place" through the "veil" or dividing curtain, and contained the "Ark of the Covenant," on the lid of which, between the "Cherubims," God took up His residence in the "Shekinah Glory." This part was called the "Most Holy Place." There were no windows in the Tabernacle, and the only entrance was through the curtained doorway into the "Holy Place." The Tabernacle and its Courtyard is a type of the "Threefold Nature of Man." The "Courtyard" represents his Body, the "Holy Place" his Soul, and the "Most Holy Place" his Spirit, and as there could be no communication between the "Courtyard" and the "Most Holy Place," only through the "Holy Place," so there can be no communication between a man's Body and Spirit only through his Soul. After the completion of the Tabernacle it remained empty of the "Presence of God" until the "Spirit of God" descended and took up His abode in the "Most Holy Place." So a man may be complete as to body, soul and spirit, but his spiritual nature will remain unregenerate until the Holy Spirit enters and takes possession of the "spirit" compartment of his nature. This happens when the "New Birth" takes place.

The "Threefold Nature of Man" is clearly brought out in the Diagram

"The Threefold Nature of Man."

The outer circle stands for the "Body" of man, the middle for the "Soul," and the inner for the "Spirit," or what Paul calls the "CARNAL" (1 Cor. 3:1-3); the "NATURAL" (1 Cor. 2:14); and the "SPIRITUAL" (1 Cor. 3:1), parts of man. In the outer circle the "Body" is shown as touching the Material World through the five senses of "Sight," "Smell," "Hearing," "Taste" and "Touch." The Gates to the "Soul" are "Imagination," "Conscience," "Memory," "Reason" and the "Affections." The "Spirit" receives impressions of outward and material things through the Soul. The "Spiritual Faculties" of the "Spirit" are "Faith," "Hope," "Reverence," "Prayer" and "Worship." In his unfallen state the "Spirit" of man was illuminated from Heaven, but when the human race fell in Adam, sin closed the window of the Spirit, and pulled down the curtain, and the "chamber of the Spirit" became a **Death Chamber,** and remains so in every unregenerate heart, until the "Life" and "Light" giving power of the Holy Spirit floods that chamber with the "**Life**" and "**Light**" giving power of the **NEW LIFE IN CHRIST JESUS.** We see then why the "natural" man cannot understand "spiritual" things. He cannot understand them until his spiritual nature has been renewed.

But the Spirit of the Natural man is not only darkened, his "Will" stands as a "guard" at the door, and prevents the entrance of the Holy Spirit, and it is not until the "Will" surrenders through the power of the "Sword of the Spirit," the "Word of God," that the Holy Spirit can enter and take up his abode in the "Spirit" of man.

When a man dies his "Soul" and "Spirit" separate from the "Body," and the "Body" is laid in the grave, but the "Spirit" is not "bodiless," it has what Paul calls its "**PSYCHICAL**" or "Soulish" Body. As this "Soulish" Body can hear, and speak, and think, and feel, it must have some "tangible" form. It is not a "ghostlike" structure. There are doubtless limitations in its use, or there would be no need for it to recover its "physical" body at the Resurrection.

That there is such a thing as the "Soulish Body" is brought out in the story of the "Rich Man and Lazarus." Luke 16: 19-31. The story is not a Parable, but a description by Christ of something that really happened in the other world to his own personal knowledge. It declares that both Lazarus and the "Rich Man" died and were buried. That is, their bodies were left on the earth. What happened to them in the "Underworld" then, is descriptive of what happened to them in their "disembodied state." In that state they were conscious and the Rich Man recognized Lazarus, which he could not have done if Lazarus had not a body, not his "physical" body, he left that on the earth, but his "Soulish" body. This is proof that the "Soulish" body is not simply a body, but that in its outward form and appearance it conforms to the earthly body of the owner, otherwise he would not be recognizable in the other world. Again the "Rich Man" could see, and feel, and thirst, and talk, and remember, proving that he possessed his senses and had not lost his personality. This proves that there is no break, as "Soul Sleep," in the Continuity of Existence, or Consciousness, in passing from the "Earth-Life" to the "Spirit-Life." Sleep in the Scriptures always refers to the "Body," not to the "Soul," and the expression "Asleep in Jesus" refers to the Believer only.

Let us trace the life of the "Soul" and "Spirit" after they have left the "Body." In the account of the "Rich Man and Lazarus" we have a description of "THE UNDERWORLD." See the Chart of "The Underworld," page 90.

"The Underworld" is made up of two compartments, "Paradise" and "Hell" (not the final Hell, that is "Gehenna" the "Lake of Fire") with an "Impassable Gulf" between. At the bottom of the "Gulf" is the "Bottomless Pit," or "Abyss." This is a place of temporary confinement for "Evil Spirits" (Demons). It has a King —"Apollyon," but is kept locked by God who commissions an angel to open it when He so desires. Rev. 9: 1-16, 17: 8, 20: 1-3. Before the resurrection of Christ the Soul

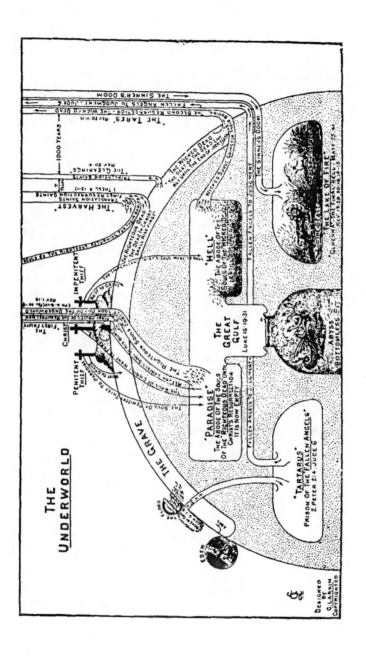

THE UNDERWORLD

Designed by
C. LARKIN
Copyrighted

and Spirit of the "Righteous Dead" went to the "Paradise" compartment of "The Underworld." There Christ met the "Penitent Thief" after His death on the Cross. On the day of His Resurrection Christ's Soul and Spirit returned from "The Underworld." But He did not return alone. He brought back with Him all the occupants of the Paradise compartment and locked it up, and He now has the "Keys of Death and Hades." Rev. 1:18. R. V. Here "Death" stands for the "grave" and "Hades" for "The Underworld." Some of those who came back from "The Underworld" with Christ got their bodies, and ascended with Him as the "First Fruits" of the resurrection "from among the dead." Matt. 27:52-53. The rest were taken up to the "Third Heaven" where Paul was caught up. 2 Cor. 12:1-4. Paul called it "Paradise." There all the "Righteous Dead" that have died since Christ's resurrection go that they may be "WITH THE LORD." Phil. 1:23. 2 Cor. 5:8. There the souls of the "Righteous Dead" shall remain until the time comes for the resurrection of their bodies, then when Christ comes back to meet His Church in the Air, He will bring back the souls of the "Righteous Dead" from the "Paradise" of the "Third Heaven," for we are told that He will bring them whose bodies "Sleep in Jesus" on the earth WITH HIM (1 Thess. 4:14), and they will continue on to the earth and get their "bodies" from the grave, and then ascend again together with the "Translated Saints" to meet the Lord IN THE AIR. See the Chart of "The Underworld."

So far as we know the souls of the "Wicked Dead" are still in the "Hell Compartment" of "The Underworld," and will remain there until the "Second Resurrection," when they will return to the earth and get their bodies, and then go to the "Great White Throne" Judgment. After judgment they will be sentenced to the "Second Death," which means that they shall die again in the sense of losing their bodies the second time, and as "disembodied spirits" be cast into the "Lake of Fire," (Gehenna, the "Final Hell"), to suffer in flames forever. As soul and spirit are impervious to flames, this explains how the wicked, after being disembodied again by the

"Second Death," can exist forever in literal fire. Mark 9: 43-48.

We are reading a great deal in these days about "Spiritualism," or the communication of the living with the dead. What is called "Spiritism" is **DEMONISM**, and is forbidden in the Scriptures. Lev. 20:6, 27. Deu. 18:10-11. Isa. 8:19 (R. V.). The "**Familiar Spirits**" of the Old Testament are the same as the "**Demons**" and "**Seducing Spirits**" of the New Testament.

SPIRITISM

Of the revival of "Spiritism" in these days we have been fully warned in the New Testament. The Apostle Paul, writing to Timothy, says—

> "Now the Spirit (Holy Spirit) speaketh expressly, that in the '**LATTER TIMES**' (the last days of this Dispensation) some **shall depart from the Faith** (that is, give up the Christian Faith) giving heed to '**SEDUCING SPIRITS**,' and '**DOCTRINES OF DEVILS**' (Demons), * * * forbidding to marry, and commanding to abstain from meats." 1 Tim. 4:1-3.

The phrase "**forbidding to marry**" does not refer to "celibacy," but to the abrogation of the marriage relation, the practice of "**FREE LOVE**" and the doctrine of "**AFFINITIES**," which Spiritism leads to. The phrase "**Abstain From Meats**" is not a reference to fasting, but the requirement of a "**vegetable diet.**" It is a well-known fact that a "vegetable diet" renders the body more susceptible to spiritual forces than a meat diet.

The close connection of this warning of the Apostle with the words—"Refuse profane and '**OLD WIVES' FABLES,**'" in verse seven, is doubtless a reference to some of the "**ISMS**" of these last days. For "Christian Science" is but an "**OLD WIFE'S**" Fable, for Mrs. Eddy was an "Old Wife" in the sense that she had been many times married. It is an indisputable fact that most of the "Witches" and "Mediums" of Scripture, and these "Lat-

ter Days," were and are women. It was through Eve
and not Adam that Satan sought to destroy the race.
The reason may be that the nervous and impressionable
character of women is better adapted to demon influence.

The revival of "Spiritism," or "DEMONISM," is one
of the "Signs of the Times," and should be a warning to
every true child of God of the approaching end of the
Age. The "Demons" belong to the "Powers of Darkness." They are not few in number, but are a great
"Martialed Host," veterans in the service of Satan. Their
central camp or abode is the "Bottomless Pit" from which
they "sally forth" at the command of their leader. Rev.
9: 1-11. They are not angels. Angels have bodies. But
the fact that demons can enter in, and take possession of,
and control human beings and animals (swine), is proof
that they are "Disembodied Spirits." They are supposed
by many to be the "spirits" of the inhabitants of the "Pre-
Adamite Earth," whose sin caused its wreck, and whose
bodies were destroyed in the catastrophe that over-
whelmed it, and their desire and purpose in entering
human bodies is to re-embody themselves again on the
earth where they once lived. That the "Demons" have a
personality is clear from the fact that Jesus conversed
with them, asked them questions, and received answers.
Luke 8: 26-33. They are possessed of more than ordinary
intelligence. They know that Jesus is the "Son of God,"
and that they are finally to be confined in a place of "Torment." Matt. 8: 29.

THE POWER OF DEMONS OVER THE HUMAN BODY

They can cause **DUMBNESS** (Matt. 9: 32-33), and
BLINDNESS (Matt. 12: 22), and **INSANITY** (Luke 8:
26-35), and the **SUICIDAL MANIA** (Mark 9: 22), and
PERSONAL INJURIES (Mark 9: 18), and impart
SUPERNATURAL STRENGTH (Luke 8: 29) and in-
flict **PHYSICAL DEFECTS AND DEFORMITIES.**
Luke 13: 11-17. Once they have got control over a human
body they can come and go at will. Luke 11: 24-26.

The Devilish character of "Demons" is seen in the use
they make of their victims. They use them as "instru-

ments of unrighteousness," (Rom. 6:13), for the proclamation of the "DOCTRINES OF DEVILS," (1 Tim. 4:1), and the teaching of "DAMNABLE HERESIES." 2 Pet. 2:1. The effect of such use of the victim is not only **unmoral**, it is **IMMORAL**. It leads to vicious and inhuman conduct. The conduct of **"demonized"** men and women seems to indicate that the "Demon" takes possession of them for the purpose of **physical sensual gratification,** thus letting us into the secret of the cause of the wreck of the Pre-Adamite Earth, the **SIN OF SENSUALITY.** This accounts for the desire of the victim to live in a state of nudity; to have lustful and licentious thoughts. In these days of increasing tendency to yield to **"Seducing Spirits"** it may account for the immodesty of fashionable attire, and the craze of dancing. The purpose of the "Demon" is often to alienate husband and wife, and break up homes by preaching the doctrine of **"FREE LOVE."** In short, the "Demon," for personal gratification, has the power, once he is in control of his victim, to derange both mind and body, and wreck the victim's health, and if deliverance is not obtained by turning to Christ, who alone has power to cast out the Demon, the victim will be lost soul and body.

Demon-possession must not be confounded with diseases, such as "Epilepsy," which causes the victim to fall in convulsions, foam at the mouth and gnash the teeth, for the Scriptures make a clear distinction between them. Matt. 4:24.

In 1 Cor. 10:20-21 we read—

> "But I say, that the things which the Gentiles sacrifice, they **SACRIFICE TO DEVILS** (Demons), and not to God; and I would not that ye should have **FELLOWSHIP WITH DEVILS** (Demons). Ye cannot drink the 'Cup of the Lord' (Communion Cup), and the 'CUP OF DEVILS'; ye cannot be partakers of the 'Lord's Table,' and of the **TABLE OF DEVILS** (Demons)."

This passage proves that behind all heathen worship there is the "Spirit of Demonism," or **"DEVIL WOR-**

SHIP," and accounts for the "wild orgies" and voluptuous and licentious mode of worship of the heathen.

The story of the rich man and Lazarus (Luke 16:19-31) reveals the fact that communication with the spirits of our departed dead, is not only unnecessary, but is not permitted. It is not necessary for we have Moses and the Prophets, that is, the Holy Scriptures, to give us all we need to know of the state of the dead. And it is not permitted, or Lazarus, or the rich man himself, would have been allowed to return to the earth and warn his brethren. The inevitable conclusion to be drawn from this story is, that the spirit of a good man **MAY** not, and the spirit of a bad man **CANNOT** return to this earth. If this be true then Spiritism is a fraud, and is one of the devices of Satan in these latter days to lead astray the unwary. Those who dabble in Spiritism are in great danger of having their **"understanding darkened"** (Eph. 4:17-19) and come under the power and control of Demons.

THY WORD IS A LAMP UNTO MY FEET
AND A LIGHT UNTO MY PATH

VIII

Satan

There are many who deny the existence of Satan. They claim that what we call Satan is only a "principle of evil." That this "evil" is a sort of "malaria," an intangible thing like disease germs that floats about in the atmosphere and attacks people's hearts under certain conditions. The existence of Satan cannot be determined by the opinions of men. The only source of information is the Bible. That is the reason why Satan tries to discredit the Word of God. He is not a "principle of evil" he is a—Person.

> "Be sober, be vigilant; because your adversary the Devil, as a roaring lion, walketh about, seeking whom he may devour." 1 Pet. 5:8.

He "walketh," he "roareth," he is to be "chained." Rev. 20:1-3. These could not be said of a "principle of evil." He has many names or aliases—"Satan," "Devil," "Beelzebub," "Belial," "Adversary," "Dragon," "Serpent." He is mentioned by one or the other of these names 174 times in the Bible.

He is a great "Celestial Potentate." He is
"The Prince of the Powers of the Air."
Eph. 2:2.
"The God of this World" (Age).
2 Cor. 4:4.

I. His Origin.

This is more or less shrouded in mystery. One thing is certain, he is a "created being," and that of the most exalted type. He was before his fall
"The Anointed Cherub That Covereth."
That is, he was the guardian or protector of the "Throne of God." He was perfect in all his ways from the day that he was created, until iniquity was found in him. In him was the "fulness of wisdom," and the "perfection of beauty," but it was his "beauty" that caused the pride that was his downfall. He was clothed in a garment that was covered with the most rare and precious gems, the sardius, topaz, diamond, beryl, onyx,

jasper, sapphire, emerald, carbuncle, all woven in with
gold. He dwelt in Eden, the "Garden of God." This
probably refers not to the earthly Eden, but to the "Paradise of God" on high, for Satan dwelt on the "Holy
Mount of God."⋅ All this we learn from Ezek. 28: 11-19,
where the Prophet has a "foreview" of the Antichrist
under the title of the "King of Tyrus," and as Antichrist
is to be an incarnation of Satan, the Prophet here describes Satan's original glory from which he fell. There
never has been as yet such a King of Tyrus as is here
described.

The cause of Satan's fall is given in Isa. 14: 12-20. He
is there called—

Lucifer, Son of the Morning.

This was his glorious title when he was created, and
this world of ours was made, at which time—

> "The 'Morning Stars,' (probably other glor-
> ious created ruling beings like himself), sang to-
> gether, and all the 'Sons of God,' (angels),
> shouted for joy." Job 38: 7.

It is well to note that the one here called "Lucifer,
Son of the Morning," is in verse four (Isa. 14: 4) also
called the "King of Babylon." As there never has been
a King of Babylon like the one here described, the description must be that of a "future" King of Babylon.
And as "Antichrist is to have for his Capital City Babylon rebuilt," this is probably a "foreview" by the Prophet
of Antichrist, as indwelt by "Lucifer," or "Satan," in that
day when he shall be "King of Babylon."

Some think that when this world was created and fit
for habitation Satan was placed in charge of it, and it
was then, as Isaiah declares, that Satan said in his heart—
"I will ascend into heaven, I will exalt my throne above
the 'Stars of God' (other ruling powers) ; I will sit also
upon the Mount of the Congregation, in the sides of the
North. I will ascend above the clouds ; I will be like
The MOST HIGH:" and that it was for this presumptuous act that the "Pre-Adamite World" became a chaos,
and "without form and void," as described in Gen. 1: 2.
This would justify the claim of Satan that this world

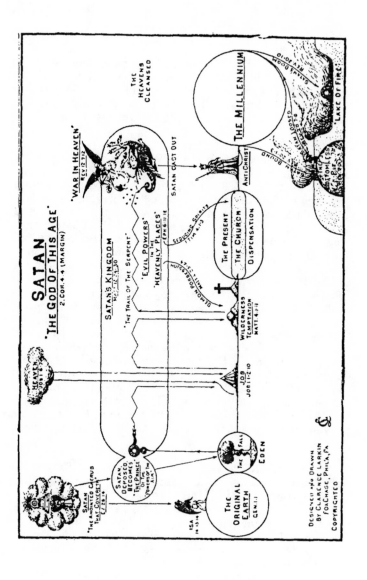

SATAN
"THE GOD OF THIS AGE"
2. Cor. 4:4 (MARGIN)

Designed and Drawn
By Clarence Larkin
Fox Chase, Phila., Pa
Copyrighted

belongs to him, and that he had the right and power to transfer the "kingdoms of the world" to Christ, if He would only acknowledge Satan's supremacy. (Matt. 4: 8, 9.) And it accounts for the persistent war Satan is waging against the Almighty to retain his possession of the earth.

II. His Present Location.

The common notion is that Satan and his angels are imprisoned in Hell. This is not true. The angels described in 2 Pet. 2:4, and Jude 6, as having left their "first estate," and being "reserved in everlasting chains under darkness," are not Satan's angels. They are a special class of angels whose sin caused the Flood. They are the "Spirits in Prison" of whom Peter speaks in I Pet. 3:18-20. See the chapter on "Ages and Dispensations," under the cause of the Flood. Satan and his angels are at liberty. We read in the first and second chapters of Job that it was the custom in Job's day for the "Sons of God" (angels), to appear at stated times in the presence of God to give an account of their stewardship, and that Satan always appeared with them. When the Lord said to Satan—"Whence comest thou?" he replied, "From going to and fro in the earth and from walking up and down in it." Job. 1:7; 2:2. Satan then was at liberty "on the earth," and has "access to God," and was "not cast out of Heaven" in Job's day, B. C. 2000, and as he has not been cast out since, he must still be at liberty in the heavenlies and on the earth. See Chart of "Satan," page 98.

III. His Kingdom.

Satan is a King, and has a Kingdom. "If Satan cast out Satan he is divided against himself; how shall then his 'kingdom' stand?" Matt. 12:24-30.

"We wrestle not against flesh and blood, but against Principalities, against Powers, against the Rulers of the Darkness of this World (Age), against Spiritual Wickedness in High Places (the Heavenlies)." Eph. 6:12.

From this we see that his Kingdom consists of "Principalities," "Powers," "Age Rulers of Darkness," and

"Wicked Spirits in the Heavenlies." These "Principalities" are ruled by "Princes," who control certain nations of our earth, as in the days of Daniel the Prophet, when a heavenly messenger was sent to Daniel, but was hindered "three weeks" from reaching him by the **"Prince of the Kingdom of Persia,"** Satan's ruling "Prince of Persia," until Michael the Archangel came to his rescue. Dan. 10:10-14.

IV. His Methods.

1. He Is the Deceiver of the World.

By the "World" is meant all those who belong to the "Satanic System," all those who are entangled in Satan's mesh.

> "And we know that we are of God, and the whole **World** (the Satanic System), lieth in the **Wicked One** (Satan)." 1 John 5:19, R. V.

Satan deceives by "blinding" the eyes of the world.

> "If our Gospel is hid, it is hid to them that 'are lost'; in whom the 'God of this World' (Satan), hath **blinded the minds of them which believe not,** lest the light of the glorious Gospel of Christ, who is the image of God, should shine unto them." 2 Cor. 4:3, 4.

To this end Satan has his preachers who preach "another gospel." Gal. 1:6-9. That gospel is the "doctrine of devils." 1 Tim. 4:1. He is the instigator of **"The Great Apostasy."** Peter, speaking of the "latter times" says—

> "There shall be false teachers among you, who **privily** shall bring in **'Damnable Heresies,'** even **denying the Lord that bought them,** and bring upon themselves swift destruction. And **many** shall follow their 'Pernicious Ways,' by reason of whom the **'WAY OF TRUTH' shall be evil spoken of."** 2 Pet. 2:1-2.

These "false teachers" are to be seen on every hand. They are those who deny the "Virgin Birth," "Deity," "Bodily Resurrection" and "Personal Premillennial Return" of the Lord Jesus Christ.

Satan is very subtle in his methods, and if it were possible he would deceive the very elect. He knows all the great Scripture subjects that are of universal interest to humanity, and he is too wise to attack them openly, so he adulterates them with false doctrine. He has tried to rob the Church of her "Blessed Hope" of the Lord's return by mixing with it a lot of false teaching and "time setting" as seen in "Millerism," "Seventh Day Adventism" and "Millennial Dawnism." To prevent mankind from turning to the Lord for healing, he has invented the systems of "Christian Science" and "New Thought." To satisfy the craving of the human mind to know what is going on in the Spirit World, Satan invented "Spiritism." Satan seeing that he could not stamp out the Church by violence and persecution has changed his tactics and is now trying to seduce her into conformity to the world, and to try to better an "Age" that God has doomed to destruction. His present purpose is to build up a "magnificent civilization," and he has deceived the Church into believing that it can bring in the "Millennium," **without Christ, by the Betterment of Society.** His hope is that the **"Gospel of Social Service"** will take the place of the **"Gospel of Grace,"** and by diverting the attention of Christian people to **"secondary"** things, they will neglect the primary work of soul saving, and thus delay the evangelization of the world, and postpone the Return of the Lord, and his own confinement in the Bottomless Pit.

2. He is the Adversary of God's People.

The warfare between **"Good"** and **"Evil,"** as recorded in the Bible from Gen. 3:15 to Rev. 20:10, is most intensely interesting reading. Satan tempts Eve. She eats and Adam with her. Result the Fall. Satan to prevent the birth of the "Promised Seed" causes Cain to kill Abel. To bring about the destruction of the human race Satan gets the "Sons of God" to marry the "Daughters of Men." Result the Flood. To destroy the unity of the race Satan suggests the building of the "Tower of Babel." Result the "Confusion of Tongues." But the story is too long. All down through the Old Testament we see Satan at work trying to frustrate the plan of God for the "Redemption of the Race." When the time came that Christ was born it was Satan who prompted Herod to destroy all the male children at Bethlehem under two years of age. It was Satan who tried to overcome Christ when weakened by fasting in the wilderness, and who suggested that He throw Himself down from the Pinnacle of the Temple. The attempt of the people to throw Christ from the hilltop at Nazareth, and the two storms on the sea of Galilee were plans of Satan to destroy Christ; and when foiled in these Satan renewed the fight through Priests and Pharisees, and succeeded at last in getting Judas to sell his Master. Then, amid the shades of Gethsemane, he sought to kill Christ by physical weakness before He could reach the Cross and make atonement for sin. When Christ was crucified Satan thought he had at last conquered, but when Christ rose from the dead Satan's rage knew no bounds. In all probability Satan and his angels contested the Ascension of Christ, and the history of the Christian Church is but one long story of the "Irrepressible Conflict" between Satan and God's people.

V. His Doom

As we have seen Satan still has his abode in the "Heavenlies" and has access to God. But the time is coming when he shall be cast out of the "Heavenlies" on to the earth (Rev. 12:9-12), and there shall be great "WOE" on the earth because of Satan's wrath, that he shall exercise through the "Beast," the "ANTICHRIST" (Rev. 13:2-8), for he will then know that his time "IS SHORT," only 3½ years. At the close of the "Tribulation Period," the "Beast" and the "False Prophet" will be cast "alive" into the "Lake of Fire," and an angel from Heaven will seize Satan and bind him with a great chain, already forged, and cast him into the "Bottomless Pit," where he shall remain for 1000 years. Rev. 20:1-3. At the end of which time he shall be loosed for a season, and then with his angels he shall be cast into the "Lake of Fire" prepared for him in the long ago to spend the Ages of the Ages. Rev. 20:7-10. Matt. 25:41.

IX

The Satanic Trinity

▬

After the Apostle John had seen and described the "Beast" that came up **out of the SEA,** he saw another "Beast" come up **out of the EARTH.** Rev. 13:11-17. This "Second Beast," while John does not say it **was a** lamb, had "Two Horns" "like a lamb," that is, it was **LAMB-LIKE.** Because of this resemblance many claim that the "Second Beast" is the Antichrist, for Antichrist is supposed to imitate Christ. While the **LAMB** (Christ) is mentioned in the Book of Revelation 22 times, the description given of Him in chapter 5:6, is that of a lamb having "**SEVEN HORNS**" and not "**TWO.**" This differentiates Him from the "lamb-like Beast" that comes up out of the earth, who, though he is "**lamb-like in appearance SPEAKS AS A DRAGON.**" See the Chart "The Satanic Trinity," page 104.

The "Second Beast" has a name. He is called the "**FALSE PROPHET**" three times. First in chapter 16: 13, then in chapter 19:20, and again in chapter 20:10. Twice he is associated with the "First Beast" (Antichrist) and once with the "Dragon" (Satan) and the "First Beast," and as they are **PERSONS** so must he be. The fact that he is called the "False Prophet" is proof that he is not the "Antichrist." Jesus had a foreview of him when He said—"There shall arise '**FALSE CHRISTS**' and '**FALSE PROPHETS,**' and shall show **GREAT SIGNS AND WONDERS**; insomuch that, if it were possible they shall deceive the very elect." Matt. 24:24. Here Jesus differentiates between "**FALSE CHRISTS**" and "**FALSE PROPHETS,**" therefore the "**ANTICHRIST**" and the "**FALSE PROPHET**" cannot be the same.

That the "Second Beast" comes up **out of the EARTH** may signify that he will be a **resurrected person.** There will be two persons who shall come back from Heaven as the "Two Witnesses," Moses and Elijah, why not two persons come up from "The Underworld," **brought up by** Satan to counteract the work of the "Two Witnesses?"

THE SATANIC TRINITY

"THE DRAGON"
THE "ANTI-GOD"
REV. 12:7-17

"THE BEAST"
THE "ANTI-CHRIST"
REV. 13:1-10

"THE FALSE PROPHET"
THE "ANTI-SPIRIT"
REV. 13:11-17

The fact that the "First Beast" (Antichrist), and the "Second Beast" (False Prophet) are cast **ALIVE** into the "Lake of Fire" (Rev. 19:20) is further proof that they are more than ordinary mortals, and that the "First Beast" is **more** than the last ruling Emperor of the revived Roman Empire. He is the **Antichrist**, Satan's **SUPERMAN.**

In the "Dragon," the "Beast," and the "False Prophet," we have the **"SATANIC TRINITY,"** Satan's imitation of the "Divine Trinity." In the unseen and invisible "Dragon" we have the **FATHER** (the **ANTI-GOD**). In the "Beast" we have the **"SON OF PERDITION"** (the **ANTI-CHRIST**), **begotten** of the Dragon, who appears on the earth, dies, and is resurrected, and to whom is given a throne by his Father the Dragon. In the "False Prophet" we have the **"ANTI-SPIRIT,"** who proceeds from the "Dragon Father" and "Dragon Son," and whose speech is like the Dragon's. The "Dragon" then will be the **"ANTI-GOD,"** the "Beast" the **"ANTI-CHRIST,"** and the "False Prophet" the **"ANTI-SPIRIT,"** and the fact that all three are cast **ALIVE** into the "Lake of Fire" (Rev. 20:10) is proof that they together form a **"Triumvirate"** which we may well call— **"THE SATANIC TRINITY."**

Again the "Antichrist" is to be a **KING** and rule over a **KINGDOM.** He will accept the "Kingdoms of this world" that Satan offered Christ, and that Christ refused. Matt. 4:8-10. He will also **EXALT** himself, and claim to be God. 2 Thess. 2:4. But the "False Prophet" is not a King, He does not exalt himself, he exalts the "First Beast" (Antichrist). His relation to the "First Beast" is the same as the Holy Spirit's relation to Christ. He causeth the earth and them which dwell therein to worship the "First Beast." He also has power to give **life,** and in this he imitates the Holy Spirit. And as the followers of Christ are sealed by the Holy Spirit until the **"Day of Redemption"** (Eph. 4:30) ; so, the followers of Antichrist shall be sealed by the False Prophet until the **"Day of Perdition."** Rev. 13:16-17.

The False Prophet will be a "Miracle Worker." While Jesus was a "miracle worker," He did all His mighty

works in the "power" of the Holy Spirit. Acts 10:38.
Among the miracles that the False Prophet will perform
he will bring down **FIRE FROM HEAVEN.** During
the Mission of the "Two Witnesses" (Rev. 11:1-14), there
will probably be a "FIRE-TEST" between Elijah and the
"False Prophet," similar to the one on Mount Carmel (1
Kings 18:17-40), to prove who is God, the Lord or Antichrist. That Satan, who will then energize the False
Prophet, can do this is clear from Job. 1:16, where Satan,
having secured permission from God to touch all that Job
had, brought down "fire from heaven" and burned up
Job's sheep and servants.

The False Prophet then commands the people to make
an

"IMAGE OF THE BEAST."

This is further proof that the "First Beast" is the Antichrist. It is a strange weakness of mankind that they
must have some **VISIBLE** God to worship, and when the
Children of Israel, who had been delivered from Egypt
under Moses' leadership, thought he had forsaken them
because he did not come down from the Mount, they
called Aaron to make them gods which should go before
them, and Aaron made for them the "GOLDEN CALF."
Ex. 32:1-6. So the False Prophet will have the people
make for the purpose of worship an "IMAGE OF THE
BEAST." But the wonderful thing about the "IMAGE"
is that the False Prophet will have power to give **LIFE**
to it, and cause it to **SPEAK,** and to demand that all
who will not worship it shall be put to death. In other
words the "IMAGE" will be a living, speaking, **AUTO-
MATON.**

This "Image" reminds us of the **"GOLDEN IMAGE"**
that Nebuchadnezzar commanded to be made and set up
in the "Plain of Dura," in the Province of Babylon (Dan.
3:1-30), before which, at the sounding of musical instruments, the people were commanded to bow down and
worship under penalty, for those who disobeyed, of being
cast into a **"BURNING FIERY FURNACE."** Doubtless there will be many in the "Day of Antichrist" who
will refuse to bow down and worship the **"Image of the**

Beast," and who will not escape as did the "Three Hebrew Children," though God may interpose in a miraculous way to deliver some. And as if this was not enough the False Prophet shall cause—**"ALL,** both small and great, rich and poor, free and bond, to receive a **'MARK'** in their **RIGHT HAND,** or in their **FOREHEAD;** and that no man might **BUY** or **SELL,** save he that has the **'MARK'** or the **'NAME OF THE BEAST,'** or the **'NUMBER OF HIS NAME.'"** This **"MARK"** will be known as the

"BRAND OF HELL."

This is what the world is fast coming to. The time is not far distant when the various "Trusts" and "Combinations of Capital" will be merged into a **"FEDERATION OF TRUSTS,"** at the head of which shall be a **"NAPOLEON OF CAPITAL."** Ultimately this "Federation of Trusts" will extend to the whole world, at the head of which shall be **THE ANTICHRIST,** and the producer and consumer will be powerless in the tentacles of this **OCTOPUS,** and no man shall be able to **BUY** or **SELL** who has not the **"MARK OF THE BEAST"** either upon his **"right hand"** or on his **"forehead."** This **"Mark"** will be **BRANDED** or burnt on. It will probably be the **"NUMBER OF THE BEAST"** or **"666."** The number **"666"** is the **"NUMBER OF MAN,"** and stops short of the perfect number **SEVEN.** Man was created on the **SIXTH** day. Goliath the opposer of God's people, a type of Satan, was 6 cubits in height, he had 6 pieces of armor, and his spearhead weighed 600 shekels. 1 Sam. 17:4-7. Nebuchadnezzar's Image, a type of the "Image of the Beast," was 60 cubits in height, 6 cubits wide, and 6 instruments of music summoned the worshippers. Dan. 3:1-7.

In that day men will doubtless prefer to have the **"MARK"** on the back of their right hand so it can be readily seen in the act of signing checks, drafts, and receipts. There will doubtless be public officials in all public places of business to see that no one buys or sells who has not the **"MARK."** This will apply to women as well as men. No one can shop, or even buy from the huckster at the door, without the **"MARK,"** under **penalty of DEATH.** Those will be awful times for those who will not **WORSHIP THE BEAST.** If they can neither buy nor sell without the **"MARK,"** they must beg, or starve or be killed. The instrument of death will be the guillotine (Rev. 20:4), and the daily papers will contain a list of the names of those who were beheaded the day before so as to frighten the people into obedience to the law. The doom of the "Satanic Trinity" will be, that at the close of that awful time of Tribulation the Lord Jesus Christ will return, and the "Dragon," the "Anti-God," will be cast into the **"BOTTOMLESS PIT"** for a thousand years (Rev. 20:1-3), and the "Beast," the **"Anti-Christ,"** and the "False Prophet," the **"Anti-Spirit,"** will be cast **ALIVE** into the **"LAKE OF FIRE."** Rev. 19:20.

Two good men, Enoch and Elijah, were translated to Heaven **without dying,** and two bad men, spoken of officially as the "Beast" and the "False Prophet," shall be cast into the "Lake of Fire" **WITHOUT DYING.**

X

The "Mystery of Godliness"
and the
"Mystery of Iniquity"

Among the "Mysteries of God" revealed in the Scriptures there stand forth two great Personages, one called the "Mystery of Godliness," the other the "Mystery of Iniquity," or Christ and Antichrist.

I. THE MYSTERY OF GODLINESS

"And without controversy great is the 'MYSTERY OF GODLINESS': GOD was manifest in the flesh, justified in the Spirit, seen of angels, preached unto the Gentiles, believed on in the world, received up into glory." 1 Tim. 3:16.

The study of the "Life and Work of Christ" is confined by most Bible students to His "Earthly Life," that is to the "Days of His Flesh."   But we must not forget that Jesus was the "ETERNAL CHRIST."   His work of Atonement on the Cross was but one phase of His work, which began in the Creation of the Universe and will continue for all eternity.   The "Greater Life and Work of Christ" is a circle of which the circumference is "Eternity" and the centre is "CALVARY."   Jesus said of Himself—"I am 'Alpha' and 'Omega,' the 'BEGINNING' and the 'ENDING,' the 'FIRST' and the 'LAST,' which IS, and which WAS, and which is TO COME, the ALMIGHTY."   Rev. 1:8, 11. See the Chart —"The Greater Life and Work of Christ," page 110. Jesus thus identifies Himself with God, and confirms His earthly statement—"I and my Father are ONE." John 10:30.   John tells us that—"THE WORD was made 'Flesh,' and dwelt among us, and we beheld His GLORY (on the Mount of Transfiguration), the GLORY as of the ONLY BEGOTTEN OF THE FATHER." John 1:14.

THE GREATER LIFE AND WORK OF CHRIST

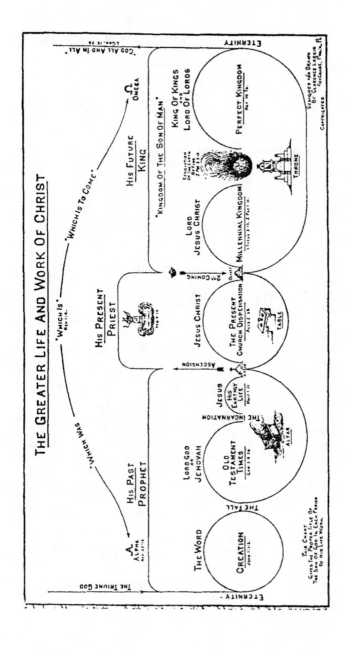

And in His prayer in the "upper room" before going out to Gethsemane Jesus prayed—"And now, O Father, glorify Thou me with Thine own self with the **GLORY** which I had with Thee **BEFORE THE WORLD WAS.**" John 17:5. Thus we see that Jesus existed before the World was and is the **ETERNAL CHRIST.***

THE SELF-EMPTYING OF CHRIST

While Jesus in Old Testament times clothed Himself in human flesh and appeared as a man to men, as He did to Abraham and Jacob (Gen. 18:1-8, 32:24-32), He did not divest Himself of His Deity, or empty Himself of His Glory. But when the time came to redeem men from the curse of sin it was necessary for Christ to lay aside His heavenly glory and become a **MAN.** Of that act the Apostle Paul says—"Have this mind in you, which was also in Christ Jesus: who, being in the '**FORM OF GOD,**' counted it not a prize to be on an equality with God, but **EMPTIED HIMSELF,** taking the form of a servant, being made in the **LIKENESS OF MEN.**" Phil. 2:5-7 (R. V.).

Of what did Christ empty Himself when He became a man? He emptied Himself of the "**FORM OF GOD.**" This "Form" consisted of the "**GLORIOUS PERSONAL BODILY FORM**" of the Godhead, revealed but for a moment on the Mount of Transfiguration. Matt. 17:1-2. It was the restoration of this "Glory" that Christ prayed for in the "upper room" before going out to Gethsemane. John 17:5. This emptying took place in Heaven in the presence of the angelic hosts. As a monarch Christ descended from the Throne, relinquished His Royal Power and Office, laid aside His crown and robes of state, and arrayed himself in the garment of a **SERVANT,** and by so doing He subjected Himself to the limitations of a servant.

That was one of the "Great Days" in the life of the Son of God. In fact it was the "Greatest Day," for without that "Day of Self-Emptying" the "Day of Crucifixion"

---

*For a full description of "The Greater Life and Work of Christ," see the chapter on "The Dispensational Work of Christ," in my larger work on "Dispensational Truth."

and the "Day of Resurrection," and all the other "Great Days" could not have been possible.

From this it is clear that the Birth of Christ is not to be understood as an ordinary human birth; which is the birth of a being that had no **previous existence,** and that had no choice as to its being born. There were only two ways Christ could become "flesh" and dwell among us, one was to be born, as the Scriptures say He was born, **of a virgin**; the other was to incarnate Himself in some man, some grand character like Samuel or Daniel, but that would be to incarnate Himself in **SINFUL HUMAN NATURE.** For Christ to have made for Himself a human body in which to dwell during His earthly life would not have fulfilled the Scriptures as to the Messiah being born of the "Seed of David," and of a Virgin (Isa. 7:14), nor would He then have been subject to the limitations of humanity with all its frailties and weaknesses. The nature of the case demanded a "Virgin Birth."

If it be said that the Virgin Mary with an inherited taint of sin in her nature could not bring forth a pure offspring, it must not be forgotten that that which was conceived in her was of the Holy Ghost, and Mary was so informed by the Angel Gabriel.

> "The **Holy Ghost** shall come upon thee, and the power of **THE HIGHEST** shall overshadow thee; therefore also that 'Holy Thing' which shall be born of thee shall be called the **SON OF GOD.**" Luke 1:35.

From this we see that the embryo that was deposited in the womb of the Virgin by the Holy Ghost contained no taint of sin, and that Mary's womb was simply the vehicle for the formation of the human body of Christ into which the "Spirit of Christ" entered at birth and thus was formed the **GOD-MAN.**

Four times in his Gospel John calls Jesus the "**Only Begotten Son of God.**" This does not refer to His Eternal origin, for He was co-existent with the Father, but refers to His Virgin Birth. God never begat another son as Jesus was begotten, so He was the only begotten "Son of God." The Apostle Paul in Col. 1:14-15, speaks of Jesus as the "Image of the Invisible God, the FIRST-BORN OF EVERY CREATURE." This cannot mean that Jesus is only a "Creature," for in the next verse Jesus is described as the Creator of all things. The probable explanation is that as Jesus became by His human birth —"God Manifest in the FLESH," (1 Tim. 3:16), thus becoming to men the "IMAGE of the Invisible God," that He thus became the "Firstborn" of the NEW CREATION of God, of which race the "Second" or "Last Adam" (Christ) is the HEAD. 1 Cor. 15:45, 2 Cor. 5:17. It is noteworthy that Jesus is not called the "Son OF GOD, or the "Son OF MAN," in the Scriptures before His Incarnation with but two exceptions, and both of these occur in the Book of Daniel, and look forward to His redemptive work at the close of this Dispensation. Dan. 3:25, Dan. 7:13.

The claim that Joseph was the natural father of Jesus is disclaimed by Scripture, for we are told that when they were only espoused, "before they came together," and Joseph learned that Mary was pregnant, he proposed to "put her away" (divorce her), but being told in a dream that she was in that condition by the Holy Ghost, Joseph, to protect her character, married her, but "knew her not" until she had brought forth her firstborn son. Matt. 1:18-25. But the Scriptures go farther than that to safeguard the Virgin Birth of Jesus. In Matthew's Gospel we have the genealogical table of Joseph's ancestry tracing him back to Abraham. In Luke's Gospel we have the genealogical ancestry of Mary tracing her back to Adam. See the Chart on the "Virgin Birth," page 114. That there are similar names in the two tables presents no difficulty as such a thing is common in tracing any long line of descent. The statement in Matthew that "Jacob begat Joseph, the husband of Mary," and the statement in Luke that "Joseph was (as supposed) the Son of Heli" are easily reconciled, for Joseph could not be the son of both Jacob and Heli. The fact that the translators of the King James version use the word "supposed." and that the word "son" is in italics (which indicates that it is not

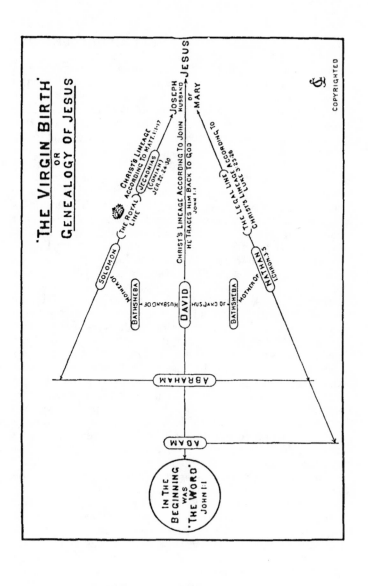

"THE VIRGIN BIRTH"
OR
GENEALOGY OF JESUS

JESUS

JOSEPH
HUSBAND

OF
MARY

CHRIST'S LINEAGE
ACCORDING TO MATT.1:1-17

JECONIAS
(CONIAH)
JER.22:24-30

CHRIST'S LINEAGE ACCORDING TO JOHN
HE TRACES HIM BACK TO GOD
JOHN 1:1

THE LEGAL LINE ACCORDING TO
CHRIST'S LINEAGE LUKE 3:23-38

(THE ROYAL LINE)

(THE LEGAL LINE)

SOLOMON
SON OF

BATHSHEBA
MOTHER OF

DAVID
HUSBAND OF

BATHSHEBA
MOTHER OF

NATHAN
1 CHRON.3:5

JO CAY
HUSBAND OF

ABRAHAM

ADAM

IN THE
BEGINNING
WAS
"THE WORD"
JOHN 1:1

COPYRIGHTED

in the original but is placed there to make sense) shows that some other word could be inserted that would make sense, and that word is "son-in-law," and so it should read, "Joseph which was the 'son-in-law' of Heli." This makes the genealogy of Luke that of Mary, for two genealogies so clearly unlike could not both be the genealogy of Joseph.

Now Jesus was to be a "Son of David," and the chart traces the lineage of Joseph through Solomon back to David, and the lineage of Mary through Nathan back to David. Solomon, as we know, succeeded his father as king, but Nathan was older than Solomon and on that ground might have contested Solomon's right of succession, though we are not told that he did. Nevertheless Solomon's title had the shadow of Nathan's claim upon it, and that there should be no cloud upon Jesus' title to the "Throne of David," God ordained that Mary, the mother of Jesus, should be a direct descendant of David through Nathan, the "legal heir" to the throne. But Jesus had no right to David's throne through Mary, for she was not in the **"Kingly Line"** of descent through Solomon. How then was Jesus' right to David's Throne to be brought about? Only by **marriage.** Here we see the wonderful way in which God safeguarded the **"Virgin Birth"** of Jesus. He saw to it that Mary married (after conception) a man who **could not be the NATURAL father of Jesus** because of a **taint** or defect in his ancestry, for while Joseph was a lineal descendant of David through the "Royal Line" of Solomon, there was one Jechonias (Matt. 1:11-12), called in Jer. 22:24-30, Coniah, of whom God had said that—"No man of his **SEED shall prosper,** sitting upon the 'Throne of David' and ruling any more in Judah." So we see that Joseph could not be the **"natural"** father of Jesus, for no descendant of his could sit on the throne of David and prosper. This forever sets at rest the claim that Joseph was the natural father of Jesus, and establishes the fact of His **"Virgin Birth."** The marriage of Joseph and Mary before the birth of Jesus made Him the adopted son and **"legal heir"** of Joseph. The title, unaffected by the curse pronounced upon Coniah, was thus conveyed to Jesus, in whom there centres through both Nathan and Solomon exclusive right to the Throne of David.

When the time came for Jesus to be born God put it into the heart of the Roman Emperor Caesar Augustus to call for an enrollment. This made it necessary for Joseph and Mary to go to Bethlehem. They could not have been enrolled unless their names were on the Register, and that they were enrolled proves that they could at that time trace their ancestry back to King David. Luke 2:1-5. It was doubtless from this register that Matthew and Luke got their genealogy. If the claim of Jesus to the "Throne of David" had not been known in Jerusalem to be absolutely without flaw, the Jews would have denounced Him as an imposter and pretender. Up to the time of Jesus' rejection as King all genealogical records were preserved in the Temple, but when Titus in A. D. 70 destroyed the city and the Temple, those records were destroyed, and the genealogical tables of Matthew and Luke alone remain to give us the lineal descent of Jesus from King David. Therefore the only living man who today can establish an unbroken genealogy directly and incontrovertibly from King David is the **MAN CHRIST JESUS.** 1 Tim. 2:5.

The Scriptures not only clearly teach that Jesus was a **MAN** (John 8:40, Acts 2:22, 1 Tim. 2:5), and also was **GOD** (John 1:1, Titus 2:13, Col. 2:19), but that these "Two Natures" were united in a single Personality, and that in a **VITAL** and **INSEPARABLE UNION.** As a man Jesus possessed a material body with all its functions. He hungered, thirsted, slept, loved, feared, groaned, wept, prayed, had compassion, suffered, and as to His body died. As God Jesus performed the works of God.

While the union of these two natures took place at the birth of Jesus, that does not imply that there was a complete consciousness of that union in the mind of Jesus at the time of His birth, for we read that as a child He "increased in wisdom and stature, and in favor with God and man." Luke 2:52. It was probably not until He was twelve years of age, on His first visit to the Temple, that the Holy Spirit revealed to Him that He must be about His Father's business. Luke 2:49. At His baptism, when the Holy Spirit, like a dove, rested upon Him, He seems to have come to the full consciousness of His Deity, and yet there were limitations to his knowledge, the self-imposed limitations of a servant, for while a servant may know much he is not supposed to know as much as his master.

While the Divine nature in Jesus kept Him from sinning and preserved Him from intellectual errors, His human nature made Him susceptible to the weaknesses and limitations of the flesh. And as the spirit of man in its union with the body suffers with the body, so Jesus the "God-Man" suffered in the flesh, and the agonies of Gethsemane and Calvary were real and agonizing to Him.

When Jesus surrendered His Spirit to the Father on the Cross, the union between the "Divine" and "human" in Jesus was not dissolved. Jesus did not go back to heaven as He came to the earth bodiless. He took His resurrected **HUMAN BODY** with Him, and we now have in Heaven the **MAN Christ Jesus.** "For there is one God, and one 'Mediator' between God and men, the **MAN Christ Jesus.**" 1 Tim. 2:5. A man can mediate between two men, but he cannot mediate between a man and a horse, because he has not the nature of both a man and a horse. So the Son of God could not mediate between God and man until He became the **"GOD-MAN,"** that is, had the nature of both God and man, and this necessitated that He not only become a man, but that He take His human nature back with Him to Heaven.

While the only account we have of the "Virgin Birth" of Christ is found in the Gospels of Matthew and Luke, this does not militate against its truthfulness. Mark had no occasion to mention it as he confines himself to the public ministry of Christ. John's Gospel was written 60 years after Christ's death and resurrection, and the "Virgin Birth" of Jesus was then well known, and John simply alludes to it in the words—"He was made flesh, and dwelt among us." If, however, we translate the first three words of John 1:13, which read—"Which were born" to **"Who was born,"** as some of the Church Fathers claim they should be rendered, the verse would read—

"Who (Jesus) was born, not of blood, nor of the will of the flesh, nor of the will of man, but of God," which would be a clear statement of the Virgin Birth as it denies a human parentage, and declares that Jesus was born of God.   As to the silence of Paul, like John, he takes it for granted that the fact of the "Virgin Birth" was then well known, and simply alluded to it in the words—"He took the form of a servant and was made **in the likeness of men.**"   Phil. 2:7.   If we accept Luke's Gospel, as Paul's Gospel, and Luke was a companion of Paul, then Luke's account of the "Virgin Birth" is in a sense Paul's. In Gal. 4:4, Paul says—"When the fulness of the time was come, God sent forth His Son, **MADE OF A WOMAN.**"   Why did he say that if he had not reference to the prophetic statement the **"Seed of The Woman"** of Gen. 3:15?   If Joseph and Mary, who were sinners by nature and practice, could have given birth to a sinless being like Christ, then a greater miracle than the "Virgin Birth" took place.   If Jesus was born as other human beings are born, He would not only have been a sinner, He would have been subject to **death.**   But death had no claim on Him.   He voluntarily surrendered His life on the Cross, and could not be "holden of death," but rose of His own power from the grave.   When Jesus at the age of twelve said to His mother—"Wist ye not that I must be about **MY** Father's Business," was there not an allusion to His "Virgin Birth," implying that God, not Joseph, was His Father?

When the fact of the "Virgin Birth" of Christ first became publicly known we are not told.   It was not made known during his lifetime.   The secret was known only to Mary and Joseph, and probably Elizabeth.   It would never have done to have told it before Christ's Ascension, as it would have reflected on Mary's chastity and on Jesus' legitimacy.   So after the death of Joseph and Elizabeth, Mary "hid all those things in her heart." But when the Deity of Christ as He hung on the Cross was witnessed to by the darkness, and earthquake, and rent veil of the Temple, and the opening of tombs, and was further evidenced by His resurrection from the dead, such a supernatural going, demanded just such a supernatural coming as that of the "Virgin Birth." As Luke gives us the detailed description of the "Virgin Birth," and he was a physician, the probability is that Mary, feeling that the time had come to disclose the miraculous manner of Christ's birth, one day after Christ's Ascension told Luke all about it and he recorded it in his Gospel, and thus it became a part of the life story of Christ, from which Matthew got his account.

As the "God-Man," Christ's mind was as lucid as the light. With Christ there never was any confusion nor hesitation in answering questions. He taught the profoundest truths in the simplest manner. He spake of things and events in which he was a participant before He came into the world, and prophesied of things that would take place after His departure and in which He would participate. He never took counsel of others. The wisdom of the ages seemed centered in Him. He exhausted every subject He touched with a single sentence, and His parables are beyond improvement. He never conjectured or supposed, and never asked questions for information but simply to fix attention on what He was about to do. He not only knew men, He knew their character and read their thoughts. Other Bible characters confess faults and sins, Jesus never. He uniformly expressed a distinct sense of faultlessness and perfection. He never once reproached Himself, or regretted anything He had ever done or said, or indicated that He had taken a wrong step or neglected an opportunity or that anything could have been done or said better than He had done or said it. He said—"I do always those things which please the Father." He never apologized or excused Himself. He asked the Disciples to watch with Him, but never to pray for Him. He never used plural personal pronouns in His prayers. He always said "I" and "Me," and "these" and "them," never "We" and "Us."

He claimed equality with God, that He was the Messiah, that He had power to forgive sins, and that He could give rest. He demanded first place, and said that no one could come to the Father only through Him. He said "I am the 'Bread of Life;'" "I am the 'Light of the World;'" "I am the 'Way,' the 'Truth,' the 'Life;'" "I

am the 'Water of Life;'" "I am the 'Resurrection and the Life;'" "before Abraham was I Am." If Jesus was not the Son of God He was the greatest "Egotist" the world has ever seen, aye! He was more, He was a bad man, an imposter, a perjurer, a blasphemer, and unworthy of acceptance or belief.

He was not a Physician. He never employed a splint, tied an artery, used a knife, nor gave a prescription, yet he cured the sick, cleansed the lepers, caused the blind to see and the deaf to hear, and the dead could not remain dead in his presence. He was not an Author. He never wrote, as far as we know, but a single line and that in the sand that the wind obliterated; but the Gospel He preached made such an impression upon the minds of His disciples that they put it into written form in which it has survived down the centuries, and is to be found in the best literature of the world. He was not an Orator, as the world speaks of oratory, but He spake as never man spake, and the common people heard Him gladly. He was a master of every form of human speech, and His parabolic form of speech has never been excelled. He was not a Poet and yet His life has inspired the world's greatest poets and given us our sublimest hymns and anthems. He was not a Musician, but to Him the great musical composers of the world owe their inspiration. He was not an Artist, but without Him the great Masterpieces of Art would never have appeared on canvas. He was not an Architect, only an humble Galilean carpenter, a maker of wooden ploughs and ox-yokes, but the most beautiful and artistic buildings in the world were designed to commemorate His memory and dedicated to His worship and service.

Who was this man? This man whose coming into the world changed the world's reckoning of the years, and gave to Christendom the festive seasons of Christmas and Easter? Was He a Fanatic? Was He a Lunatic? Was He a Dreamer? There never was another man like Him. No writer could ever invent such a character. Who was He then? He was a **FOREIGNER**. He was not of the type of men that this world produces. He came from some other realm. He came to make us a

"**Kinsman,**" and having done that He went back to His own country again taking our nature with Him. The supernatural manner of His coming demanded the supernatural manner of His going. He was what He claimed to be the "**Mystery of Godliness**"—GOD MANIFEST IN THE FLESH.

II. THE MYSTERY OF INIQUITY.

Jesus said to the Jews—"I am come in my **Father's name,** and ye receive me not; if **ANOTHER** shall come in his own name, him ye will receive." John 5:43. Who is this "**OTHER**" who is to come? In both the Old and New Testament we are told of a "**Mysterious and Terrible Personage**" who shall be revealed in the "**Last Times.**" He is described under different names and aliases. In the Old Testament he is called the "**ASSYRIAN**" (Isa. 10:5, 12, 24; 30:27-33); "**LUCIFER**" (Isa. 14:12); the "**LITTLE HORN**" (Dan. 7:8; 8:9); a "King of **FIERCE COUNTENANCE**" (Dan. 8:23); the "**PRINCE THAT SHALL COME**" (Dan. 9:26); the "**WILFUL KING.**" Dan. 11:36. In the New Testament he is called the "**MAN OF SIN,**" the "**SON OF PERDITION,**" the "**MYSTERY OF INIQUITY,**" "**THAT WICKED**" (2 Thess. 2:3-8); the "**ANTICHRIST**" (1 John 2:18); the "**BEAST.**" Rev. 13:1-8.*

The difference between Christ and Antichrist is clearly brought out in the following contrasts.

1. **Christ** came from **Above.** John 6:38.
   Antichrist ascends from **The Pit.** Rev. 11:7.
2. Christ came in His **Father's** name. John 5:43.
   Antichrist comes in his **Own** name. John 5:43.
3. Christ **Humbled** Himself. Phil. 2:8.
   Antichrist **Exalts** himself. 2 Thess. 2:4.
4. Christ **Despised.** Isa. 53:3; Luke 23:18.
   Antichrist **Admired.** Rev. 13:3, 4.
5. Christ **Exalted.** Phil. 2:9.
   Antichrist **Cast Down to Hell.** Isa. 14:14, 15; Rev. 19:20.

*For a full description of the Antichrist, see the chapter on the Antichrist in my larger book, "Dispensational Truth."

6.   Christ to do His **Father's** will.   John 6:38.
     Antichrist to do his **Own will.**   Dan. 11:36.
7.   Christ came to **Save.**   Luke 19:10.
     Antichrist comes to **Destroy.**   Dan. 8:24.
8.   Christ is the **Good Shepherd.**   John 10:14-15.
     Antichrist is the Idol **(evil) Shepherd.**   Zech. 11: 16, 17.
9.   Christ is the "**True Vine.**"   John 15:1.
     Antichrist is the "**Vine of the Earth.**"   Rev. 14:18.
10. Christ is the "**Truth.**"   John 14:6.
     Antichrist is the "**Lie.**"   2 Thess. **2:11.**
11. Christ is the "**Holy One.**"   Mark 1:24.
     Antichrist is the "**Lawless One.**"   **2** Thess. 2:8 (R. V.).
12. Christ is the "**Man of Sorrows.**"   Isa. 53:3.
     Antichrist is the "**Man of Sin.**"   2 Thess. 2:3.
13. Christ is the "**Son of God.**"   Luke 1:35.
     Antichrist is the "**Son of Perdition.**"   2 Thess. 2:3.
14. Christ, "**The Mystery of Godliness,**" is **God** manifest in the flesh.   1 Tim. 3:16.
     Antichrist, "**The Mystery of Iniquity,**" will be **Satan** manifest in the flesh.   2 Thess. 2:7.

Let us examine Paul's description of the Antichrist.

"Let no man deceive you by any means; for '**that Day**' (the Day of the Lord) shall not come, except there come a '**falling away first,**' and that

'MAN OF SIN'
be revealed, the
'SON OF PERDITION;'

who opposeth and exalteth himself above all that is called God, or that is worshipped; so that he **as God** sitteth in the 'Temple of God' (the rebuilt Temple at Jerusalem), showing himself that he is God. . . . For the

'MYSTERY OF INIQUITY'

doth already work (in Paul's day): only He (the Holy Spirit) who now letteth (restraineth R. V.) will let (restrain), until He be taken out of the way. And then shall

THE ANTICHRIST

Fourth Wild Beast
Dan. 7, 7, 8, 11, 19, 23, 24

Daniel's Foreview
The Little Horn Of The He-Goat
Dan. 8, 9-12, 23-25

The Wilful King
Dan. 11, 36-39

Paul's Foreview
2 Thess. 2, 3-12

John's Foreview
Beast Out Of The Sea
Rev. 13, 1-7

"SON OF PERDITION"

"MYSTERY OF INIQUITY"

"THAT WICKED"

'THAT WICKED'

be revealed, whom the Lord shall consume with
the spirit (breath) of His mouth, and shall destroy with the brightness (manifestation R. V.)
of His Coming: even him, whose coming is after
the working of Satan with all power and signs
and lying wonders, and with all deceivableness
of unrighteousness in them that perish; because
they received not the love of the truth (Christ),
that they might be saved." 2 Thess. 2:3-10.

In this passage of Scripture Paul gives the Antichrist
four different names, the "Man of Sin," the "Son of Per-
dition," the "Mystery of Iniquity," and "That Wicked."
The name that the Apostle Paul gives the Antichrist—the
"SON OF PERDITION," is not without significance.
The Apostle also calls the Antichrist in this passage the
"MYSTERY OF INIQUITY." What does that mean?
In 1 Tim. 3:16, Christ is spoken of as the "MYSTERY
OF GODLINESS." That is, that He was GOD MANI-
FEST IN THE FLESH. How did He become "manifest
in the flesh?" By being born of the Virgin Mary by the
Holy Spirit. Thus it was that Jesus became the "SON
OF GOD." Luke 1:35. Now as iniquity is the opposite
of Godliness, then the "MYSTERY OF INIQUITY"
must be the opposite of the "MYSTERY OF GODLI-
NESS." That is, if Christ is the "MYSTERY OF GOD-
LINESS," Antichrist must be the "MYSTERY OF
INIQUITY," and as Christ was the "SON OF GOD,"
then Antichrist must be the "SON OF PERDITION,"
that is of SATAN. And as Christ was born of a virgin
by the Holy Spirit, so Antichrist will be born of a
WOMAN (not necessarily a virgin) by Satan. This is
no new view for it has been held by many of God's spiritually minded children since the days of the Apostle John,
and there is warrant for it in the Scriptures. In Gen. 3:
15, God said to the Serpent (Satan), "I will put enmity
between thee and the woman, and between 'THY SEED'
and 'HER SEED.'" Now the Woman's SEED was
CHRIST, then the Serpent's SEED must be ANTI-
CHRIST. In John 8:44 Jesus said to the Jews—"Ye are

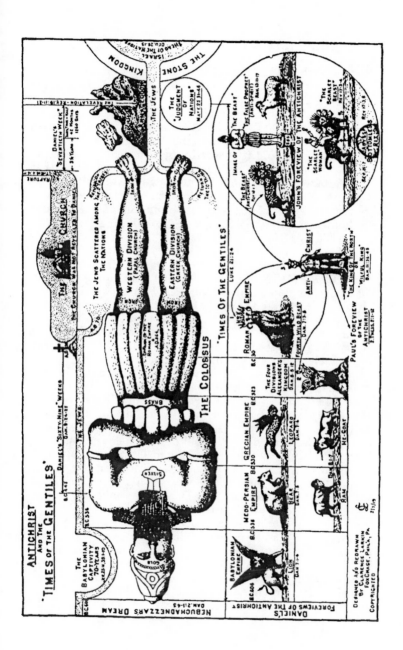

of your father **THE DEVIL** . . . When he speaketh a lie, he speaketh of his own; for he is a **liar**, and the father of **IT**." In the Greek there is the definite article before "lie," and it should read **"THE LIE,"** so when the Devil speaks of **"THE LIE,"** he is speaking of his own (child), for he is a liar, and the **FATHER OF "IT"**— **"THE LIE."** And it is worthy of note that in the verse (vs. 11) that follows the passage we are considering that the Apostle says—"And for this cause God shall send them strong delusion that they should believe **a lie**." Here again the definite article is found in the Greek, and it should read **"The LIE,"** the **"SON OF PERDITION,"** the **ANTICHRIST**.

The character of the **"Mystery of Iniquity"**—THE **ANTICHRIST**, was revealed to Daniel. Daniel saw a **"LITTLE HORN"** (the Antichrist) come up among the **"Ten Horns"** on the head of the **"Fourth Wild Beast,"** that had **"eyes like the eyes of a man, and a mouth speaking great things."** Dan. 7:7-8. Daniel was told that this **"Little Horn"** was a king that should arise and that he would be a "person" of remarkable intelligence and great oratorical powers, having a "mouth speaking great things." That he would be audacious, arrogant, imperious, and persecuting, and change "times and laws," and that the "Saints of the Most High" (Daniel's own people, the Jews) would be given into his hands for a "Time," and "Times," and the "Dividing of Time," or 3½ years, after which his dominion would be taken away from him. Dan. 7:23-26. In the next chapter Daniel has another vision of this "Little Horn," as it appeared on one of the "four horns" of the "He Goat." This "Little Horn" waxed exceedingly great, and Daniel was told that in the "latter time" of the "Fourth World Kingdom" (the revived Roman Empire, yet future), that a "King of Fierce Countenance," and understanding dark sentences shall stand up, but not in his own power (he shall be indwelt by Satan): and he shall destroy wonderfully, and shall prosper, and practice, and shall destroy the mighty and the Holy People (the Jews), and through his policy also he shall cause craft to prosper in his hand (no one shall be able to buy without the "Mark of the Beast," Rev. 13:

17) ; and he shall magnify himself in his heart (2 Thess. 2:3-4), and by peace shall destroy many; he shall also stand up against the "Prince of Princes" (Christ), "but he shall be broken without hand." Dan. 8:23-25.

The "Mystery of Iniquity" will be Satan's "**SUPER-MAN.**" As to ability he will be a "composite man," embracing the powers of Nebuchadnezzar, Xerxes, Alexander the Great, and Caesar Augustus. He will have the marvellous gift of attracting unregenerate men, and the irresistible fascination of his personality, his versatile attainments, superhuman wisdom, great administrative and executive ability, along with his powers as a consummate flatterer, a brilliant diplomatist, a superb strategist, will make him the most conspicuous and prominent of men. All these gifts will be conferred on him by Satan, whose tool he will be. He will pose as a great humanitarian, the friend of men, and the especial friend of the Jewish race, whom he will persuade that he has come to usher in the "Golden Age" as pictured by the prophets, and who will receive him as their Messiah. He will intoxicate men with a strong delusion and his never-varying success. And when he shall be slain and rise again from the dead (Rev. 13:3), in imitation of the resurrection of Christ, he will have lost none of these powers, but will be in addition the embodiment of all kinds of wickedness and blasphemy.

There has never as yet appeared on this earth a person who answers the description given above. Such a character is almost inconceivable. No writer would have invented such a character. He shall reign for seven years, at the end of which time the Lord Jesus Christ shall return to the earth and destroy the allied armies of Antichrist, and he shall be cast with the False Prophet alive into the Lake of Fire. Rev. 19:19-20. Thus will end the "Mystery of Iniquity"—**THE ANTICHRIST.**

XI

Resurrection of Jesus

The Resurrection of Jesus is the foundation fact on which Christianity is built. "If Christ be not raised, your faith is vain; ye are yet in your sins." 1 Cor. 15: 17. The proof of Jesus' "Deity" depended on His Resurrection from the dead. Five different times He declared that He would be crucified and buried and on the third day would rise from the dead. Matt. 12: 39-40; 20: 17-19; 26: 30-32; Luke 18: 31-33; John 2: 19-22. If He had not risen we would not have known whether He was what He claimed to be or not, but the Apostle Paul says He was "declared (demonstrated) to be the **SON OF GOD . . .** by the **RESURRECTION FROM THE DEAD."** Rom. 1: 4. Jesus came to take the sinner's place and satisfy the Law. If Jesus had not risen from the dead we should not have known whether this had been done. When the criminal has served out his full time he cannot be held in confinement a moment longer. According to the Scriptures Jesus' sentence was that He should remain in the grave three days, when the time was up no power in heaven, earth, or hell could hold Him there a minute longer. This is clearly brought out in Acts 2: 24—"Whom God raised up from the dead, having loosed the pains (power) of death because it was not possible that He should be **HOLDEN OF IT."** The Psalmist said of Jesus—"Thou wilt not suffer Thine 'Holy One' to see **CORRUPTION."** Psa. 16: 10. Acts 2: 29-32. Therefore Jesus had to rise before the fourth day when corruption is supposed to set in. The Resurrection of Jesus is proof that **"DEATH"** has been conquered. When Jesus appeared to John on the Isle of Patmos He declared—"I am He that **liveth,** and was **dead**; and behold, I am alive **for evermore,** Amen: and have the **KEYS** of 'Hell' (Hades, the Underworld) and of 'Death' (the Grave)." Rev. 1: 18. We can picture "Death" saying to Captain Sepulchre, "Hold on to that man in Joseph's Tomb until 'corruption' shall have seized upon Him, for if He comes out He will make a breach in the walls of 'Hades' (the Underworld) through which all the prisoners of 'Hades' will escape." But it was not "Death" that had taken Christ captive. Christ simply pursued "Death" into his own dominions, and then conquering him came forth leading captivity captive, and crying "I am the **RESURRECTION** and the **LIFE.**" John 11:25. When Jesus rose from the dead He—"**ABOLISHED DEATH**, and brought 'Life' and 'Immortality' to light." 2 Tim. 1:10. That is, He took from Death its terrors, and made provision by which we shall be freed from the bonds of Death by the resurrection of our bodies, so that ultimately there will be no more Death. Rev. 21:4. Therefore because the Tomb could not hold Jesus it shall not be able to hold us, for—"If the Spirit of Him who raised up Jesus from the dead **dwell in us,** He that raised up Christ from the dead shall **quicken our mortal bodies** by His Spirit that dwelleth in us." Rom. 8:11. That is raise us from the dead.

THE FACT OF THE RESURRECTION OF JESUS

There can be no question as to Jesus' death on the Cross. All four Evangelists tell us that Jesus "yielded up His spirit." Death did not conquer Him. He yielded up His life of His own accord. He said "I have power to lay down my life and I have power to take it again." John 10:17-18. The Roman soldiers did not break the limbs of Jesus because they saw He was dead. John 19:33. And the Centurion testified to Pilate that Jesus was dead. Mark 15:43-45. If Jesus had not yielded up His life on the Cross the "spear thrust" would have killed him, for we read that when the soldier thrust his spear into Jesus' side there came forth water and **blood,** showing that the spear had pierced His heart. John 19:34. If Jesus had not actually died on the Cross but only swooned away He would have been smothered to death by the napkin that was wrapped about His head. Every precaution was taken not only to see that Jesus was dead, but that His body should not be secretly removed from the Tomb. The Tomb was sealed and a guard of Roman soldiers placed to watch it. Matt. 27:62-66. But there were other "Watchers" than the Roman soldiers. Unseen angels kept watch over the resting place of the Son of God. Thus past Friday night, Saturday, Saturday night, but as the sky began to purple in the east on that first Easter Morn there was a great earthquake and an angel descended from Heaven and rolled away the stone from the door of the Sepulchre, and so dazzling was his appearance that the Roman guard became as dead men. Matt. 28:2-4. Whether the angel rolled away the stone to let Jesus out, or simply to reveal the fact that the Tomb was empty, we are not told, but the empty Tomb of Joseph of Arimathea bore witness to the fact that Jesus had risen as He said He would.

There were many witnesses who saw Jesus die on the Cross, but there was not an eye-witness to His Resurrection. That is, no one actually saw Him come out of the Sepulchre. The Roman soldiers did not see him come forth for they were as dead men during the rolling away of the stone and for some time afterward. The story that the Elders put in their mouth, that His Disciples came by night and stole Him away while they slept (Matt. 28:11-15), was to discredit the Disciples if they should claim that Jesus had risen, and is absurd upon its face, for it was death for a Roman soldier to sleep on duty, and if they were all asleep how could they know whether Jesus' body was stolen or arose, and if stolen who stole it? It would have been noisy work breaking the seal and rolling back the stone and would have aroused the soldiers if asleep. More, it was a bright moonlight night, and many pilgrims who had come to the Passover Feast were camped about the city, and it would have been difficult to have carried away the body of Jesus without being seen. If the chief priests had really believed that Jesus' body had been stolen, they would have offered a reward for its recovery, for the recovery of the body would have set at rest for all time the question of Jesus' resurrection. But they did not, thus proving that they believed a miracle had taken place.

But the most remarkable testimony to the physical resurrection of the body of Jesus is found in the statement of the Apostle John, that when he and Peter came to the empty tomb and went in and examined it, they found the linen cloths, in which the body of Jesus had been wrapped, lying on the stone slab on which it had been laid, "and the napkin that was about His head not lying with the linen cloths, but wrapped together in a place by itself." John 20:6-7. That is, the grave clothes of Jesus were not taken away from the Sepulchre, nor tossed to one side as if discarded, but like a hollow cocoon, stiffened by the emblaming material, they were left lying on the stone slab, and the napkin was lying by itself, just the distance of the head from the body, revealing the fact that when Jesus arose He just slipped out of His burial clothes as a locust sheds his skin, and left His clothes behind as a silent witness that His body was not stolen, for if His body had been stolen the thieves would not have tarried to remove His grave clothes, and if for any reason they did, they would not have left them in order, but would have thrown them down anywhere and anyhow.

We have still further evidence that the disciples did not steal the body in the fact that they were so hard to convince that Jesus had really risen from the dead. To us it is a mystery that every one of the disciples was not at the Sepulchre on the morning of the third day to see their Master rise. He had told them so often that He was to be crucified and rise again the third day, but they either forgot it in their sorrow or disbelieved it, for of all His disciples only a few women went to the Sepulchre that morning, and they went not expecting to see Him rise, but to further embalm His body, and they seemed not to have known that a guard had been placed at the Sepulchre for they wondered who would roll away the stone that they might reach the body of Jesus. Mark 16:1-3. We see now the wisdom of their unbelief. If the disciples had hung around the Sepulchre it would have added plausibility to the charge that they had stolen His body, but their very absence and unbelief disprove the charge.

But while no one actually saw Jesus rise from the dead, there were many witnesses who saw Him after His

Resurrection, and that not weeks and months after, but the very day He arose. If He had not been really dead when He was laid in the Sepulchre and revived, and in some way escaped from the Tomb there would have been the pitiable spectacle of His dragging himself about a physical wreck, with wounds in His hands and feet and side. But Jesus when He appeared to His disciples was in robust health, and able to walk half a dozen miles to Emmaus with two of His disciples on the afternoon of the day He arose. The miracle of Christ's Resurrection was twofold, restoration to LIFE, and restoration to HEALTH.

On the day of His Resurrection Jesus appeared to His disciples five times. First to Mary Magdalene (John 20: 11-18), then to the women (Matt. 28:9-10), then to Peter (Luke 24:34), then in the late afternoon to the two disciples on the road to Emmaus (Luke 24:13-35), and then in the evening to a number of the disciples in the "Upper Room." John 20:19 (Luke 24:36-48). A week later, in the same room, He again appeared to His disciples, Thomas being present. John 20:24-29. Later He appeared to seven disciples on the shore of the Sea of Galilee (John 21:1-25), then to the "Eleven" on a mountain in Galilee (Matt. 28:16-20; Mark 16:14-18), then to 500 brethren at once (1 Cor. 15:6), then to James (1 Cor. 15:7), and then, forty days after His Resurrection, He ascended to Heaven in the presence of His Disciples from the Mount of Olives. Luke 24:50-53. Paul tells us in his letter to the Corinthians (1 Cor. 15:6), written 27 years after the Resurrection, that of 500 witnesses that saw Him at one time, the greater part were still alive. It stands to reason that all these persons could not have been deceived, and if there had been collusion among them to perpetrate a fraud, it is improbable to suppose that all of them could have kept the secret or that it would not have leaked out in some way.

But someone may ask—"Why did not Jesus appear to His enemies, as well as to His disciples?" That is, to the Chief Priests, and to Pilate. He did not appear to them because He told the Jews that they should not see Him again until they should say—"Blessed is He that cometh in the name of the Lord" (Matt. 23:37-39), and that will not be until the Revelation Stage of His Second Coming, when they shall again look upon Him whom they pierced. But the fact is He did appear to one of his greatest enemies—"Saul of Tarsus," who has confirmed in his wonderful chapter on the Resurrection, the 15th of First Corinthians, that Jesus did rise from the dead.

Sixty-six years after His Resurrection Jesus appeared to the Apostle John on the Isle of Patmos, and thus we have from the testimony of these many witnesses, indisputable evidence as to the Resurrection of Jesus. This testimony comes from His enemies as well as His friends, and the appearances were not made in secret, but in the open where fraud was impossible. As further proof that Jesus did not revive, but actually rose from the dead, we have the fact that He did not die again but **ASCENDED TO HEAVEN IN THE PRESENCE OF HIS DISCIPLES.**

For over eighteen centuries that "idle tale" of the Roman soldiers, that the Disciples of Jesus stole His body, has been the only explanation of the miraculous fact that on Sunday morning, April 9, A. D. 30, the virgin Sepulchre of Joseph of Arimathea was found **TENANTLESS.** The most astute legal minds of the centuries have weighed the evidence for the Resurrection of Jesus and pronounced it to be flawless.

There is no discrepancy between John and the other evangelists as to the visit of the women to the Sepulchre. Mary with the other women, at dawn, started to the Sepulchre. They found the stone rolled away and the Sepulchre empty. Mary left the other women and hastened back to tell the Disciples. After she had gone the other women entered the Sepulchre when they saw a young man in white who told them that Jesus was risen, and commanded them to go and tell His Disciples. Mark 16:4-7. They at once left the Sepulchre to look for the Disciples. Meanwhile Mary met Peter and John who left her and ran to the Sepulchre, which, after hurriedly investigating, they left and returned to Jerusalem. John 20:3-10. Mary returned to the Sepulchre after Peter and John had left, and finding herself alone began to weep.

Jesus appeared to her and called her by name. At once she recognized the Master and wanted to **touch Him**, but Jesus said—"Touch me not; for I am not yet ascended to my Father." He then commanded her to go and tell the brethren, and then He disappeared. Mary at once left the Sepulchre to do the Master's bidding. Shortly after, Jesus met the other women on their way to tell the Disciples. To them He said—"All Hail," and they fell at His feet, upon which they laid their hands, and worshipped Him. Matt. 28:9-10. At once the question arises why did Jesus forbid Mary to touch Him, and shortly after permitted the women to do so? The only possible answer is that in the meantime, with the swiftness of light, Jesus had ascended to the Father and returned. On the "Day of Atonement," after the High Priest had offered on the Altar the "Blood of the Atonement," if any one touched him before He could carry the "blood" into the Most Holy Place and make Atonement, the Offering was of no avail. So Jesus having offered His own blood on the Altar of the Cross, for Mary to have touched Him before He ascended to the Most Holy Place on high and offered His blood there would have vitiated the work of the Cross.

The fact that the women held Jesus by the feet, that that afternoon He walked for miles and talked with two of His disciples, that in the evening he ate a piece of broiled fish and a honeycomb, that a week later He told Thomas to thrust his hand in His side, and that some time later He breakfasted with His Disciples on the shore of the Sea of Galilee, all prove that Jesus' Resurrection body was not a phantom, but had a physical form and could perform the functions of a human body, and while it was not a glorified body like He had on the Mount of Transfiguration, it had the power to enter a closed room, and to appear and disappear at will, and remain unrecognized until He disclosed Himself by the tone of His voice. This gives us a hint of what our resurrection bodies will be like, as far as their capabilities and powers are concerned, when it will be necessary during the "Age to Come" for us to visit the earth on missions of love and service.

The Resurrection of Jesus changed the whole attitude of the disciples toward Him, and completely revolutionized their lives and became the central theme of their preaching. The "Standard of God's Power" in the Old Testament was the "EXODUS." The "Standard of God's Power" in the New Testament is the "RESURRECTION OF JESUS." It was the culmination of all of Jesus' miracles. As God He laid down His life on the Cross, and as God He rose from the dead. Why then should we think it incredible that GOD should raise the dead? Acts 26:8.

As a testimony to the fact that Jesus rose from the dead we have the observance of the "First Day of the Week" or the "Lord's Day," and the ordinance of baptism. The command to observe the Sabbath was given to Israel exclusively. It was not given to the Gentiles. It was given to Israel as the "Sign" of the "Mosaic Covenant." "Verily my Sabbaths ye shall keep; for it is a SIGN between me and you throughout your generations." Ex. 31:13. Ezek. 20:12, 19-21. The Sabbath Day then belongs to the Jews alone and is not binding on the Gentiles (the world), or on the Church (Christians). Nowhere in the Bible do you find God finding fault with a nation or people, except the Jewish nation, for not observing the Sabbath. As a Jewish ordinance it has never been abrogated, changed, or transferred to any other day of the week, or to any other people. It is now in abeyance as foretold in Hosea 2:11 it would be. It is resumed when the Jews are nationally restored to their own land. Isa. 66:23. Ezek. 44:24; 46:1-3. The fact then that the Christian Church observes the "First Day of the Week," the day on which Jesus rose from the dead, as a day of rest and worship is a proof of the Resurrection of Jesus. As to the relation of Baptism to the Resurrection of Jesus, see the Chapter on "Regeneration and Baptism."

XII

The Resurrections

The Scriptures speak of three kinds of resurrection. **1. NATIONAL.** This refers to Israel who are now nationally dead and buried in the "Graveyard of the Nations," but who are to be revived and restored to their own land. Hosea 6:1-2. See the Chapter on "The Jews," page 33. **2. SPIRITUAL.** This refers to those who are spiritually dead in "Trespasses and Sins." Eph. 2:1-6. Eph. 5:14. Rom. 6:11. This is a **"Present Resurrection"** and is going on continually. Every time a soul is "born again" there is a passing from **"death"** unto **"life,"** a **"Spiritual Resurrection."** John 5:24. **3. PHYSICAL.** This is of the dead body. The "Spirit" of man does not die, it goes back to God who gave it. All that goes into the grave is the **body,** and all that can come out of the grave is the **body.** See the Chapter on the "Spirit World."

THE RESURRECTION OF THE BODY

Jesus clearly and distinctly taught a resurrection "from the grave."

"Marvel not at this; for the hour is coming in the which all that are **in the graves** shall hear His voice, and shall **come forth;** they that have done good unto the **'Resurrection of LIFE,'** and they that have done evil unto the **'Resurrection of DAMNATION.'"** John 5:28, 29.

Here Jesus teaches the resurrection of both the "Righteous" and the "Wicked." The Apostle Paul taught the same thing.

"And have hope toward God, which they themselves also allow, that there shall be a **resurrection of the Dead,** both of the **Just** (justified), and of the **Unjust** (unjustified)." Acts 24:15.

"For as in Adam all **die** (physically), even so in Christ shall **all be made alive** (physically)." 1 Cor. 15:22.

That the Apostle means "physical" death, and "physical" resurrection here is clear, for it is the body, and

THE RESURRECTIONS

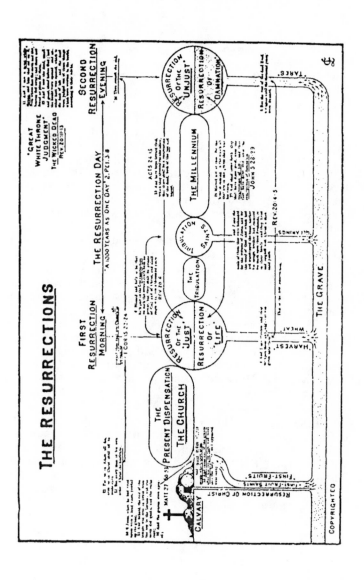

not the spirit that he is discoursing about, and so the Universalist has no "proof text" here for the doctrine of "Universal Salvation."

These passages clearly teach that there is to be a resurrection of "all the dead," and if we did not look any further, we would be led to believe that the Righteous and the Wicked are not only to rise, but that they are to rise at the "same time." But when we turn to the Book of Revelation we find that the Righteous are to rise "before" the Wicked, and not simply precede them, but there is a space of a 1000 years between the two Resurrections. Rev. 20:4, 5.

"And I saw thrones, and they sat upon them,
and judgment was given unto them."

This refers to the saints of the First Resurrection, who, represented by the "Four and Twenty Elders" of Rev. 4:4, are seen seated on thrones surrounding the Throne of God.

"And I saw the souls of them that were beheaded for the witness of Jesus, and for the Word of God, and which had not worshipped The Beast, neither His Image, neither had received His Mark upon their foreheads, or in their hands; and they LIVED and Reigned With Christ a THOUSAND YEARS."

These are the "Tribulation Saints." John first saw them in their "martyred" condition (as souls), then he saw them rise from the dead (they lived again), and they, with the First Resurrection Saints, reigned with Christ a Thousand Years.

"But the rest of the dead (the wicked), lived not again until the 'Thousand Years' were finished."

The rest of the verse—"This is the 'First Resurrection,'" refers not to the "rest of the dead," but to those in verse 4, who lived and reigned with Christ for a 1000 years, for:

"Blessed and holy is he that hath part in the First Resurrection, on such the Second Death (the doom of the Wicked, Rev. 20:14, 15), hath no power, but they shall be **Priests of God and of Christ,** and shall **Reign With Him a THOU- SAND YEARS."** Rev. 20:6.

That the Dead are to rise in different bands or co- horts, with an "interval of time" between, is beautifully brought out in 1 Cor. 15:22-24.

"For as in Adam all die (physically), even so in Christ shall all be made alive (physically). But every man in his **own order."**

The word translated "order" is a military expression, and means a band, cohort, brigade or division of an army. Paul then gives the order:

1. "Christ the **First Fruits."**
2. "Afterward they that **Are** Christ's At His Coming."
3. "Then cometh **The End."**

Now we know that between "Christ the First Fruits," and they that "are Christ's at His Coming," there has already been nearly 1900 years, and as we have seen there will be 1000 years between the resurrection of those that "are Christ's at His Coming" and the "Wicked dead," therefore there is not to be a **simultaneous resurrection** of the Righteous and the Wicked. Already there has been an **"OUT Resurrection"** from **"among the dead."** When Jesus expired on the Cross "the earth did quake, and the rocks rent; and the **graves were opened;** and many **BODIES OF THE SAINTS** which slept **AROSE,** and **came out of their graves AFTER HIS RESURREC- TION** (they could not precede Him), and **WENT INTO THE HOLY CITY** (Jerusalem), **AND APPEARED TO MANY."** Matt. 27:50-53. They with Jesus made up the **"FIRST FRUITS,"** and they are now in their resurrec- tion bodies with Him in glory. See Chart.

It has been objected that the passage in Rev. 20:4, 5, is the **"only"** place in the Bible where a **"length of time"** is given between the resurrection of the Righteous and the Wicked, and that it is not fair to base such an im- portant fact upon a single statement found in such a symbolic Book. But we do not have to depend on Rev. 20:4-6 to prove that there is to be an **"out"** Resurrection "from among the dead." There are a number of passages referring to the resurrection of the dead that are unexplainable only on the supposition that there is a "time space" between the resurrection of the Righteous and the Wicked.

In the reply that Jesus made to the Sudducees in answer to their question as to whose wife the woman would be in the next world who had had seven husbands in this, He said—

> "They which shall be accounted worthy to obtain that world (Age), and the resurrection from the dead, neither marry, nor are given in marriage; neither can they die any more (Second Death); for they are equal unto the angels; and are the 'Children of God' being the children of THE (out) Resurrection." Luke 20:35, 36.

This is a very important statement. The use of the Greek word "Aion," translated "world," but which means "Age," shows that Jesus is speaking of a "class of dead" who are to be raised "before" the next or "Millennial Age," and that those thus raised can "die no more," there is no "Second Death" for them. Why? Because they are "equal unto the angels" and are the "Children of God," having been "born again," and are the "Children of THE Resurrection," the "Out FROM AMONG The Dead" or FIRST RESURRECTION, for only the "Children" of the "First Resurrection" shall live again "before" the Millennium.

In Luke 14:14 Jesus speaks of a "special" resurrection that He calls the Resurrection of the "JUST." This is an "Out Resurrection" from "among the dead," and is only for the "Justified," and must refer to the "First" Resurrection.

The writer to the Hebrews (Heb. 11:35) speaks of a "better" Resurrection, and it is a significant fact that the Apostles preached through Jesus the Resurrection "from the dead." Not the Resurrection "of" the dead, that they always believed, but the Resurrection "from among" the dead, that was a "New Doctrine."

There is no question but that Paul believed in the resurrection "of" the dead, and that he expected to rise "some time," but in his letter to the Philippians (3:11) he expresses the hope that he might "attain unto 'THE' resurrection of the dead." Paul must therefore have had in mind some "special" Resurrection. What Paul meant is clear when we turn to 1 Thess. 4:15-17, where he speaks of the resurrection of the "dead in Christ" and "translation of the living saints," at the Second Coming of the Lord, and as Christ is to come back to usher in the Millennium, then that event must "precede" the Millennium, and be an "Out Resurrection from among the dead," for the "rest of the dead" live not again until the 1000 years "are finished."

But the resurrection of the Righteous and the Wicked is not only to be different as to "time" but as to **CHARACTER.** They that have done "good" (the Righteous) shall rise unto the **"Resurrection of LIFE,"** while they that have done "evil" (the Wicked) shall rise unto the **"Resurrection of DAMNATION."** John 5:28-29. And we read in Rev. 20:12-15, that those who are raised at the Second Resurrection, or the "Resurrection of Damnation," must appear at the **"GREAT WHITE THRONE JUDGMENT,"** and that their names shall **not** be found written in the "Book of Life," and they shall be cast into the **"Lake of Fire,"** which is the **"SECOND DEATH."**

THE MANNER OF THE RESURRECTION

It is claimed by many that the departure of the Soul and Spirit from the body at death is what is meant by the Resurrection. But that cannot be so for the dead (the body) are to rise from their **"GRAVES."** John 5:28-29.

The objection to the resurrection of the **body** is based on the supposition that bodies that have been eaten by animals, blown to atoms, or destroyed by fire or quicklime cannot be restored. But nothing is **impossible** with **GOD.** Luke 1:37. Acts 26:8. Paul reveals the manner of the Resurrection in 1 Cor. 15:35-54. It is called—

THE GERM THEORY.

That is, that in every human body there is a **"LIVING GERM"** that is **indestructible,** and though the body turn to dust that "Living Germ" will continue to exist in the grave, or wherever it may have been deposited, and like the seed in the ground will spring into "immortal life" when the time for the resurrection of the body shall come.

But while the resurrection body shall be alike in kind, it will be different in character and possess different qualities. This Paul declares when he says that "All 'flesh' is not the same flesh; but there is one kind of flesh of 'men,' another flesh of 'beasts,' another of 'fishes,' and another of birds.'" That is, the flesh of God's creatures is adapted to their environment. "Fish flesh" cannot fly in the air, nor "Bird flesh" swim in the sea. So there are bodies "terrestrial" and bodies "celestial." The human body as it is now constituted could not exist in Heaven. There must be a change, and this change is brought about by the resurrection. This change Paul portrays. He says—

"So also is the **Resurrection of the Dead.** It is sown in **corruption**; it is raised in **incorruption**; it is sown in **dishonor**, it is raised in **Glory**; it is sown in **weakness**; it is raised in **Power**; it is sown a **Natural body**; it is raised a **Spiritual** body." I Cor. 15:42-44.

This does not mean that it will have no "substance." We cannot conceive of a "body" that is to have the faculties of the "Spirit Body" not having "form" and "substance." Christ's resurrection body is a "sample" of what ours is to be. While it is true that His body did not see "corruption" and He rose in the "same body" that was laid in the grave; while it was the same in "identity," it was different in "character." While the "nail prints" and 'spear wound" were visible it could pass through closed doors, and appear and disappear at will. It had "flesh" and **"bones"** (Luke 24:39-43), but not **"blood,"** for "flesh and **blood**" cannot enter the Kingdom of God (1 Cor. 15:50), for **"blood"** is that which causes "corruption." To preserve a body it must be drained of blood, or the blood chemically preserved by an embalming fluid. As the sacrifice was to be bled, so Jesus left His blood on the earth.

As our resurrection bodies will have visible "form" and "shape" it stands to reason that they will have a framework of "flesh" and "bones," but it will be "flesh" and "bones" adapted to its new environment. We must not forget that Enoch and Elijah went up in their **"bodies."** Presumably their bodies were "glorified" in the transit, but they were not "disembodied," and if they have use for a "body" in Heaven why not we? Is it reasonable to suppose that only those two saints shall be in Heaven in their bodies? Why did Michael the Archangel contend with the Devil over the "body" of Moses, if Moses had no further need of it? Did not he and Elijah have use for their bodies when they appeared on the Mt. of Transfiguration with Jesus? And if they were "the" two men that stood by in "white apparel" when Jesus ascended (Acts 1:9-11), and are to be the "Two Witnesses" of Rev. 11:3-6, we see that as they are the "type" of the Resurrected and Translated Saints, that the Saints at the Rapture will have "bodies" like Moses and Elijah now have.

The Resurrection of Christ with those who arose with Him was the **"First Fruits,"** the Resurrection of the "Righteous" is the **"Harvest,"** of the "Tribulation" Saints the **"Gleanings,"** and the "Wicked" are the **"Tares."**

It has been objected that if all the dead that have ever lived on this earth were to be raised at one time there would not be standing room. But as we have seen they are not to be all raised at the same time, for the Righteous shall rise and be taken off the earth a 1000 years before the Wicked. But suppose they were. The present population of the world is 1,700,000,000. A generation is generally counted as 33 years. Suppose for argument there had been 1,700,000,000 on the earth in Adam's day, and that that many had died every 33 years since, that would make the dead up to 1900 A. D., 4000 B. C. years + 1900 A. D. years = 5900 years ÷ 33 = 178 generations of 1,700,000,000 people each = 302,600,-000,000 dead, who if they were raised and were each given a square yard to stand on, could stand on less than one-half of the state of Texas.

XIII

The Judgments

―

The common opinion that the Millennium is to be ushered in by the preaching of the Gospel, and that after the Millennium there is to be a "General Resurrection" followed by a "General Judgment," and then the earth is to be destroyed by fire, is not scriptural.

There can be no "General" Judgment because the Scriptures speak of one Judgment as being in the **"Air"** (1 Thess. 4:16, 17; 2 Cor. 5:6-10); another on the **"Earth"** (Matt. 25:31-46); and a third in **"Heaven,"** the earth and its atmosphere having fled away. Rev. 20:11-15. And to make sure that these three separate Judgments should not be combined in one General Judgment scene, three different Thrones are mentioned.

1. The "Judgment Seat of Christ." 2 Cor. 5:10. "In the Air." For "Believers" only.
2. The "Throne of Glory." Matt. 25:31, 32. "On the Earth." For "The Nations."
3. The "Great White Throne." Rev. 20:11, 12. "In Heaven." For the "Wicked Dead."

The Scriptures speak of

Five Separate Judgments.

They differ in five general aspects. As to "Subjects," "Time," "Place," "Basis of Judgment" and "Result."

JUDGMENT NO. 1

1. Subjects—Believers as to "SIN."
2. Time—A. D. 30.
3. Place—Calvary.
4. Basis of Judgment. Christ's "FINISHED WORK."
5. Result—
   1. **Death** as to Christ.
   2. **Justification** as to the Believer.

This Judgment is **PAST.** The Bible proofs of the results of this Judgment are Rom. 10:4.

"For Christ is the **END OF THE LAW** for righteousness to **every one that Believeth.**"

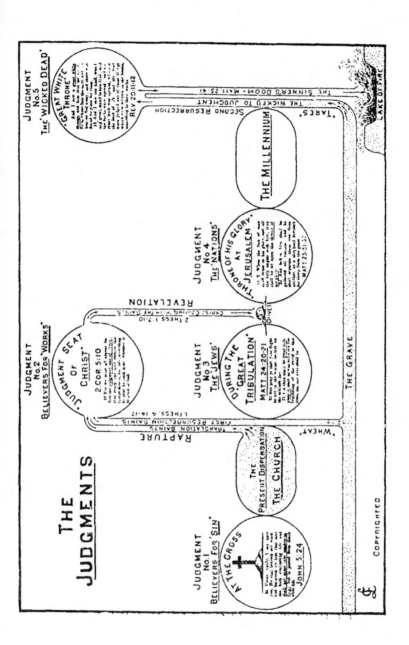

"There is therefore **NOW no condemnation** (Judgment) **to them which are in CHRIST JESUS,** who walk not after the flesh, but after the Spirit. For the **Law of the 'SPIRIT OF LIFE'** in Christ Jesus hath made me **FREE From the Law** of 'Sin and Death.'" Rom. 8: 1, 2.

"Verily, verily, I say unto you, He that heareth my word, and believeth on Him that sent me, **HATH EVERLASTING LIFE and shall not come into condemnation** (Judgment) but **IS PASSED From Death Unto Life.**" John 5:24.

The "Believer's" Judgment for **Sin** then is **PAST.** and was settled at the **Cross.** But we must not forget that the Judgment of the Believer is **threefold.**

1. As a "Sinner."
2. As a "Son."
3. As a "Servant."

As we have already seen his Judgment as a "Sinner" is **Past.** Let us look at his judgment

2. **As a "Son."**

As soon as the sinner accepts Christ as his personal Saviour that settles the **"Sin"** question for him. For if our iniquities are laid on **Him** (Jesus), then they are **not on Us.** Isa. 53:5, 6. But the **"Sin"** question, and the **"Sins"** question are two different things. Christ died on the Cross to atone for **"sin,"** to pay the penalty of Adam's disobedience in the Garden of Eden. **"Sin"** is that tendency in mankind to do wrong which we call "Natural Depravity." We do not get rid of this "tendency" by the "New Birth," but we get a "counteracting force" called the "New Nature." We become a "dual personality." composed of the "Old" and "New Natures," and which shall predominate depends on which we feed and which we starve. This explains the "warfare" that Paul describes as his experience, after his conversion, in Rom. 7:1-25. This warfare will continue until the "Old" nature is eradicated at death. **"Sins"** are the outward acts of wrongdoing that we commit as the result of our tendency to sin.

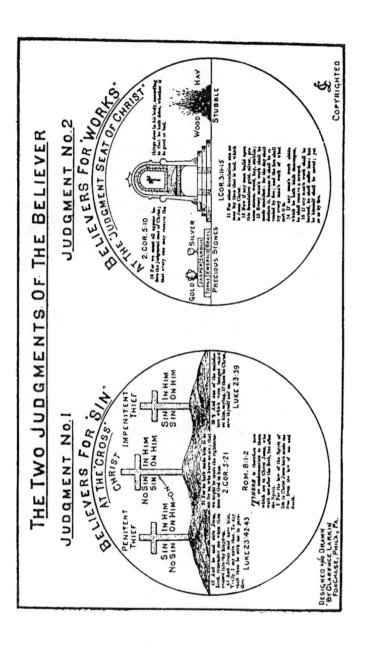

THE TWO JUDGMENTS OF THE BELIEVER

JUDGMENT No.1

BELIEVERS FOR "SIN".

AT THE "CROSS".

PENITENT THIEF

CHRIST

IMPENITENT THIEF

SIN IN HIM
NO SIN ON HIM

NO SIN
SIN IN HIM—ON

SIN IN HIM
ON HIM

42 And he said unto Jesus, Lord, remember me when thou comest into thy kingdom.
43 And Jesus said unto him, Verily I say unto thee, To day shalt thou be with me in paradise.

LUKE 23:42,43

21 For he hath made him to be sin for us, who knew no sin; that we might be made the righteousness of God in him.

2.COR. 5:21

ROM. 8:1-2

THERE is therefore now no condemnation to them which are in Christ Jesus, who walk not after the flesh, but after the Spirit.
2 For the law of the Spirit of life in Christ Jesus hath made me free from the law of sin and death.

39 And one of the malefactors which were hanged railed on him, saying, If thou be Christ, save thyself and us.

LUKE 23:39

JUDGMENT No.2

BELIEVERS FOR "WORKS".

AT THE "JUDGMENT SEAT OF CHRIST"

2.COR. 5:10

10 For we must all appear before the judgment seat of Christ; that every one may receive the things done in his body, according to that he hath done, whether it be good or bad.

GOLD SILVER

JASPER [2.AGUE]
TOPAZ [EMERALD]BERYL

PRECIOUS STONES

WOOD HAY STUBBLE

1.COR. 3:11-15

11 For other foundation can no man lay than that is laid, which is Jesus Christ.
12 Now if any man build upon this foundation gold, silver, precious stones, wood, hay, stubble;
13 Every man's work shall be made manifest: for the day shall declare it, because it shall be revealed by fire; and the fire shall try every man's work of what sort it is.
14 If any man's work abide which he hath built thereupon, he shall receive a reward.
15 If any man's work shall be burned, he shall suffer loss: but he himself shall be saved; yet so as by fire.

DESIGNED AND DRAWN
BY CLARENCE LARKIN
FOX CHASE, PHILA., PA.

These sins must be put away daily by "confession."

"My little children, these things write I unto you, that ye sin not. And if any man sin, we have an 'Advocate' with the Father, Jesus Christ the righteous." 1 John 2:1.

"If we confess our sins, He is faithful and just to forgive us our sins, and to cleanse us from all unrighteousness." 1 John 1:9.

Our Judgment as "Sons" is for "unconfessed sins." The punishment is chastisement. This explains much of the chastisement of Christians, and should show them that they are "Sons" and not "Bastards." Heb. 12:5-11. Paul says—

"If we would 'judge ourselves' we should not be judged. But when we are judged we are chastened of the Lord, that we should not be condemned (Judged) with the world." 1 Cor. 11:31, 32.

Our duty then as "Sons" is to "self-judge" ourselves daily, "confess our sins," and so avert the chastisement of our Heavenly Father.

3. As a Servant. This leads us to—

JUDGMENT NO. 2

1. Subjects—Believers as to "WORKS."
2. Time—After The Church is caught out.
3. Place—"Judgment Seat of Christ" (in the Air).
4. Basis of Judgment—Their "WORKS."
5. Result—Reward or Loss.

This Judgment is FUTURE.

"We must all appear before the 'Judgment Seat of Christ,' that every one may receive the things 'done in the body' according to that he hath done, whether it be 'good' or 'bad' (worthless)." 2 Cor. 5:10.

The pronoun "We" occurs 26 times in the chapter, and in every instance it means the Believer, and the Epistle is addressed to the "Church" and "Saints" at Corinth, so the Judgment here spoken of is for Believers "only." The "Time" of the Judgment is when the Lord comes (1 Cor. 4:5), and the "Place" is "in the air" (1 Thess. 4:17) and before the Judgment Seat of Christ.

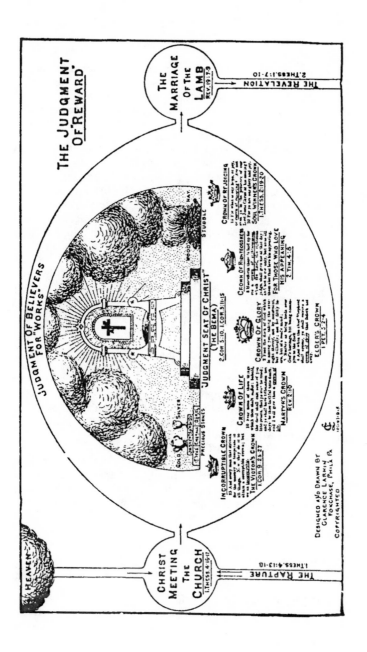

THE JUDGMENT OF 'REWARD'

JUDGMENT OF BELIEVERS FOR "WORKS"

THE MARRIAGE OF THE LAMB
REV. 19:7.9

2.THESS.1:7-10
THE REVELATION

HEAVEN

CHRIST MEETING THE CHURCH
1.THESS. 4:16-17

1.THESS.4:13-18
THE RAPTURE

DESIGNED AND DRAWN BY
CLARENCE LARKIN
FOXCHASE, PHILA, PA.
COPYRIGHTED

JUDGMENT SEAT OF CHRIST
(THE BEMA)
2.COR. 5:10, 1.COR. 3:11-15

INCORRUPTIBLE CROWN
1.COR. 9:25,27
THE VICTOR'S CROWN

CROWN OF LIFE
THE MARTYR'S CROWN
REV. 2:10

CROWN OF GLORY
ELDER'S CROWN
1.PET. 3:7-4

CROWN OF RIGHTEOUSNESS
FOR THOSE WHO LOVE HIS APPEARING
2.TIM. 4:8

CROWN OF REJOICING
SOUL WINNER'S CROWN
1.THESS. 2:19-20

GOLD   SILVER   PRECIOUS STONES

WOOD   HAY   STUBBLE

It will not be a Judgment in the sense of a "trial" to see whether the judged are innocent (saved) or guilty (lost), for it is a Judgment of the **"saved only."** It will be like the Judges' stand at a Fair, or Race Track, where rewards are distributed to the successful contestants. Paul describes such a scene in 1 Cor. 9 : 24-27.

It is not a Judgment for sin, but for "works." This Judgment is described in 1 Cor. 3 : 11-15.

"Other foundation can no man lay than that is laid, which is Jesus Christ. Now if any man build upon this foundation **gold, silver, precious stones** (valuable building stones, as marble, etc.), **wood, hay, stubble**; every man's 'Work' shall be made manifest; for the 'Day' (Judgment Day) shall declare it, because it shall be revealed by 'fire,' and the fire shall try every man's 'work' of what sort it is. If any man's work 'abide' which he hath built there upon he shall receive a 'reward.' If any man's work shall be 'burned' he shall suffer 'loss;' but 'he himself shall be saved;' yet so as by fire."

The result of this Judgment is **"reward"** or **"loss."** All our "bad" and "dead works," represented by the wood, hay and stubble, will be consumed, and only our "good works" shall remain. There is much which passes for Christian service which is merely human and secular, and does not count in our eternal reward. For those who deserve a "reward" it will be

The Crowning Day.

After the Grecian games were all over the runners, wrestlers, and successful contestants assembled before the **"Bema,"** or Judges' stand, which was an elevated seat on which the Umpire sat, and the winners received a "corruptible crown" of "laurel leaves." Some had no reward, they had lost the "Victor's Crown." But while there was no reward there was no punishment, they were not cast out.

The New Testament speaks of Five Crowns. See Chart.

1. The Crown of "LIFE."

This is the "Martyr's" crown, and is mentioned twice.

"Blessed is the man that endureth temptation (testing), for when he is 'tried' (at the Judgment Seat of Christ), he shall receive the 'Crown of Life' which the Lord hath promised to them that love Him." James 1:12.

"Fear none of those things which thou shalt suffer; behold, the Devil shall cast some of you into prison, that ye may be tried (tested) and ye shall have tribulation ten days; be thou faithful 'unto death,' and I will give thee a 'Crown of Life.'" Rev. 2:10.

Notice it does not say "until" death, but "unto" death. They were not to recant but to remain faithful unto a martyr's death. To recant was to lose the crown. This refers to the martyrs of the Tribulation Period.

2. The Crown of "GLORY."

This is the "Elder's" or "Pastor's" crown, given by the Chief Shepherd when He shall appear. But it is not for those who serve for "filthy lucre" or "lord it over God's heritage." 1 Pet. 5:2-4.

3. The Crown of "REJOICING."

This is the "Soul Winner's" crown. Those brought to Jesus by us will be our "crown of rejoicing" at His Coming. 1 Thess. 2:19, 20. Phil. 4:1.

4. The Crown of "RIGHTEOUSNESS."

This is the crown of those who "love His appearing" and will be given in "that day"—the Day of His Appearing. 2 Tim. 4:8.

5. The Crown "INCORRUPTIBLE."

This is the "Victor's" crown, and is for those who "keep under their body" (1 Cor. 9:25-27); who do not yield to their fleshly lusts; who do not permit themselves to be diverted from the Master's work by worldly amusements and pleasure, nor saturate their body with drugs.

If we do not want to be "ashamed at His Coming," (1 John 2:28), let us see to it that we keep our body "under" and so live that we shall secure a crown.

JUDGMENT NO. 3

1. Subjects—The JEWS.
2. Time—"The Great Tribulation."
3. Place—Jerusalem and Vicinity.
4. Basis of Judgment—Rejection of the Godhead.
5. Result—Their Conversion and Reception of Christ as Their Messiah.

This Judgment is **FUTURE**.

While the Church is being judged at the Judgment Seat of Christ in the air, the Jews will be judged under Antichrist on the earth. The Jews are an "earthly" people; and as all the promises to them are "earthly," it follows that their Judgment must be of an "earthly" character. The basis of their Judgment is their "rejection of the Godhead." In the days of Samuel they rejected God the Father. 1 Sam. 8:7. In the days of Christ they rejected God the Son. Luke 23:18. In the days of Stephen they rejected God the Holy Spirit. Acts 7:51, 54-60. For their sin they have been scattered among the nations until the "Times of the Gentiles" are fulfilled. When the "Times of the Gentiles" are about to end the Jews will be gathered back to the Holy Land "unconverted," and caused to "pass under the rod." Ez. 20:34-38. They will be cast into God's "Melting Pot" (Ez. 22:19-22), and pass through an experience spoken of by Jeremiah and Daniel as the "TIME OF JACOB'S TROUBLE." Jer. 30:4-7. Dan. 12:1. Christ calls it "The Great Tribulation," and He and Zechariah the Prophet associate it with the "Return of the Lord." Matt. 24:21-31. Zech. 14:1-11. The human agent the Lord will use will be Antichrist, the awfulness of whose rule will be supplemented by the pouring out of the "Vials of God's wrath" upon the earth. Rev. 15:1, 5-8—16:1-21.

The result of these terrible Judgments will be that the Jews will call in their misery upon the Lord. Zech. 12:10. Then Christ will come back to the Mt. of Olives (Zech. 14:4) and the Jews will look upon Him whom they "pierced" (Zech. 12:10), and a nation, the Jewish Nation, shall be "born (converted) in a day." Isa. 66:8. This will complete the Judgment of the Jews.

JUDGMENT NO. 4

1. Subjects—The NATIONS (Gentiles).
2. Time—The "Revelation of Christ."
3. Place—The "Throne of His Glory." On the Earth —"Valley of Jehoshaphat."
4. Basis of Judgment—Their Treatment of Christ's Brethren—The Jews.
5. Result—Some Nations "SAVED," Others "DE-STROYED."

This Judgment is FUTURE.

The account of this Judgment is given in Matt. 25: 31-46. The description of this Judgment, and of the one given in Rev. 20:11-15 are combined by many, and taken to teach the doctrine of a general Judgment. But when we compare them they differ so widely that it is evident that they do not describe the same event. What God has put asunder let no man join together. The following comparison will show the difference in the two accounts:

Matt. 25:31-46.

1. No Resurection.
2. Living Nations Judged.
3. On the Earth. Joel 3:2.
4. No Books Mentioned.
5. Three Classes Named. "Sheep," "Goats," "Brethren."
6. Time—Before the Millennium.

Rev. 20:11-15.

1. A Resurrection.
2. Dead Judged.
3. Heaven and Earth Gone.
4. Books Opened.
5. One Class Named. "The Dead."
6. Time—After the Millennium.

This comparison reveals the fact that one of these Judgments is "on the earth," the other in the "heavens," and that they are separated by 1000 years.

The Greek word "ethnos" here translated "Nations" occurs 158 times in the New Testament. It is translated "Gentiles" 92 times, "Nation" or "Nations" 61 times, and "The Heathen" 5 times, but it is never in any instance (unless it be this) applied either to the "dead" or the "resurrected."

As this is a Judgment of nations only, the Jews cannot be in it, for they are not reckoned among the nations. Num. 23:9. And as the Church will be associated with Christ in this Judgment, for the "Saints" (the Church) shall judge the "World" (the Nations) (I Cor. 6:2), the Church cannot be in this Judgment either. As we have seen the Church and the Jews have been already judged, so the "Judgment of the Nations" cannot be a general Judgment. Who then, is asked, are meant by the Sheep? Do they not represent the Righteous, and all the Righteous from the beginning of the world to the end of Time? And do not the Goats in like manner represent all the Wicked?

If the Sheep are the Righteous, and the Goats the Wicked, then who are the Brethren? If they are the "followers of Christ," as some claim, they should be classed with the Sheep. The Scriptures teach that the Righteous are saved by "faith," and the Wicked are lost because they "reject Christ," but in this Judgment scene the Sheep inherit a "Kingdom" and the Goats are commanded to "depart," because of their **treatment of the Brethren.**

All the confusion is caused by trying to make a Judgment of "nations" mean a Judgment of "individuals." The Sheep represent one class of Nations, and the Goats another class, while the Brethren represent the Jews (Christ's brethren). We must bear in mind the **time** and **place** of this Judgment. The **time** is at the "Revelation of Christ" when He comes to set up His "Millennial Kingdom" on the earth. The **place** is the "Valley of Jehoshaphat" in the vicinity of Jerusalem.

> "For, behold, in **those days,** and in **that time,** when I shall bring again **the captivity** of Judah and Jerusalem, I will also gather **ALL NATIONS,** and will bring them down into the 'Valley of Jehoshaphat,' and will plead with them there for **MY PEOPLE** and for my heritage **ISRAEL,** whom they have scattered among **the Nations,** and parted my land." Joel 3:1, 2.

This prophecy clearly states that there is to be a "Judgment of Nations" on the earth in the "Valley of Jehoshaphat" at the time of the restoration of the Jews to their own land, and that the basis of Judgment is the treatment by the nations of Christ's brethren—The Jews.

During the "Tribulation Period" the Nations that treat the Jewish People kindly, feeding and clothing them, and visiting them in prison, will be the "Sheep Nations," while those who neglect to do so will be the "Goat Nations." At the "Judgment of Nations" the King (Christ) will say to the "Sheep Nations," inasmuch as ye have been kind to My brethren (the Jews), "Come, ye blessed of my Father, inherit the Kingdom prepared for you from the foundation of the world." This Kingdom is the "Millennial Kingdom" that the "Sheep Nations" as Nations will "inherit" and possess during the Millennium. And as they are to be among the "saved nations" of the New Earth (Rev. 21:24) it can be said of them that they, or at least the righteous individuals of them, shall enter into life eternal. Matt. 25:46. Christ's sentence upon the "Goat Nations" will be—"Depart from Me, ye cursed, into everlasting fire, prepared for the Devil and his angels," and "these shall go away into everlasting punishment." The "Goat Nations" will at once be destroyed as Nations, not one of them shall get into the Millennium, and the wicked individuals that compose them will perish and be eternally lost.

JUDGMENT NO. 5

1. Subjects—The WICKED DEAD.
2. Time—During the Renovation of the Earth by Fire.
3. Place—Before "The Great White Throne."
4. Basis of Judgment—Their "Works."
5. Result—Cast Into the "Lake of Fire."

This Judgment is FUTURE.

The account of it is given in Rev. 20:11-15. It will take place at the close of the Millennium a 1000 years after the Judgment of the Nations, and before the "Great White Throne." The "Great White Throne" will not be on the earth, for the "Great White Throne Judgment" will take place during the renovation of the earth by fire, for the "renovation" of this Earth is reserved or kept until the time of that Judgment, which **Peter** calls "The **Day of Judgment** and **Perdition of Ungodly Men**" (2 Pet. 3:7), because the Judgment of the "Great White Throne' is the Judgment of the **wicked dead.**

All the Righteous dead will arise at the First Resurrection. If any Righteous die between the First Resurrection and the Resurrection of the "wicked" or Second Resurrection, they will rise with the wicked dead at that Resurrection. The words—"Whosoever was not found written in the Book of Life" (vs. 15), imply that there will be "some," probably very few, Righteous at the Second Resurrection.

At the close of the Millennium and just before the renovation of the earth by fire, the living Righteous will probably be translated, and the living Wicked or Ungodly will be destroyed in the flames that will consume the earth's atmosphere and exterior surface.

The Wicked or Ungodly will not be judged to see whether they are entitled to Eternal Life, but to ascertain the "**degree**" of their punishment. The sad feature of this Judgment will be that there will be many kind and lovable people there who were not saved, and who will be classed among the "ungodly" because they rejected Christ as a Saviour. The "Books" will be opened in which the "Recording Angel" has kept a record of every person's life, and they will be judged every man according to his "works." Some will be sentenced to a more severe punishment than others, but none will escape. The worst of all is, that those who were not so bad must spend eternity with the ungodly, and that in the "Lake of Fire." Their punishment includes the **second death,** which means that they shall lose their resurrection bodies, in which they were judged, and become "disembodied spirits" again, and so exist in the "Lake of Fire" **FOREVER.**

The "Fallen Angels" (not the Devil's angels), who are "reserved in everlasting chains under darkness,"will be judged at this time, which Jude calls the Judgment of the "Great Day." Jude 6.

XIV

The Two Adams

The Scriptures speak of two "Representative Men." The first is called "**ADAM**," the second is called the "**LAST ADAM**" (1 Cor. 15:45), or the "**Second MAN**," the "Lord from Heaven." 1 Cor. 15:47. This identifies Him with the Lord Jesus Christ. The "First Adam" is charged with bringing sin into the world. "By one man sin entered into the world, and death by sin; and so death passed upon all men, for that all have sinned." Rom. 5:12. The "Last Adam" came to reverse what the First Adam did, and to "put away sin." Heb. 9:26.

"For if by one man's offence death reigned by one: much more they which receive abundance of grace and of the gift of righteousness shall reign in life by one, Jesus Christ." Rom. 5:17. To understand the work of these two "Representative Men" we must study their history.

I. THE FIRST ADAM.

After the earth had been restored from its "formless and void" condition, and the air, sea, and earth been re-populated with bird, fish, and animal life, we read—

"And God said, Let **US** make man in **OUR IMAGE**, after **OUR LIKENESS**: and let them have dominion over the fish of the sea, and over the fowl of the air, and over the cattle, and over all the earth, and over every creeping thing that creepeth upon the earth. So God **created** man in His **OWN IMAGE**, in the **IMAGE OF GOD created** He him; male and female created He them." Gen. 1:26-27.

From this we see that man is a **CREATED** being. That he was made in the "**IMAGE OF GOD**," not in the image of an "Ape," and was formed not from a brute, but of the "dust of the earth." There is an "Impassable Gulf" between the lowest order of man and the highest type of beast that science has failed to bridge. The "Missing Link" has never been found. That the whole human race is of "One Species" and had a common origin (Acts 17:26) is clear from the fact that, when the different races of the earth's inhabitants intermarry, their offspring are not sterile but fertile. There is no contradiction between the first and second chapters of Genesis as to the creation of man. The first chapter (Gen. 1:26-28) gives the **FACT** of his creation, the second, the **MANNER OF IT."** Gen. 2:7. One is supplementary to the other. In Gen. 2:7, we are told that—"the **LORD GOD** formed (fashioned) man of the **dust of the ground,** and breathed into his nostrils the '**Breath of Life;**' and man became a '**Living Soul.'**" From this we see that the creation of man was "Threefold." (1) The formation of the **BODY.** (2) The impartation of the **SPIRIT.** (3) The unification of the two through the **SOULISH** part of man. The two principal parts of man are the **BODY** and the **SPIRIT,** but as the functions of these are separate, one being physical and the other spiritual, a third part had to be supplied called the **SOUL,** intermediate between them, and through which they may communicate. This makes man a "Threefold Being." 1 Thess. 5:23, Heb. 4:12. See the Chapter on "The Spirit World," and the Chart "The Threefold Nature of Man," page 86.

In Adam as originally created the "Soul" was such a perfect medium of communication between the "Body" and the "Spirit" that there was no conflict between them. The three blended together in one harmonious whole. When man fell the "Soul" became the "Battlefield" of the "Body" and the "Spirit," and the conflict began that Paul so graphically describes in Rom. 7:7-24.

Eve was not fashioned in the same way as Adam. She was **"made"** later. "The Lord God caused a '**deep sleep**' to fall upon Adam and he slept; and He took one of his '**RIBS,**' and closed up the flesh thereof: and the '**RIB,**' which the Lord God had taken from man, made (builded) He a **WOMAN,** and brought her unto the man. And Adam said, this is now '**bone of my bones,**' and '**flesh of my flesh;**' she shall be called **WOMAN,** because she

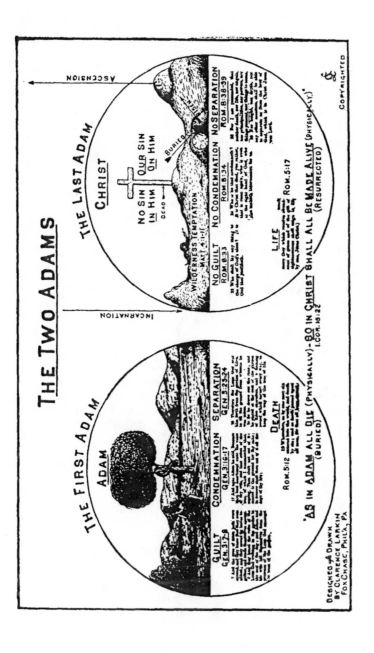

THE TWO ADAMS

THE FIRST ADAM

THE LAST ADAM

ADAM

CHRIST

ASCENSION

INCARNATION

WILDERNESS TEMPTATION
MAT. 4:1-11

NO SIN IN HIM
OUR SIN ON HIM

DEAD

BURIED

GUILT
GEN. 3:7-9

CONDEMNATION
GEN. 3:16-17

SEPARATION
GEN. 3:23-24

NO GUILT
ROM. 8:33

NO CONDEMNATION
ROM. 8:34

NO SEPARATION
ROM. 8:38-39

DEATH
ROM. 5:12

LIFE
ROM. 5:17

"AS IN ADAM ALL DIE (PHYSICALLY)—SO IN CHRIST SHALL ALL BE MADE ALIVE (PHYSICALLY)."
(BURIED)   (RESURRECTED)
I. COR. 15:22

DESIGNED & DRAWN
BY CLARENCE LARKIN
FOX CHASE, PHILA., PA.

COPYRIGHTED

was taken **OUT OF MAN."** Gen. 2:21-23. The reason why Eve was not fashioned separately from Adam, but was taken out of Adam's side, was to show that in their relation to each other as man and wife they were to be **ONE FLESH.** That is in their interests, sympathies, etc., they were to be one, and physically they were to be counterparts of each other. In this respect Adam and Eve, are a type of the Last Adam and His Eve—**THE CHURCH.** Eph. 5:25-32.

Adam was not created a baby or a primitive savage, but a full grown man perfect in intellect and knowledge, else he could not have named the beasts of the field and the fowls of the air. And the fact that his descendants had such skill in the invention of musical instruments and mechanical devices and could build cities and towers and such a vessel as the Ark, proves that the men of Antediluvian times were men of gigantic intellect and attainments, and that instead of man having **"evolved upwards"** he has **"DEGENERATED DOWNWARDS."**

The first pair were happy in their sweet companionship, and doubtless believed that it would last forever. They knew nothing of the ruins of the Primeval Earth beneath their feet, now covered with the Edenic verdure of a renewed earth. Neither did they know that the heavens above them swarmed with fallen beings under the leadership of Satan, and that their happiness was to end in a **"Fall"** that would necessitate their expulsion from that "Garden of Delights," and that sooner or later they should taste of physical death.

If it be charged that God should have forewarned Adam of his danger of an attack by Satan, let it not be forgotten that the commandment not to eat of the "Tree of Knowledge of Good and Evil" should have caused him to beware of any being who should tempt him to disobey the command of God and eat of it. To have plainly told him of the plan of Satan would have frustrated God's purpose in the testing of Adam. True obedience is to obey without knowing why.

How long after Adam was created Eve was given to him we do not know. It must have been some time, for Adam required time to name all the living creatures that were brought to him, of cattle, of fowl, and of the beasts of the field. Neither are we told how long after Eve was given to Adam before the Temptation. It is hardly likely that it was immediately, for while they were mature physically they were but as children in experience, at least Eve was, and she was unfit to cope with the seductive wiles of the Serpent, the most powerful enemy of God and man.

Satan's purpose in the "Temptation" was to thwart God's purpose in the creation of man (the peopling of the earth with a holy race of beings), and to regain the earth, which he had lost by his rebellion. His hope was to excite God to destroy the first pair for their sin before they could populate the earth. He played his game with consummate skill. Fearing that if they were approached together they might withstand him, he awaited the time when Eve should be alone.

It is not improbable that Eve, curious to know the cause of the prohibition, had stolen away from Adam and gone off by herself to examine the Tree, and that Satan, discovering her there, was not slow to take advantage of his opportunity.

If Eve had avoided the vicinity of the Tree, she would not have been able to cast that look at it which made her desire to eat of its fruit. Satan saw that Eve was disgruntled about something. He wisely surmised that it was because God had forbidden Adam and Eve to eat of the Tree, so he approached her and spoke to her. The fact that Eve was not afraid to talk with the Serpent is an indication that it was not a loathsome creature, and that it was no stranger to her. She had seen it often, and probably talked with it before, for Satan does not make his supreme effort until he has first prepared the way. What the Serpent was like before it was cursed and caused to crawl instead of stand upright, we do not know, but it must have been a beautiful creature. Whether it had the power to talk, or simply became the mouthpiece of Satan we are not told. What we do know is that Satan incarnated himself in it.

Observing that Eve was casting longing glances at the "Fruit" of the Tree, the Serpent (Satan) opened the conversation by craftily asking—"Yea, hath God said, Ye shall not eat of **every** tree of the Garden?" The subtility of this question is seen in its insinuating suggestion that God did not love them, and was unfair and unkind to forbid them **anything.** In her answer Eve betrays her feeling toward God by adding to the prohibition, saying —"Neither shall ye **TOUCH** it," as if God was afraid to trust her. She also altered the penalty from—"thou shalt **surely die,**" to "lest ye die," thus expressing doubt as to the **certainty** of death. It is a dangerous thing to add to or subtract from God's word. Rev. 22:18-19. The commencement of the Fall was the "deceitful handling" of the Word of God. 2 Cor. 4:2.

Satan was the first **"Higher Critic."** He was the creator of the **"SEED OF DOUBT."** It was deposited in the heart or mind of Eve by Satan's question—"Yea, hath **GOD** said?" This led Eve to question the love of God. This **"MICROBE OF UNBELIEF"** the human race has inherited from Eve. Men do not openly deny the goodness of God so much as they **question** the statements of the Word of God. They say—"Has God really said we must not do thus and so? Have we not misunderstood what He has said, or misinterpreted His meaning? Surely God is too loving and merciful to eternally punish the wicked."

Satan having sown the "Seed of Doubt" and perceiving that the poison was working, next declared that God was a liar by saying—**"Ye shall not surely die."** This is the **"DEVIL'S LIE,"** and it has been incorporated into the religious systems of today that teach that man shall not be eternally punished. Satan then impugned God's motive by declaring that God did not want them to have a knowledge of "Good" and "Evil" lest they become **"gods"** like Himself. This appealed to Eve's curiosity and ambition, and stirred up a **"torrent of desire"** in her heart, and when she saw that the "Tree" was **"good for food"** (the Lust of the Flesh), and **"pleasant to the eyes"** (the Lust of the Eye), and **"desirable to make one wise"** (the Pride of Life), she did not wait to consult her husband, but put forth her hand and plucked and ate the fruit, and the days of her innocence were ended; and when Adam appeared, without contrition of heart, she in turn tempted him, and he not willing to be separated from her also ate, the result the ruin of the race. The Woman was deceived, but Adam was not deceived, nevertheless, the Apostle tells us, it was the **"woman's"** fault. 1 Tim. 2:13-14.

The inducement that Satan held out to Eve, that the **acquisition of knowledge** would put her and Adam on the same plane with God, and make them **GOD-LIKE,** is the same inducement that Satan offers to ambitious men today, and he is seeking through his dupes to build up a magnificent civilization on the discoveries and inventions of men, and exalt man without God, and his aim is the final

"DEIFICATION OF MAN,"

that will find its culmination in his

"SUPERMAN,"
"THE ANTICHRIST,"

who will sit in the Temple at Jerusalem and proclaim himself **GOD.** 2 Thess. 2:3-4. This accounts for all the "World Systems" of today, for the social, religious, political and commercial betterment and advancement of the race.

Adam and Eve were created **"INNOCENT."** "Innocence" is not **"RIGHTEOUSNESS."** "Innocence" cannot become "Righteousness" until **TESTED.** If Adam and Eve had stood the **"Test"** they would have become "Righteous" or "Holy," they failed and became **SINNERS.** There is but one **step** from "Innocence" to **"HOLINESS,"** or from "Innocence" to **"SIN."** Adam and Eve took the step from "Innocence" to **SIN** and became **SINNERS.** If they had taken the opposite step they would have become "Holy" and been beyond the possibility of "Sin." Now man cannot become "Holy" without the New Birth.

In the Fall of man the triumph of Satan was complete. The first effect of the disobedience of Adam and Eve was **"SELF-CONSCIOUSNESS."** "They saw that they were **NAKED.**" The result of this knowledge led them to invent clothing made of **"FIG LEAVES."** All living creatures are clothed by nature. Fish have scales, birds have feathers, beasts have hair, or fur, or wool; even serpents have a beautifully colored skin. Many are naked when ushered into existence, but it is not long until nature provides clothing. Man alone of all God's creatures is left without clothing, and is compelled to have recourse to artificial covering. Why is this? It is the result of SIN.

Adam and Eve at first wore no clothing, nor did they need to. Their state of innocence made them not ashamed. Some claim that their unfallen nature was clothed in a veil of radiant glory that hid their nakedness. This they lost in the Fall. At once, conscious of their shame, they resorted to artificial clothing. Clothes are the trappings of guilt. The style and character of clothing may change, but the guilt remains. Clothing may hide our shame from the eyes of man, but not from the eyes of God. A black heart may hide behind a white vest.

The sun set that day upon a scene that witnessed the downfall of the human race. It was a dark and fearful night. They both dreaded to meet God and so hid themselves in the forest when the Lord God came down to take His usual walk in the Garden in the cool of the day. Heretofore they had looked forward to the daily visit of the Lord God, but now they feared to face Him. Thus sin makes cowards of us all.

By questioning them the Lord God got them to sit in judgment on their own conduct. Adam blamed his fall on Eve, she blamed her fall on the Serpent. God patiently listened to them and gave them an opportunity to justify their conduct, then He passed judgment on them. But to the Serpent He gave no opportunity for justification, but said—

> "Because thou hast done this, thou are cursed above all cattle, and above every beast of the field; upon thy belly shalt thou go, and dust thou shall eat all the days of thy life; and I will put enmity between thee and the woman, and between THY SEED and HER SEED, IT (her

seed—CHRIST) shall bruise thy HEAD, and THOU shalt bruise His HEEL."

In the expression **THY SEED** (Satan's seed) we have a prophetic reference to **THE ANTICHRIST** who as Satan's seed is called in 2 Thess. 2:3 the "**SON OF PERDITION.**"

These are the words of a Judge to a condemned criminal who is awaiting sentence, and is a confirmation of Satan's previous rebellion, who here hears his doom. At once the Serpent, the tool of Satan, is changed into a crawling, loathsome, venomous reptile. The Woman's sentence was that she should lose her position as man's equal and become subject to him, and that untold sorrow and misery in motherhood should be her lot. Unto Adam God said, "Cursed is the ground for thy sake, . . . thorns also and thistles shall it bring forth to thee, . . . in the sweat of thy face shalt thou eat bread, till thou return unto the ground." So what had been a pleasure to Adam, the care of the Garden, was henceforth to be a task, for driven out from the Garden he must make a living by tilling a soil that brought forth naturally nothing but thorns, thistles and weeds.

The Edenic Dispensation was perfectly unique. It was characterized by the "**absence of sin,**" and the "**presence of God.**" There will be nothing like it again until "The Tabernacle of God is with men," and He will dwell with them on the New Earth. Rev. 21:3. In the Edenic Dispensation God dealt with Adam on the basis of "**INNOCENCE,**" and He can never treat with man again on the same basis until the curse of sin shall be removed from the earth. Man is no longer under probation, but under condemnation. John 3:18. Ever since the Fall God has had to deal with man as a guilty, lost, helpless and ruined **sinner.** And not only a ruined **sinner,** a ruined **CREATURE.** There is no good thing in him, he is at "**enmity with God,**" and is not "**subject to the law of God, neither indeed can be.**" Rom. 8:6-7.

In mercy God drove the guilty, but forgiven pair, from the Garden lest they eat of the "Tree of Life" and be doomed to live "forever" in their sinful mortal bodies. Men claim that innocence and a perfect environment are safeguards against wrong-doing, but the catastrophe of Eden proves that this is not true.

II. THE LAST ADAM

The Fall of the "First Adam" demanded the coming of the "Last Adam." It is self-evident that a fallen creature cannot redeem itself. It must be redeemed by a power outside itself. Therefore no human being of the Adamic race could redeem the race. Such a redemption demanded a Divine interposition. But the Redeemer must have the same nature as the Adamic race. He must be a **MAN**. To this end he must be born into the human race and yet be free from the **"taint of Sin."** This was accomplished by the "Virgin Birth." See the Chapter on "The Mystery of Godliness."

The "Last Adam" having taken upon Himself human nature it was necessary that He be put to the same test as the "First Adam." To this end we read that immediately after His Baptism, before He had preached a sermon or called a disciple, He was led of the Holy Spirit into the "Wilderness" to be tempted (tested) of the Devil. Matt. 4:1. It was not then a case of it "happened so." It was a part of God's plan as to the "Last Adam." The Temptation was not planned by the Devil. He doubtless would have avoided it, for he knew who Jesus was, but Jesus having been led into the rendezvous of the Devil, the Devil could not well avoid the meeting. That he was not over-anxious to make the test is evident from the fact that he waited until Jesus was physically worn out from fasting.

Notice the "Place of Temptation." It was not in a "Garden" like that in which the "First Adam" was tested. It was in the "Wilderness," a place uninhabited except by wild beasts, and with no means of satisfying hunger. It is profitable to compare the "Forty Days" of fasting with those of Moses and Elijah. Moses and Elijah both had **GOD** with them. Jesus had the **DEVIL**.

THE FIRST TEMPTATION

Mark says He "was in the Wilderness 40 days tempted of Satan." Luke says "being 40 days tempted of the Devil." Matthew says "and when he had fasted 40 days

and 40 nights, He was afterward an hungered, and when the Tempter came to Him, he said," etc. The probability is that the Devil skirmished from ambush with Jesus during the 40 days, and then when he saw Jesus weakened by fasting, and believing the "Psychological Moment" had come he attacked him in the open. The matter of hunger was neither **incidental** nor **accidental.** It was **ordained.** If it had not been a feature of the Temptation Jesus might just as well have been tempted in Capernaum or at Jerusalem after a feast. While the Temptation of Jesus was to show that He was qualified to be the Head of a New Race, the time of the Temptation, between the declaration of His Sonship and the proclamation of the Kingdom, is not without significance, for it explains the character of the Temptations as having a bearing on the setting up and feeding the subjects of the Kingdom.

The "First Temptation" is similar to the one in Eden. It raised the question of doubt. "**IF** Thou be the **SON OF GOD.**" It had been but six weeks since God the Father had said at Christ's Baptism—"This is my beloved **SON** in whom I am well pleased," and the force of the Devil's argument lay in the fact that Jesus, being hungry, and with no visible means of supplying His need, could test the fact of His Sonship by performing a **miracle,** for that was the Old Testament sign of Messiahship. The Devil may have gone farther and said—"You will die if you do not eat, how then can you carry out your Kingdom plans? Do you not know that the way to get the ascendency over men is to feed them? How can you set up a Kingdom without a 'Commissary Department?' If you know that you have power to turn stones into bread, all you will have to do is to say—'Come unto me all ye that are hungry and I will give you food and supply your needs,' and you will have a multitude of followers." Was not this true when Jesus fed the 5000 and they wanted to take Him and make Him King and he had to flee to prevent the premature setting up of the Kingdom?

For Jesus to have turned a stone into bread to satisfy His own need would have been illegitimate, for the power to work miracles was given Him not to supply His own needs but the needs of others. For Jesus to have turned a stone into bread to satisfy His own hunger would have been disobedience. God's purpose in having the Holy Spirit drive Jesus into the Wilderness was that He might be made to hunger, and He had no right to satisfy His hunger until God saw fit to satisfy it Himself, so to have turned stones into bread would have been an act of disobedience. This is clear, for when the purpose of the Temptations was fulfilled angels came and ministered unto Him and supplied all His physical needs.

In Jesus' reply to the Devil—"It is written **MAN** shall not live by bread alone, but by every word that proceedeth out of the mouth of God," Jesus, by the use of the word **MAN**, classes Himself with humanity and takes the position of trust and dependence upon His Heavenly Father, declaring that man needs something more than physical food, he needs the kind of food of which Jesus spake at the well of Samaria, "I have **meat** to eat that ye know not . . . my **meat** is to **do the will of Him that sent me.**" Jesus in His reply took the "**impregnable position**" that what God the Father had said as to His **SONSHIP** needed not the corroborative proof of a miracle.

THE SECOND TEMPTATION

No length of time is given between the Temptations, and the inference is that they followed one another in quick succession as suggested by the word—"then." It would be interesting to know what the second and third Temptations of Adam and Eve would have been if they had not fallen to the first. Probably they would have been different. Having failed in his effort to get Jesus to disobey the "Will of God," the Devil changes his tactics. He takes Jesus from the Wilderness to Jerusalem and sets Him on a Pinnacle of the Temple, and says— "**IF** Thou be the **SON OF GOD,** cast Thyself down; for it is written, He shall give His angels charge concerning Thee; and in their hands they shall bear Thee up, lest at any time Thou dash Thy foot against a stone." Psa. 91 : 11-12.

This Temptation is a challenge to Jesus to make His faith in God's protecting care **visible**. If He trusted God in all things let Him cast Himself down from the Pinnacle of the Temple and test the promise of God to give His angels charge over Him and bear Him slowly down to the ground. The Kingdom idea is also seen in this Temptation. The Prophet Malachi (Malachi 3:1) had foretold that the Messiah would suddenly come to His Temple. What could then be more spectacular than for Jesus to float down, apparently out of the heavens, into the Court of the Temple filled with the representatives of the people. Surely such an apocalypse would dazzle the multitude and they would at once accept Him as their Messiah. This was a temptation for Jesus to test His Deity and Sonship by presuming on the protective care of God. The Devil's hope was that if Jesus yielded and threw Himself down from the Pinnacle of the Temple, that His presumption would have put Him outside the pale of angelic assistance and that He would have been dashed to death on the marble pavement of the Temple.

Jesus' reply was—"It is written again, Thou shalt not tempt the Lord thy God." This was a rebuke and for the second time the Devil found himself foiled.

THE THIRD TEMPTATION

"Again, the Devil taketh Him up into an exceeding high mountain, and sheweth Him all the Kingdoms of this world, and the glory of them; and saith unto Him, All these things will I give Thee, if Thou wilt fall down and worship me." Matt. 4:8-9.

This was the Devil's **"TRUMP CARD,"** his Masterpiece of Temptation. Having failed to get Jesus to satisfy His hunger in an illegitimate way, or to test His Father's protecting care, the Devil bluntly offers Him the Kingdoms of This World if He will transfer His allegiance from His Father and fall down and worship him. It is clear that this was a **compromise offer**. The Devil knew that he was doomed to defeat and he wanted to make the best bargain he could. It is worthy of note that Jesus did not dispute his claim of Lordship over the "Kingdoms of this World." In fact, Jesus called him, the "Prince of this World." And it is further worthy of note that when Jesus refused the offer it was to still leave the "Kingdoms of this World" under the Devil's dominion, and they will remain there until He comes whose right it is to rule and reign over them in Millennial Glory.

The Devil knew that Jesus had come into the world to get control of the "Kingdoms of the World," and what he practically said to Jesus was—"You came into the world to die on the Cross that you might win back these Kingdoms to God. Now if you will bow down and by worshipping me acknowledge my supremacy over these Kingdoms, I will give them to you without the sufferings of the Cross."

To dazzle Jesus with the grandeur of his proposition the Devil took Jesus up on to an exceedingly high mountain, and in a "moment of time" (Luke 4:5), as if he feared a prolonged view would dispel the illusion and disclose the worthlessness of those Kingdoms, the Devil showed Jesus the "Kingdoms of the World" and the "Glory of them." But Jesus saw farther than the Devil. He saw the Kingdom that He Himself was destined to set up and that in comparison with those Kingdoms would far excel them, and He knew the offer was not worth the price. Furthermore He knew the promise— "Ask of **ME** (the Father), and I shall give Thee the Heathen for Thine inheritance, and the uttermost parts of the earth for Thy possession" (Psa. 2:7-9), so it was not necessary that He accept the Devil's offer.

The Devil's proposition was his undoing. Immediately Jesus said—"Get thee hence, Satan." This was a command, and at once Satan, now unmasked and called by his right name, like a whipped cur, foiled and defeated, slunk away, and the angels came and ministered to Jesus. By His victory over Temptation Jesus passed from the **"FULNESS** of the Spirit" to the **"POWER** of the Spirit." Luke 4:1, 14.

We are told that Jesus was "tempted in 'all points' like as we are, yet without sin." Heb. 4:15. These "**all points**" may be summed up under three heads, represented by the "Three Temptations" of Jesus, and were included in the "One Temptation" of Eve—(1) "The Lust of the FLESH," (2) "The Pride of Life," and (3) "The Lust of the EYES." 1 John 2:16. All the temptations of mankind may be summed up under three heads, represented by the Wilderness Temptations.

1. The Temptation to Secure the Supply of Our Natural needs by ILLEGITIMATE MEANS.

2. The Temptation to Presume on God's Protection When We WILFULLY RUN INTO DANGER.

3. The Temptation to Secure This World's Goods and Honors, Without Toil or Suffering, by Entering Into a League With the FORCES OF EVIL.

The lessons for the Christian Church are—(1) Do not turn your church into a "Soup Kitchen" or a place of "Suppers" to get the funds to supply the needs of the Church. (2) Do not use spectacular and sensational methods to get an audience. (3) Do not enter into an alliance with the powers of state, wealth and society, or into Federations of Antichristian Forces for world supremacy. Eve, the bride of Adam, was tempted first, fell, and pulled her husband down with her. Christ the Last Adam was tested first and because of His victory over temptation He is able to keep His Bride the Church from falling. The Last Adam will recover the Kingly Sceptre the First Adam lost. The Devil tempts us to make us UNUSABLE. God tests us to show that we are USABLE. The instrument of victory is the "WORD OF GOD." We must be able to answer the Devil with—"IT IS WRITTEN."

COULD JESUS HAVE SINNED?

There are those who claim that Jesus could not have been tempted in all points like as we are if it were not possible for Him to sin. Others claim that while it was possible for Jesus to sin there was no probability that He would, and therefore there was no risk incurred in His Temptation. Those who claim that it was possible for Jesus to sin compare Him with Satan and Adam, who, though created pure and sinless, had in them the possibility of sinning as is evidenced by their fall. But

Satan and Adam were created beings, while Jesus was the Only Begotten **SON OF GOD,** born of the "Virgin Mary," and it was said of the body of Jesus that it was **"THAT HOLY THING."** Therefore the humanity of Jesus was **SINLESS,** and when joined to the Eternally Holy Personality of the **SON,** there could have been no possibility of Jesus sinning.

If Jesus could have sinned then the whole scheme of Salvation **hung in the balance** until after the Wilderness Temptation. Such a thought is not only unthinkable but unscriptural. Jesus was the Lamb—"**foreordained before the foundation of the world** (1 Pet. 1:18-20), and a lamb accepted for sacrifice must be "without spot or blemish." The Scriptures declare that "Whosoever is **born of God CANNOT SIN.**" 1 John 3:9. Therefore Jesus could not sin. If He could have sinned at the Temptation, since there has been no change in His nature since then, for He took His humanity back with Him to Heaven, what is there to prevent His yielding to Temptation in the future? What guarantee have we that the whole plan of Salvation shall not yet be upset? The thought is contrary to the whole trend of the Scripture.

What then was the purpose of the Temptation if it were not possible for Jesus to have fallen? The purpose was simply to show that Jesus was a **PERFECT SAVIOUR,** and that there was **NO SIN IN HIM,** nor possibility of failure. He was thus set before us, not as an example to be followed when we are tempted, but as an object of Faith to whom to look as our **DELIVERER** when we are tempted. A simple illustration will make this plain. We will suppose that a double track "Suspension Bridge" has been built over a deep canyon connecting two mountain ranges. To the people in the valley the Bridge seems to be but an "airy nothing" hardly capable of carrying its own weight and they are afraid to trust themselves to it, but one day to their amazement two long trains of freight cars loaded with pig-iron approach from opposite directions, and when both have reached the centre of the Bridge they stop. At once they expect the Bridge to collapse. But no, it remains intact. And when, after remaining 24 hours on the Bridge, the trains continue on their way, they no longer lack faith in the safety of the Bridge. So with the Temptation of Jesus. It was the test of His Sonship and of His power to overcome and destroy the works of the Devil, and we need no longer fear but that He is a Perfect and All-Powerful Saviour.

As we have seen, the First Adam brought upon the human race guilt, condemnation, separation, so the Last Adam reverses all these and the standing of the Believer is that of "not guilty," no longer under condemnation, and for him there shall be "no separation" from God. Rom. 8:33, 34, 38-39. The "wages of sin" is **Death**, but we read in Paul's immortal chapter on the Resurrection of the body (1 Cor. 15:22), and he is speaking only of the body and not of the soul, so the Universalist cannot find an argument here for universal salvation, "As in Adam all **die** (physically), so in Christ shall all be made **alive** (physically)." So as the First Adam brought death into the world, the Last Adam brought "Resurrection," "Life," and "Immortality" to light through the Gospel.

XV

Atonement and Redemption

The Christian Religion has been charged with being a **"BLOODY"** Religion; that it savors of the Abattoir, turned the Temple into a "Slaughter House," and is a "Religion of the Shambles" because it demands the "Blood of Christ," and therefore is revolting to persons of refined sensibilities. What the blood is to our bodies (life), the "Blood of Christ" is to the Bible. Take the "scarlet word" out of the Bible, and the Bible is a **DEAD** book. If you were to take a brush and dip it in red ink and go carefully through your Bible from Genesis to Revelation and mark out all the passages that refer to the "Blood," and are associated with it in any way, you would be surprised at how little of the Bible you would have left. In fact its value would be gone. The historical portions would be meaningless, the ethical teaching powerless, and the prophetical statements unfulfilled. Every doctrine in the Bible is dependent on the "Blood." Without it there would be no "Forgiveness," no "Regeneration," no "Justification," no "Sanctification," no "Peace," no "Joy," no "Rest," no "Hope," no "Resurrection," no "Heaven," no "Robes Washed," no "New Song." Twenty-eight times in the Book of Revelation Jesus is called **THE LAMB**, and that title is always associated with His atoning work. So we see if we take the "Blood" out of the Bible the Doctrine of the Atonement must go

I. THE ATONEMENT

The word means **"AT-ONE-MENT."** The "Fall of Man" put man and God **"AT-TWO-MENT,"** that is, alienated and separated them. The purpose of the Atonement is to make them one again. It is a principle of law that the "Penalty" of a broken law must fall on the breaker of the law or on his substitute or bondsman, otherwise the law is of no effect. A law without a penalty would be useless. It is not the law but the penalty that men stand in fear of. An "Atonement" then is any

"Provision" that may be introduced into the administration of a Government, whereby that Government may, upon just, safe, and honorable grounds, release an offender from the "Penalty" of a broken law. Now God made a "Law" to govern the conduct of Adam and Eve in the Garden of Eden. The "Law" was—"Of every tree of the Garden thou mayest freely eat: but of the 'Tree of the Knowledge of Good and Evil' thou **SHALT NOT EAT.**" The "Penalty" was—"In the day that thou eatest thereof thou shalt surely **DIE.**" Gen. 2:16-17. When Adam and Eve ate of the forbidden fruit they broke that "Law" and were doomed to die. But their death would frustrate God's purpose in their creation, which was to repopulate the restored earth. Gen. 1:28. Now God could not withhold the "Penalty" of **death** without breaking His Holy Word, and in the future cause Adam and Eve to doubt his truthfulness. It became necessary therefore that the "Penalty" of the Law, if it was not to fall on Adam and Eve, should fall on some one who should take their place. The substitute that God in His love and justice provided was **HIMSELF** in the person of His Son Jesus, for Jesus was no other than God manifest in the flesh. 1 Tim. 3:16. But this substitute was not provided immediately. It was not until 4000 years later that Jesus paid the "Penalty" of Adam's disobedience by His **death** on the Cross.

But during those 4000 years, by the shedding of the blood of bullocks, goats, and innocent lambs, whose bodies were laid smoking and quivering on Hebrew altars, God, in one great "Object Lesson," kept before the people the fact that without the **SHEDDING OF BLOOD** there could be no remission for sin. The sprinkling of the blood of every Passover Lamb was a reminder of Him who was to be the "Lamb of God" who should take away the sin of the world. John 1:29. And when the hour had come for the offering up of **THE SACRIFICE,** we see Justice and Mercy standing on the Hill Calvary, and hear Justice say to Mercy—"Where is He who, over 4000 years ago, in the Garden of Eden, offered Himself a **SUBSTITUTE** for the sin of the world?" "Behold Him," says Mercy, "coming up the Hill bearing His Cross." When He reached the top of the Hill Justice presented the "Bond," executed centuries before, and demanded its payment. The Son of God replied—"I will this day cancel it." Soon all the preparations for the sacrifice were complete, and the "Lamb of God" was laid on the **ALTAR OF THE CROSS**. As Jesus laid His hand upon the crossbar of the Cross, He held in it, invisible to human eyes, the "Bond" to be cancelled, and when the Roman soldier drove the nail through that hand there were fulfilled the words of the Apostle—

> "And you, being dead in your sins and the uncircumcision of your flesh, hath He quickened together with Him, having forgiven you all trespasses; **BLOTTING OUT THE HAND-WRITING OF ORDINANCES** that was against us, which was contrary to us, and took IT out of the way, **NAILING IT TO HIS CROSS**." Col. 2:13-14.

By the cancellation of the "Bond" the Law and Justice of God were satisfied, and it was possible for God to—"Be **JUST** and the **JUSTIFIER** of them who **BELIEVE IN JESUS**." Rom. 3:26.

But some one may say, "How could an innocent person assume the guilt of another?" This can only be done by the innocent person entering into **"Corporate Oneness"** with the guilty person, and thus becoming **IDENTIFIED WITH HIM**. For illustration, the debts of a poor widow could not be justly charged up to a millionaire neighbor, but if he entered into "Corporate Oneness" with her by marrying her, and thus assuming all her obligations, then he could justly and legally be held responsible for her debts. Now this is just what the Apostle says—

> "Wherefore, my brethren, ye also are become **DEAD TO THE LAW** (our first husband) by the body of Christ (that is by Christ's death); that ye should be **MARRIED TO ANOTHER**, even to Him (Christ) who is **RAISED FROM THE DEAD**." Rom. 7:4.

This union with Christ results in a "**LEGAL AN-SWERABLENESS**" by Him for all our debts to the Law, and Jesus recognized the justice of all His sufferings on the Cross, when He said to the two disciples on the Road to Emmaus—"O fools, and slow of heart to believe all that the prophets have spoken: **OUGHT NOT CHRIST TO HAVE SUFFERED THESE THINGS,** and to enter into His Glory?" Luke 24:25-26. We see then that the Atonement of Christ means more than mere "**Substitution,**" it means a "**CORPORATE ONENESS,**" a union in which it was perfectly just for God to exact from His Son the penalty of death in satisfaction of the broken Law. We are therefore as believers to "**RECKON OURSELVES DEAD TO THE LAW.**" (Rom. 7:4.) That is, we are to believe and act as those who have been freed from the Law, for "there is therefore now **NO CONDEMNATION** to them who are in Christ Jesus" (Rom. 8:1), for we were judged for sin in Christ on the Cross, and our Judgment for "**Sin**" **IS PAST.**

The efficacy and "Substitutionary" character of the Atonement is beautifully illustrated in the story of Barabbas. Barabbas had been condemned to die, he was to have suffered the penalty of his crime on the cross between the two thieves, but when the multitude was given the choice between Christ or Barabbas, they chose Christ, and He as a **SUBSTITUTE** took Barabbas' place on the central cross, and His death **satisfied the Law,** and Barabbas was free. If Barabbas had gone out to Calvary that day and witnessed Christ's death in his stead, and had accepted Jesus as his personal Saviour from sin, he would have been the first man to understand the substitutionary character of the Atonement.

As sinners we were under the "curse of the Law," but as believers—"Christ hath redeemed us from the **CURSE** of the Law, being made a **CURSE** for us: for it is written, **CURSED IS EVERY ONE THAT HANG-ETH ON A TREE.**" Gal. 3·13. The "**Tree**" that Christ hung on was the **CROSS.** We are therefore **DEAD** to the Law: not physically dead, but **JUDICIALLY** dead, for the "Penalty" of a law cannot be exacted twice. If Jesus "bare our sins in His own body upon the Tree"

(1 Pet. 2:24), then they are no longer upon us and we are free from sin. The death of Christ was no mere accident or incident, it was predetermined. "Ye were not redeemed with corruptible things, as silver and gold . . . but with the **PRECIOUS BLOOD OF CHRIST**, as of a lamb without blemish and without spot: who verily was foreordained **BEFORE THE FOUNDATION OF THE WORLD**." 1 Pet. 1:18-20.

From this we see that there was a purpose in Christ's death; that Calvary and the Cross were a necessity, and that the mission of Christ was not simply to bear witness to the Father, and reveal God to men, but to die upon the Cross for the Salvation of the World.

THE EXTENT OF THE ATONEMENT

Some would limit the Atonement to the elect only. They look upon the Atonement as a "Commercial Transaction," and quote the words—"Ye are bought with a price" (1 Cor. 6:19-20), and claim that as in a commercial transaction there must be a buyer and seller, a thing to be bought and sold, and a price to be paid, that God was the "Buyer," that the Law was the "Seller," that the "elect" were the "Thing" sold, and that the "Blood of Christ" was the "Purchase Price." Now as in a commercial transaction there must be a mutual understanding as to the price to be paid, and the quality and quantity of the articles to be delivered, the "Commercial View" of the Atonement implies that God bargained for a certain number of persons that He personally would choose, and that He would insist on the delivery of not only the exact number, but the same ones. To illustrate if a man bought 100 horses, it would not suffice when the animals were delivered to merely count them to see whether there were 100, but he would want to know if they were the same horses that he had purchased.

From this we see that the "Commercial View" of the Atonement limits the "purchasing value" of Christ's Blood to the elect only. But Christ did not die to save a few individuals, He died to pay the "Penalty" of Adam's disobedience, which was **DEATH**. In other words He died to redeem the human race from the "curse of sin," and put it in a salvable position. "He is the propitiation of our (the Righteous) sins: and not for ours only, but also for the sins of the **WHOLE WORLD.**" 1 John 2:2. The word "Propitiation" means the "**act of reconciliation.**" The "Death of Christ" was the ground on which God can deal, and does deal in mercy with the whole world. "For if, **when we were enemies,** we were **RECONCILED TO GOD** by the 'Death of His Son,' much more, **BEING RECONCILED,** we shall be saved by His life." Rom. 5:10. Or as Paul puts it in Col. 1:20. Christ "**MADE PEACE** through the 'Blood of the Cross,' and has reconciled **ALL THINGS** unto Himself, whether they be on earth or in Heaven." We see then that the Atonement of Christ on the Cross is sufficient for the whole human race and places it in a **SALVABLE** position. But this does not mean "Universal Salvation," for all men are not saved, because they do not comply with the condition of Salvation, which is to accept the **FINISHED WORK OF CHRIST.**

II. REDEMPTION

The words Atonement and Redemption are used as if they meant the same thing, but they are different as to **time** and **act** though they are both the result of the "Finished Work" of Christ on the Cross. Redemption means to redeem a thing that is rightfully our own, but for the time being is in the possession of another, whose claim upon it must be legally met. Writing to the Ephesians Paul said—"Ye were sealed with the Holy Spirit of promise, which is the **earnest** of our inheritance until the **REDEMPTION** of the **PURCHASED POSSESSION.**" Eph. 1:13-14. Then there is a **POSSESSION** to be **REDEEMED.** What this is Paul tells us in Rom. 8:22-23—"We know that the **WHOLE CREATION GROANETH AND TRAVAILETH IN PAIN TOGETHER UNTIL NOW.** And not only they, but ourselves also, which have the 'First-fruits of the Spirit,' even we ourselves also groan within ourselves, waiting for the **adoption,** to wit, the **REDEMPTION OF OUR BODY.**" From this we see that something belonging to "Creation" and to "Man" has slipped out of their possession and needs to be redeemed. What this was we are told in the third chapter of Genesis. When Adam sinned he lost the **immortality of his body,** and his **inheritance of the earth.** The latter passed into the possession of Satan to the disinheritance of all of Adam's seed. Adam was impotent to redeem what was lost, but the Law (Lev. 25:23-34) provides that a **kinsman** may redeem a lost possession. That **"Kinsman"** has been provided in the person of **JESUS CHRIST.** To become a kinsman He had to be born into the human race. This the "Virgin Birth" accomplished. Jesus paid the **REDEMPTIVE PRICE,** which was His own **BLOOD** on the Cross (1 Pet. 1:18-20), but He has not as yet claimed that which He then purchased. Redemption is not the act of a moment, but requires a period of time. This is the "Day of Salvation," but it has extended over nearly nineteen centuries. The "Day of Redemption" will be at least a 1000 years long. It will begin with the Resurrection of the bodies of the Righteous dead, and continue until the New Heaven and Earth appear.

THE REDEMPTION OF THE BODY

We cannot conceive of the glory of the "Resurrection Body." The Transfiguration of Christ gives us a faint conception of it, for we are told that when He shall appear we shall be like Him. Paul attempts to give us an idea of it in his immortal chapter on the Resurrection. 1 Cor. 15. He says—1. "It is sown in **'corruption;'** it is raised in **INCORRUPTION."** That is the unvarnished truth, it is sown in foul rottenness. Paul called it a **"VILE BODY."** Phil. 3:21. Whence cometh this corruption? It is simply **SIN MATERIALIZED AND CONSUMMATED.** But it is to be raised in **INCORRUPTION.** O happy day, when the bodies of the "Dead in Christ" shall come forth from the tomb in immortal bodies and fadeless beauty, and the living saints shall be changed and clothed in the garments of Glory, and caught up to meet their Redeemer in the air!

2. "It is sown in **'dishonor,'** it is raised in **GLORY."** How many a body has been sown in dishonor through sin, that has caused disfigurement, but the Resurection

will change all this, for we shall then be raised in **GLORY,** and have a body like unto His "Glorious Body."

3. "It is sown in '**weakness**;' it is raised in **POWER.**" A corpse is the very embodiment of weakness. Nothing else seems to have such a dead weight as a lifeless body. But if that lifeless body be the body of one of God's saints He will raise it with **POWER.** Not only shall God display power in the breaking of the tombs of the dead, but the raised body shall be possessed of power. Not simply power as to strength, but new powers of sight, hearing, memory, etc. It shall be able to travel with the speed of light, and run and not be weary, and walk and not faint.

4. "It is sown a '**natural**' body; it is raised a **SPIRITUAL** body.'" This does not mean that our "Spiritual Body" shall be an "Etherealized Spiritlike Structure," but a real body of "flesh and bones," not **blood,** for it is the blood that causes corruption, but a body like Christ's resurrection body, of which He said—"Handle me and see, for a Spirit hath not **flesh** and **bones** as ye see me have." Luke 24:36-43. Now our bodies are controlled by natural laws; then they will be governed by the laws of the Spirit World. Then we shall bask in the sunshine of God's presence in a land where there is no sorrow, pain or death.

But Jesus did not die simply to redeem our bodies but to redeem the brute creation, and the earth. We read that in the "Day of Redemption"—"The wolf also shall dwell with the lamb, and the leopard shall lie down with the kid; and the calf and the young lion and the fatling together; and a little child shall lead them. And the cow and the bear shall feed; their young ones shall lie down together; and the lion shall eat straw like the ox. And the sucking child shall play on the hole of the asp, and the weaned child shall put his hand on the cockatrice' den." Isa. 11:6-8.

The effect of the Fall of Man was far-reaching. Not only was the human race involved, but the whole earth and atmosphere was affected. "And unto Adam He (the Lord God) said, Because thou hast hearkened unto the voice of thy wife, and hast eaten of the tree, of which I commanded thee, saying, Thou shalt not eat of it: **cursed is the ground** for Thy sake; in sorrow shalt thou eat of it all the days of thy life: **THORNS** also and **THISTLES** shall it bring forth to thee." Gen. 3: 17-18. From this we see that "Thorns" and "Thistles" are the result of sin. And from other scriptures we learn that animal life suffers, and the land fails to give its increase on account of sin. It is not without significance that the one who is to be the Redeemer of the earth from its sin-cursed state was crowned with **THORNS**. It was symbolic of His office as Redeemer. But the day is coming when the earth shall be redeemed from its sin-cursed condition and the exterior surface of the earth go through a "Baptism of Fire," that will consume and destroy the thorns and thistles and all disease germs and insect pests, all the result of sin, and the Atmosphere will also be purified with fire, and cleansed of evil spirits, and out of it all will come the "New Heaven" and the "New Earth" wherein shall dwell righteousness, and on it shall rest the "New City," the home of the redeemed of God. Then all **discord** shall cease, and **Eternal Harmony** shall prevail throughout the Universe of God. No, God is not going to destroy this earth on which His Son died. It is too sacred and holy a spot. So he saw to it that the work of the Cross should include not only the Salvation of man's **SOUL**, but the Redemption of his **BODY** and of the **EARTH** as well.

XVI

Sin and Salvation

It takes no Bible, or standard of morals, to make a man realize that when he would do good evil is present with him. We all recognize that there is a conflict between our conscience and our conduct, between our better judgment and our natural disposition. Men may call this "Moral Inharmony" or what they will, the Bible calls it **SIN**. Every careful and thoughtful observer will note that there is a difference between the animal creation and man. Animals do not have to contend against inherited tendencies to do evil. They are governed by instinct which naturally leads them to their highest possible attainments. But man has an inveterate tendency to go astray, to sin, to entertain all kinds of misleading errors, and it is an endless struggle with him to do good. Why this difference? Something has happened to man that has not happened to the animal creation. Something has happened to change his nature. What that thing is we would not have known if the Scriptures had not revealed to us the "Fall of Man" in Eden. Now we know what has caused the difference, it is **SIN**.

I. SIN

Sin is the world's "BLOOD POISON." Bad blood manifests itself in the human body in two ways. Inwardly as diabetes, and outwardly in inflammation, boils, carbuncles and ulcers. The former is invisible and may for a time be unsuspected, while the latter are evident to the eye. We must distinguish between **"SIN"** and **"SINS."** **"SIN"** is that tendency or disposition to sin that we inherit from Adam. **"SINS"** are the "specific acts" of sin that we commit as the result of our tendency to sin. The first like diabetes is internal, the second like boils and carbuncles are external. Jesus came to make an Atonement for **"SIN,"** not for **"SINS."** He came to remove the "Natural Depravity," or tendency to sin, of the human heart. That is to impart a "New Nature" in which there will be no tendency to sin, and therefore no desire to commit specific acts of sin. By "Natural Depravity" is not meant that there is nothing good in human nature at all, that men are never kind, affectionate generous, lovable, but that the tendency of the human heart is naturally toward evil. It is because people do not understand the nature of sin that they are offended when we speak of them as sinners. They think that a sinner is one guilty of some specific crime, as murder, theft or adultery, whereas a sinner is one who has a sinful disposition.

We have five definitions of sin in the New Testament.

1. LAWLESSNESS is Sin.

"Whosoever committeth sin transgresseth also the law: for sin is the **transgression of the law."** 1 John 3: 4. To break any law of God or man is to sin.

2. NEGLECT is Sin.

"To him that knoweth to do good, and **doeth it not,** to him it is sin." James 4: 17.

3. DOUBT is Sin.

"And he that doubteth is damned if he eat, because he eateth not of faith: for whatsoever is **not of faith** is sin." Rom. 14: 23. That is, to do anything we doubt the rightfulness of is **SIN.**

4. UNBELIEF is Sin.

"And when He (the Holy Spirit) is come, He will reprove the world of sin, and of righteousness, and of judgment: of **sin,** because they believe not on **ME."** (Jesus.) John 16: 8-9. The crowning sin of all sins is to not believe in Jesus. Men and women are not lost because they are sinners, but because they will not accept Jesus as their Saviour.

5. ALL UNRIGHTEOUSNESS is Sin.

"All unrighteousness is sin." 1 John 5: 17. This is a blanket mortgage that covers every kind of sin.

Let us for a few minutes turn the "Search Light" of God's Word on our lives. The Psalmist said—"Thou hast set our 'iniquities' before Thee, our 'secret sins' in the light of Thy countenance." Psa. 90:8. Here the Psalmist speaks of two classes of sins, "Open" and "Secret." The "open sins" are such as are publicly committed, as profanity, intemperance, lying and theft. The "secret sins" are such as are committed in secret. Would you like the Almighty to turn the "X-RAY" of His omniscient "Eye" on your heart, and search every "Chamber of Imagery," and bring to light every impure and murderous thought, every feeling of envy, pride, jealousy, hatred, and revenge? The Apostle John says that "Whosoever **hateth** his brother is a **MURDERER.**" 1 John 3:15. Do you wish that someone was dead that you might possess their property? Then you are a murderer. Jesus said that to merely look at a woman to lust after her is adultery. Matt. 5:27-28.

What does the Bible say about the human heart? Listen. "The heart is **deceitful above all things** and **desperately** wicked: who can know it." Jer. 17:9. One day Jesus dissected the human heart for the benefit of His Disciples. Read what He said—"For from within, out of the heart of men, proceed **evil thoughts, adulteries, fornications, murders, thefts, covetousness, wickedness, deceit, lasciviousness, an evil eye, blasphemy, pride, foolishness.**" Mark 7:21-22. Here are 13 specifications that outline the character of the human heart; can any one read them and say, "That does not describe my heart?"

In fruit there is a tendency to rot and decay, and unless preserved it will soon perish. So it is with the "root principle" of sin in the human heart. Out of Christ there is no difference between men. Take a man honest, honorable, truthful, upright, benevolent; take a woman pure, chaste, amiable, gentle, meek, the embodiment of all loveliness: take some sweet girl, pure as a lily, the light of the household, a living joy: take a little child, innocent, the heaven-sent prattler of the fireside, and as unspotted as the new fallen snow; and what is the difference between any of these and the lost spirits, the sin-saturated souls hating and hated, cursing and cursed, blaspheming and damned that writhe in Hell? It is simply the difference between meal into which the leaven has been placed, and meal in which the leaven has done its work. It is simply a difference as to time and development. The batch of meal that has been leavened cannot take the leaven out of itself, neither can it prevent the leaven from doing its work. Its final state is only a question of Time. If men and women go into the other world without having the leaven of sin eradicated by the **"BLOOD OF JESUS,"** the leaven of sin will continue to work on down the Eternal Ages, and they will grow worse and worse as eternity rolls on, until they shall become as bad as the demons in Hell. The leper was just as truly a leper the moment the first taint of leprosy entered his system, as he was when he sat a loathsome creature outside the city walls and cried "Unclean! Unclean!"

What does sin do? It produces shame and leads to separation. It drove Adam and Eve out of the Garden. Of the wicked it is said—"He shall be driven from light into darkness, and chased out of the world." Job. 18:18. And Peter said to Jesus—"Depart from me; for I am a sinful man, O Lord." Luke 5:8.

What are the Wages of Sin? **DEATH.** Sin does not ask us to sin for nothing. It pays wages, and it pays on the instalment plan, and it pays in full, and we cannot avoid taking the wage. And the wage is **DEATH.** Not physical death, for animals and the righteous die. If the wages of sin were mere physical death it would be a blessing rather than a curse, for many a sinner would be glad to die a physical death if that was all the punishment he had reason to expect. It is not spiritual death for sinners are already spiritually dead. Eph. 2:1-3. It is **"ETERNAL DEATH."** What is that? We are told in Rev. 20:11-15, that after the Wicked shall have been judged and found guilty they shall be sentenced to the **"Second Death."** What is the "Second Death?" What is the "First Death?" It is the separation of the soul and spirit from the body. At the resurrection of the Wicked, the Wicked get back their bodies, but when they are sentenced to the "Second Death" they die again in the sense that they lose their bodies again, and in their soul and spirit, that are indestructible by fire, they go to the Lake of Fire where they remain separated from God for all eternity and that is what is meant by "Eternal Death."

Sin is not a misfortune, it is perverseness. To claim that we ought not to be held responsible for having been born with a nature tainted by sin is no excuse. Our sin is in refusing to accept the provision God has made to get rid of that nature by accepting Christ as our Saviour. By my rejection of Jesus Christ as my Saviour I elect to bear the penalty of sin myself.

SIN is the most expensive thing in the Universe. It cost Satan the loss of his exalted position before the Throne of God and led to rebellion in Heaven. It cost the human race the loss of Paradise. It cost God the "Life Blood" of His Only Begotten and Beloved Son. It cost Jesus the agony and "blood sweat" of Gethsemane, and the excruciating sufferings of the Cross, and the tasting of Eternal Death when He took the place of the sinner and realized what it meant to be forsaken by God.

II. SALVATION

Every rational human being recognizes that he has a "Threefold Need." (1). In regard to **YESTERDAY.** Why? Because "yesterday" was the day of **SIN.** What are we to do with the past years? We cannot live them over again, nor balance them by "Works of Supereroga-tion." (2). In regard to **TO-DAY.** If I have managed to provide for the sin of yesterday, what am I to do for **today?** For today if there is no change in my nature I will sin as yesterday. (3). In regard to **TOMORROW.** Suppose that I have been able to make provision for the past and the present, for yesterday and today, what am I to do for **tomorrow?** for tomorow will come with the same old forms of temptation, the same old suggestions to evil, the same helplessness to overcome sin as in the past. From this we see that we need **PARDON** for the Past, **PURITY** for the Present, and **POWER** for the Future. Where are we to get them?

If, as we have seen, **SIN** is the World's "**BLOOD POISON,**" and every human being born into the world has inherited the disease, then as there is a remedy some-where for every disease, there must be a remedy for the "Disease of Sin," and this remedy is found in the Gospel. "For I am not ashamed of the 'Gospel of Christ;' for it is the **POWER OF GOD UNTO SALVATION** to every one that believeth." Rom. 1:16. The "Power" of the Gospel lies in the **"BLOOD OF JESUS."** "The **BLOOD OF JESUS CHRIST** His Son, cleanseth us from all sin." 1 John 1:7. This is fully explained in the Chapter on "Atonement and Redemption," and so need not be more fully dwelt on here.

Salvation is a "threefold process." It begins in "Justification," proceeds through "Sanctification," and ends in "Glorification." Titus 2:11-13. So we can say that we **are** saved, that we are **being** saved, and that we **will be** saved.

1. **We are saved from the PENALTY of Sin.**

This we get by "Faith." Faith leads to our **JUSTIFICATION.** "Therefore being **JUSTIFIED BY FAITH,** we have peace with God through our Lord Jesus Christ." Rom. 5:1. The word "Justification" is a legal term and means to declare not guilty. It can best be defined by an illustration. We will suppose that a man has been charged with murder and tried and found guilty and been sentenced to die. Before the hour of execution a man appears at the prison and asks to see the Sheriff, to whom he hands an official document, which when the Sheriff reads he finds to be a pardon. The man at once is set at liberty and walks out of the prison a **free** man, but not a justified man for the guilt of the crime still remains on him. He is simply a **pardoned CRIMINAL.** On the other hand we will suppose that the condemned criminal was really innocent, having been condemned on circumstantial evidence, and that before the date set for execution the real murderer surrenders himself to the Sheriff and produces evidence that he is the real criminal. What then must the Sheriff do? He cannot any longer hold the first man, for he is not guilty, he therefore sets him free, and he walks out of the prison a **JUSTIFIED** man because he is **innocent of the crime** charged against him. That is the legal meaning of "Justification" and that is the Scriptural meaning. Here is the "Mystery of Salvation." It would be impossible for an innocent man to satisfy the law, for while he might take the criminal's **place** he could not take his **GUILT**. But this is what Jesus Christ does. "He hath made Him to be **SIN FOR US, who know no sin**: that we might be made the righteousness of God in Him." 2 Cor. 5:21.

The moment a sinner accepts by faith the Lord Jesus Christ as his personal Saviour he is **JUSTIFIED**. "Verily, verily, I say unto you, He that heareth my word, and **BELIEVETH** on Him that sent me, **HATH EVER-LASTING LIFE,** and shall not come into condemnation (Judgment), but **IS PASSED** from death unto life." John 5:24. The result of Justification is that we have peace **WITH** God. Rom. 5:1. We must distinguish between "peace **WITH** God," and the "peace **OF** God." Phil. 4:7. Here an illustration will best serve our purpose. We will suppose that during the Civil War President Lincoln had issued a proclamation that any person in rebellion against the Government would be pardoned the moment that, coming from the South, he should step over the "Mason and Dixon Line." Suppose such a person had crossed the line at 12 o'clock midnight unknown to himself, at once he would have been at peace **WITH** the Government, but not knowing that he had crossed the line he continued on in fear of arrest and imprisonment until, as the day began to dawn, he realized that for hours he had been safe. What joy and peace of mind would then fill his soul. So the very moment we accept with saving faith the Lord Jesus Christ as our Saviour we have "peace **WITH** God," but it may be days, weeks, and even years before we know this, and have the "peace **OF** God" that passeth all understanding.

2.   We are saved from the POWER of Sin.

When the angel announced to Joseph that Mary was to have a son, he said—"Thou shalt call his name **JESUS;** for He shall save His people from their **SINS.**" Matt. 1:21. So we see that Jesus is not only a Saviour from **SIN,** but also from **SINS.** From our daily besetting, or as the colored preacher said, **upsetting** sins. Writing to the Philippians Paul said—"Work out your own salvation with **fear** and trembling, for it is **GOD WHICH WORKETH IN YOU** both to **WILL** and to **DO** of His good pleasure." Phil. 2: 12-13. Now this does not mean that we are to be saved by our works. It means that having received Salvation through faith we are to now **work it out.** That is, having been saved from the "Penalty" of Sin, we must work to be delivered from its "Power." And in this, though we do it with **fear** and **trembling,** conscious of our own weakness, we will be aided by God, for it is God who **worketh in us,** to **WILL** and **DO** of His good pleasure. What we need to do then is to co-operate with God in His work of Sanctification, to let Him will and do in us what is necessary to save us from the "Power" of Sin.

The revelation of sin is progressive. It is not until after conversion that we really begin to realize what sin is. When you awake in the morning twilight you see a few conspicuous articles of furniture. As the light increases you see taking form the pictures on the wall and the toilet articles on the dressing table; but it is not until the sun is up that you see smaller articles as pins, pieces of thread and particles of dust. When we came to Christ we were conscious of a few sinful habits. We gave them up. But as we grew in grace other things in our lives were seen as wrong and laid aside. And so it has gone on. Things that we did five years ago we would not do today, and what we do today, we will not do five years from now. Writing to the Corinthians eighteen years after his conversion, Paul said—"I am not meet to be called an Apostle." 1 Cor. 15:9. Six years later he wrote to the Ephesians—"I am less than the least of all saints." Eph. 3:8. And five years later he wrote to Timothy—"I am the **chief of sinners.**" 1 Tim. 1:15. What was the matter with Paul? Had he grown worse? No, he only realized more than ever his own sinfulness. Paul never professed complete sanctification. He said that he was not "already perfect" or had "attained" unto that for which he had been "apprehended by Christ" but he was "reaching forth" and "pressing toward" the mark. Phil. 3:12-14. From this we see that Sanctification is a progressive act. and that our complete deliverance from the "Power" of Sin will not be until the death of the body. though we may have to a large extent "Victory over Sin" if we surrender absolutely to the "Will of God," and permit Him to **will** and to **do** of His good pleasure in us.

3. **We are to be saved from the PRESENCE of Sin.**

Jesus died on the Cross to save our **soul** from death, He is coming back to complete our salvation by redeeming our **body** from the grave, or to change it into an immortal body at the Rapture. Not until then shall we be saved from the "Presence" of Sin. So we see that Salvation is a "threefold process." That it begins in "Justification" and ends in "Glorification." Justification being instant and complete deliverance from the "Penalty" of Sin; "Sanctification" being a progressive deliverance from the "Power" of Sin, and "Glorification" our final deliverance from the "Presence" of Sin.

XVII

Law and Grace

The Scriptures make a clear distinction between "Law" and "Grace," putting "Law" in one Dispensation and "Grace" in another. "The 'Law' was given by (through) Moses, but 'Grace' and 'Truth' came by (through) Jesus Christ." John 1:17. By the "Law" we are to understand the "MOSAIC LAW," the "Law" given to Moses by God on Mount Sinai. It was three-fold.

1. **THE MORAL LAW.** Ex. 20:1-17.
   (The Ten Commandments.)
2. **THE CIVIL LAW.** Ex. 21:1-24:18.
3. **THE CEREMONIAL LAW.** Ex. 25:1-40:38.

We are not to understand that there was no "Law" before Moses, or no "Grace" before Jesus Christ, for "sin" is the "transgression of the law," (1 John 3:4), and Adam's sin was the transgression of the law that God laid down as to the eating of the fruit of the Garden, and "Grace" was revealed and exercised when Adam and Eve were spared the penalty of their sin. In Rom. 2:12 the Apostle Paul speaks of those who were "without law" from Eden until Moses. He does not mean that they were not accountable for their conduct, for by their actions they showed that there was an "unwritten law" in their hearts that their conscience bore witness to. Rom. 2:14-15. What Paul meant was that there was no "Written Law," that is, no "MOSAIC LAW," before the days of Moses. Let it be understood then in this discussion that by "Law" is meant the "Mosaic Law," and that there can be no mixing or blending of "Law" and "Grace" in this or any other Dispensation.

I. THE LAW

1. THE "LAW" WAS NOT GIVEN TO THE GENTILES.

"When the Gentiles, **WHICH HAVE NOT THE LAW** do by nature the things contained in the Law,

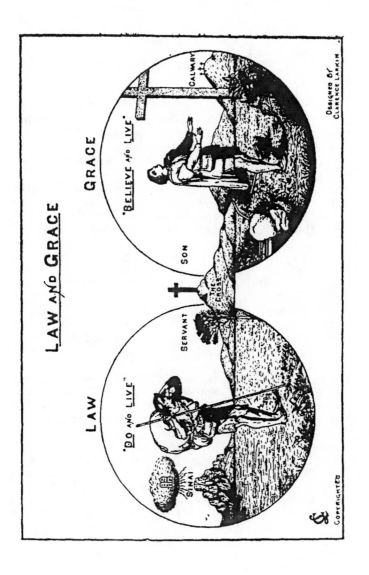

these, having **NOT THE LAW,** are a law unto themselves." Rom. 2:14.

The "Law" was given to Israel exclusively. For illustration take the "Law of the Sabbath." It was not given to the Gentiles. It was given as the **"SIGN"** of the **"Mosaic Covenant."** Ex. 31:13. Ez. 20:12, 19-21. The "Sabbath Day" belongs to the Jews alone and is not binding on the Gentiles (the World), or on the Church (Christians), though Christians are expected to observe the "First Day of the Week" for rest and worship. Nowhere in the Bible do we find God finding fault with any nation or people, except the Jews, for not observing the Sabbath. As a Jewish ordinance it has never been abrogated, changed, or transferred to any other day of the week, or to any other people. It is now in abeyance as foretold in Hosea 2:11, 3:4-5, it would be. It is to be resumed when the Jews are nationally restored to their own land. Isa. 66:23. Ez. 44:24, 46:1-3.

2. THE PURPOSE OF THE LAW.

The "Law" was not given to **JUSTIFY** men, for by the "deeds of the Law" shall no flesh be **justified in God's sight.** Rom. 3:20. Gal. 2:16. The "Law" was given that men might **know what sin is,** "for by the 'Law' is **the knowledge of sin,"** (Rom. 3:20), for men would have not known that **"covetousness"** was sin, if the "Law" had not said—**"Thou shalt not COVET."** Rom. 7:7. The "Law" was given to **"stop men's mouths,"** and keep men from boasting of their own righteousness, and see themselves guilty before God. Rom. 3:19. The "Law" was given to be a **"Schoolmaster"** to lead men to Christ. Gal. 3:24-25. All the rites and ceremonies of the "Ceremonial Law" pointed to Christ, such as the Feasts and Offerings. Now that Christ has come neither Jew nor Gentile is under the "Mosaic Law," for He fulfilled the "Law," that is, all the rites and ceremonies of the "Law" found their fulfilment in Him. Christ then "is the 'END OF THE LAW' for Righteousness** to every one that **BELIEVETH."** Rom. 10:4. Therefore Believers are **"DEAD TO THE LAW,"** (Rom. 7:4. Gal. 2:19), that is, they are no longer under the bondage of **"Legalism,"** but under **GRACE.**

II. GRACE

"By **Grace** are ye saved **through** faith; and that not of yourselves; it is the **GIFT OF GOD**; not of works, lest any man should boast." Eph. 2:8-9.

From this scripture we see that "**Grace**" is a **GIFT**. If a man receive salvation in exchange for his works, then salvation is but another word for "**wages**." Or if Salvation is given in exchange for benefits bestowed, then it is simply a "reward." Now if a man receive Salvation as **wages**, or as a reward, then Salvation is not a **GIFT** but something that he was entitled to, and therefore is not of **GRACE**. Grace is not something given us to help us keep the Law, Grace is **UNDESERVED MERCY**.

The "Source" of Grace is **GOD'S LOVE**. "For God **SO LOVED** the world, that He gave His only begotten Son, that whosoever believeth in Him should not perish, but have everlasting life." John 3:16.

The "Channel" of Grace is **CHRIST**. . "**Grace** and **Truth** came **BY JESUS CHRIST**." John 1:17. Titus 2:11.

The "Instrument" of Grace is **FAITH**. "By Grace are ye saved **THROUGH FAITH**." Eph. 2:8. Not faith in a thing, as some good deed we have done, but faith in a **PERSON**, and that person **JESUS CHRIST**.

That we may the better see the difference between "Law" and "Grace" let us contrast them.

1. "BLOOD" AND "WINE."

The first miracle that Moses performed as the representative of the "Law" was to turn water into **BLOOD**, typical of **DEATH**. Ex. 7:19-21. The first miracle that Jesus performed as the representative of "Grace" was to turn water into **WINE**, typical of **LIFE**. John 2:7-11.

2. "DARKNESS" AND "LIGHT."

All the "Law" can do is to produce **DARKNESS**, as when Moses caused a "thick darkness" to cover the land of Egypt. Ex. 10:22-23. But "Grace" gives **LIGHT**. Jesus said—"I am the **LIGHT of the World**." John 9:5. Jesus came to give not only sight to the physically blind but to the spiritually blind as well.

3. "DEATH" AND "LIFE."

The last scene in Egypt was **DEATH**. The death of the first-born. Ex. 12:29-30. The **"End of the Law"** is **DEATH**. Rom. 6:23. One of the last miracles of Christ was to give **LIFE**, the resurrection of Lazarus. John 11:41-44. Jesus came to bring **LIFE** and **IMMORTALITY** to light, through the "Gospel of Grace." The first time the "Law" was proclaimed 3000 were **KILLED**. Ex. 32:26-28. The first time that "Grace" was preached 3000 were **SAVED**. Acts 2:41.

4. "STRIPPED" AND "CLOTHED."

We are by nature like the man in the Parable of the Good Samaritan robbed and stripped and left by the way-side to die. Luke 10:30-37. The "Law," like the "Priest" and the "Levite," passes by and gives no help, while "Grace" comes where we are, and like the "Good Samaritan" pours in oil and wine, and puts us in his place on his beast, and provides for our future.

5. "SEEK" AND "SAVE."

The "Law" says—**"SEEK** the Lord while He may be found." "Grace" says—"The Son of Man is come to **'SEEK AND TO SAVE'** that which was lost." Luke 19:10. What a vista the Parable of the "Lost Sheep" opens up. It was not so much the sheep that was lost, as that a **man** had **LOST A SHEEP**. When Adam sinned and wandered away, God said—"Adam, if you can do without me, I cannot do without you." Then it was that "Grace" began its work.

6. "DO AND LIVE," AND "LIVE AND DO."

The "Law" says—**"DO** and thou shalt **Live."** Lev. 18:5. "Grace" says—**"IT IS FINISHED."** No man is **justified** by his works, but as a Believer he will be **rewarded** for his works. We are not to work **to** the Cross, but **from** the Cross.

7. "SERVANTS" AND "SONS."

The "Law" said to Moses at the "Burning Bush"—"Put **OFF** thy **shoes."** Ex. 3:3-5. Why? Thou art a **SERVANT**. Heb. 3:5. "Grace" said to the "Prodigal"

when he returned home—"Put **ON** thy shoes." Luke 15:
22. Why? Because he was a **SON**. Luke 15:24.

THE LAW SAYS	GRACE SAYS
"Keep Off."	"Embrace Him."
"Bow the Knee."	"Kiss Him."
"Punish."	"Forgive."
"Strip Him."	"Best Robe."
"Kills."	"Makes Alive."

Under the "Law" the "SHEEP" died for the "Shepherd." Under "Grace" the "SHEPHERD" died for the "Sheep." John 10:14-15.

THE LAW demands holiness.

GRACE gives holiness.

THE LAW says—Cursed is every one that continueth not in all things which are written in the book of the law to do them.

GRACE says—Blessed is the man whose iniquities are forgiven, whose sin is covered; blessed is the man to whom the Lord will not impute iniquity.

THE LAW says—Thou shalt love the Lord thy God with all thy heart, and with all thy mind, and with all thy strength.

GRACE says—Herein is love: not that we love God, but that He loved us, and sent His Son to be the propitiation for our sins.

THE LAW speaks of priestly sacrifices offered year by year continually, which could never make the comers thereunto perfect.

GRACE says—But this Man, after he had offered **one** sacrifice for sins forever . . . by one offering hath perfected forever them that are sanctified.

THE LAW declares—That as many as have sinned in the Law, shall be judged by the Law.

GRACE declares—That there is no condemnation (Judgment for Sin) for those who are in Christ Jesus for they **HAVE PASSED** from Death unto Life. John 5:24.

THE PURPOSE OF GRACE

The "Purpose" of God's Grace is revealed in Eph. 2:7, as being—"That in the 'Ages to Come' He might show the **EXCEEDING RICHES OF HIS GRACE.**" In the British Museum there are gathered from every nation and land under the sun specimens of all kinds of animal, vegetable, and mineral life. No expense has been spared to make the collection complete. So God is gathering from every tribe, people, and nation specimens of His "Grace," so that in the "Ages to Come" He may exhibit these trophies of "Grace" as samples of what the Gospel can do, and the sweet thought of it is, that there are no **duplicates.** You may think that you are too bad, too vile, too cranky, too odd and peculiar to be saved, but that is why God wants you, for there will only be **SPECIMEN SINNERS** up there, and God wants to show the Universe that the Gospel is the **"POWER OF GOD UNTO SALVATION TO EVERY ONE THAT BELIEVETH."** Rom. 1:16.

XVIII

Faith and Works

We hear a great deal about "Faith" and "Works." Some say we are saved by "Faith" alone, others make a great deal of "Works." Some say that **both** are necessary to salvation for the same reason that a bird cannot fly without two wings, or that you cannot make progress in a boat without two oars. One quotes Paul, who says— "That a man is **justified** by FAITH, WITHOUT THE DEEDS OF THE LAW " (Rom. 3:28), the other quotes James, who says—"Ye see then how that by **WORKS** a man is justified, and not by **faith only**." James 2:24. But the Apostle James is not speaking of the "Doctrine of JUSTIFICATION," but of a man justifying himself **before men**. The illustration he uses is that of Abraham offering up his son Isaac. Abraham was a man of faith, but the only way he could make it **visible** to the men of his generation was by his **WORKS**, so God commanded him to offer up his son Isaac. Gen. 22:1-2. Abraham's works had nothing to do with his salvation, but simply bore witness to his **faith**, for Abraham believed God, and it was imputed to him for righteousness. James 2:21-26.

So great was Abraham's faith in God's promise as to Isaac being the one through whom the promised seed was to come, that he believed that if he offered him up as commanded, that God would raise him from the dead. Heb. 11:17-19. In like manner Rahab's faith was justified or made visible by her works when she tied the "Scarlet Cord" in her window. Josh. 2:15-21. And to show the relation of "Works" to "Faith" the Apostle ends by saying—"For as the 'body' without the 'spirit' is **dead**, so faith without 'works' is **dead also**," that is, is DEAD FAITH, for if a man does not make his faith visible by his works it is a question whether he has any faith at all.

Now it is noteworthy that the Apostle Paul uses this same incident of Abraham offering up his son Isaac to prove that Abraham was justified by "Faith" **without "Works."**

"If Abraham were justified by works, he hath whereof to glory; **BUT NOT BEFORE GOD.** For what saith the Scripture? Abraham **BELIEVED GOD, and it was COUNTED UNTO HIM FOR RIGHTEOUSNESS.**" Rom. 4:2-3. Gen 15:6. So we see that it was Abraham's "Faith" that justified him before **GOD**, and his "**Works**" that justified him before **MEN.**

But I think I hear some one ask—"Does not the Bible say—That we are to '**WORK OUT OUR OWN SALVATION?**'" Yes, the Apostle Paul in writing to the Philippians says—"**Work out your own salvation** with fear and trembling; for it is **GOD WHO WORKETH IN YOU** both to will and to do His good pleasure." Phil. 2:12-13. But a man cannot work out what he has not got. He must first **have** "Salvation" before he can work it out. Paul was writing to the "Saints" at Philippi, to those who were already saved. The doctrine the Apostle desired to express was that "Salvation" included more than the mere escape from the "Penalty of Sin," it meant also escape from the "Power" and "Presence of Sin," and this meant that they must work or strive with "fear and trembling" to overcome indwelling sin, for it was God who would work in them, if they would let Him, to make the fruits of Salvation complete in their lives. So we see that we are **saved** by "Faith" and not by "Works," but "Works" have their place in the Believer's life as we shall see.

I. FAITH

The Bible definition of "Faith" is—"Faith is the **SUBSTANCE of things hoped for, the EVIDENCE of things not seen**" (Heb. 11:1), and in the remaining verses of the chapter the Apostle illustrates his definition by the conduct of the Old Testament worthies that he names. I hold in my hand a check, it is the **substance** (on paper) of the money I hope to get when I cash it, and the **evidence** (in black and white) of the money that I have not as yet seen.

One of the most remarkable illustrations of "Faith" in the Scriptures is that of the Prophet Jeremiah when he was told to purchase the "Field of Anathoth." Jer. 32:

6-44. At first sight it seems to be the wildest real estate speculation on record. Jeremiah had just prophesied that the Children of Israel were to be carried away into captivity to Babylon for 70 years, then why should he purchase the "Field of Anathoth," for he would not live to return and claim it, and probably none of his relatives would. But to show his faith in the Divine promise that at the end of the "Seventy Years" the Children of Israel would return and claim their possessions, he tells us that he paid the money for the "Field," and took the "evidences of the purchase" or deeds, and put them in an **earthen** vessel. Why in an **earthen** vessel? Because an iron vessel would have rusted, or a wooden vessel decayed in the "Seventy Years." Now we learn from this transaction that Faith is an **INVESTMENT IN THE DIVINE PROMISES.**

This is beautifully illustrated in the lives of the Old Testament patriarchs. Noah invested in the "Divine Promise" when he built the Ark. Abraham invested in the "Divine Promise" when he left his home at Ur and journeyed to Canaan, and when his beloved Sarah died, he bought the "Cave of Machpelah" to bury her in rather than take her remains back to Ur of the Chaldees, because he believed the promise that his seed should inherit the Land of Canaan forever. Jacob invested in the same "Divine Promise," when on his deathbed in Egypt he charged his sons to carry his body back to Canaan and entomb it in the "Cave of Machpelah." Gen. 49: 29-31. And Joseph did the same when he took an oath of his brethren that they would carry his bones back with them when they returned to Canaan. Gen. 50: 24-26. Moses invested in the same "Promise" when by faith, when he was come to years, he refused to be called the son of Pharoah's daughter, choosing rather to suffer affliction with the people of God, esteeming the reproach of Christ greater riches than the treasures of Egypt, for he had respect unto the recompense of reward, for he endured as seeing Him who is invisible. Heb. 11: 23-27.

As Christians we should invest in the "Divine Promises" as to our **PRESENT SALVATION.** There are three elements in "saving faith." (1). **KNOWLEDGE.**

A man cannot believe in something he knows nothing about. (2). **BELIEF.** A man may know about a thing but not believe in it. (3). **DEPENDENCE.** A man may know about a thing and believe in it, and yet put no dependence on it. To illustrate, you are on a sinking ship, a lifeboat puts out from the shore and approaches the ship unknown to you. Some one tells you of the lifeboat, that is **knowledge.** You watch the lifeboat as it carries load after load of passengers safely to the shore and you are convinced of its saving power, that is **belief.** But your knowledge of the existence of the lifeboat, and your belief in its ability to save you, will not save you unless you get in the boat and depend on it to save you, that is **FAITH.**

Let us take a promise of Christ as to the **PRESENT SALVATION** of the Believer.

> "Verily, verily, I say unto you, He that **HEARETH MY WORD** (Knowledge), and **BELIEVETH ON HIM** that sent me (Faith), **HATH** (not will have some time) **EVERLASTING LIFE,** and shall not come into condemnation (Judgment); but **IS PASSED** from **death** to **LIFE.**" John 5:24.

Now can you invest in that promise of Christ as to your heavenly inheritance like Abraham, Jacob and Joseph did as to their earthly inheritance? If so you have saving faith.

But you say I do not **feel** saved. Well, I do not know that when a man receives the "Title Deed" to a property that he has any **peculiar sensation** or feeling about it. It is not **feeling** but the **"Title Deed"** that evidences his right to the property. You cannot expect interest (feeling) until you have invested the principal, and then you have to wait until the interest is due. Feeling does not come first. Feeling **is** not the **root,** faith is the root, feeling is the **FRUIT.** See the diagram, page 204.

We must not only **invest** in the "Divine Promises" as to our Salvation, but we must **TRAFFIC** in them, conduct our Christian work and service in dependence on them. If God has promised to supply all our **need** in Christian Service "according to **HIS RICHES IN**

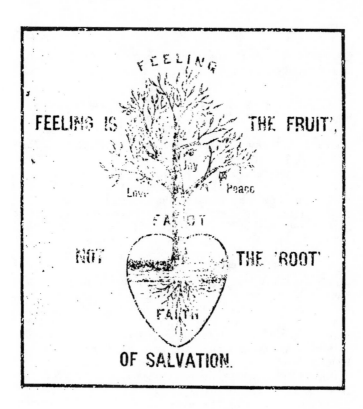

"GLORY " (Phil. 4 : 19), then let us bank on that promise and we will never lack the means to carry on His work.

II. WORKS

While a Christian is not saved by **"Works,"** he is to be **rewarded** for his "works." "For the Son of Man shall come in the glory of His Father, with His angels; and then He shall **reward** every man **ACCORDING TO HIS WORKS."** Matt. 16 : 27. Believers will be rewarded at the "Judgment Seat of Christ." "For we (Believers) must all appear before the 'Judgment Seat of Christ;' that every one may receive the things **DONE IN HIS BODY** (that is while he was alive), **according to that he hath done,** whether it be **GOOD or BAD."** 2 Cor. 5 : 10.

The character of these works must be Christian. "For other foundation can no man lay than that is laid, which is **JESUS CHRIST.** Now if any man build upon this **foundation** (with) **gold, silver, precious stones, wood, hay, stubble;** every man's work shall be made manifest: for the day (Judgment Day) shall declare it, because it shall be revealed **BY FIRE;** and the fire shall **try every** man's work of what sort it is. If any man's work **abide** which he hath built thereupon, he shall receive a **REWARD.** If any man's work shall be **burned, he shall** suffer **LOSS;** but he himself **SHALL BE SAVED; yet so as by fire."** 1 Cor. 3 : 11-15.

We see from this that even the works of the Believer are not all good or worthy of reward. Some may have been done with the wrong motive, or the "Hireling Spirit," and they shall be consumed as wood, hay and stubble, while the good works, likened unto gold, silver, and precious stones, will pass through the "fiery test" untarnished. The rewards that will be given are **"crowns."** See the account of the "Judgment Seat of Christ" in the chapter on "The Judgments."

Such "works" as "penance," "crucifixion of the flesh," "fastings," etc., done for the purpose of winning merit, are not counted on the balance sheet of works. The sad feature of the "Judgment of Rewards" is, that while those whose works are burned up are **SAVED, they must** remain **rewardless,** and therefore **crownless,** for all eternity.

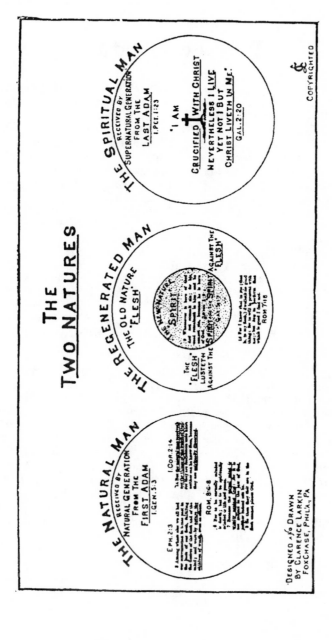

THE
TWO NATURES

THE NATURAL MAN

RECEIVED BY
NATURAL GENERATION
FROM THE
FIRST ADAM
I. GEN. 5:3

EPH. 2:3

I COR. 2:14

ROM. 8:6-8

THE REGENERATED MAN

THE OLD NATURE
"FLESH"

THE NEW NATURE
"SPIRIT"

GAL. 5:17

THE
"FLESH"
LUSTETH
AGAINST THE
"SPIRIT"

"SPIRIT" AGAINST THE
"FLESH"

ROM. 7:18

THE SPIRITUAL MAN

RECEIVED BY
SUPERNATURAL GENERATION
FROM THE
LAST ADAM
I. PET. 1:23

"I AM
CRUCIFIED WITH CHRIST
NEVERTHELESS I LIVE
YET NOT I BUT
CHRIST LIVETH IN ME."
GAL. 2:20

DESIGNED AND DRAWN
BY CLARENCE LARKIN
FOX CHASE, PHILA., PA.

XIX

The Two Natures

It is very important that every Christian Believer should understand what the Scriptures teach as to the "Two Natures." Because of a lack of knowledge of the "Dual Nature" of the "New Born" Soul many a new convert, after rejoicing for a while in his new found hope and then suddenly awakening to the fact that his old fleshly inclinations are not dead, is led to believe that he was never converted, and disheartened and discouraged he begins to drift and finally backslides.

When Nicodemus made his night visit to Jesus, Jesus said unto him, "Except a man be born of **water** (the Word of God. 1 Pet. 1:23. James 1:18), and of the **SPIRIT** (Holy Spirit), he cannot enter into the Kingdom of God." John 3:5. And He gave the reason why. For "that which is born of **FLESH** is **FLESH**; and that which is born of **SPIRIT** is **SPIRIT**." John 3:6. Here we see two lines of **HEREDITY**. The "Flesh" line, and the "Spirit" line. The Scriptures speak of the first as the **"Natural Man,"** and the second as the **"Spiritual Man."**

I. THE NATURAL MAN

Of the "Natural Man" the Scriptures say, "That his understanding is darkened." Eph. 4:18. That he cannot receive (perceive) the things of the Spirit of God, for they only can be spiritually discerned. 1 Cor. 2:14. That he is the child of wrath. Eph. 2:3. That he is at enmity with God, and cannot please Him. Rom. 8:7-8. That his heart is deceitful and desperately wicked (Jer. 17:9), and out of it proceedeth "evil thoughts, adulteries, fornications, murders, thefts, covetousness, deceit, lasciviousness, an evil eye, blasphemy, pride and foolishness." Mark 7:21-22. That he is spiritually dead in trespasses and sins. Eph. 2:1. That there is no good thing in him. Rom. 7:18. That as the Ethiopian cannot change his skin, or the Leopard his spots, so the "Natural Man" without supernatural help cannot change his character. Jer. 13:23.

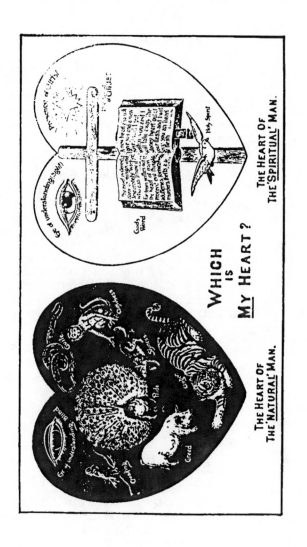

Now God does not say in this description of the "Natural Man" that none are refined, or cultured, or sweet-tempered, or generous, or charitable, or honest, or truthful, or **religious**, but that **none are RIGHTEOUS**, for **"ALL have sinned, and come short** of the **GLORY OF GOD."** Rom. 3:23.

II. THE SPIRITUAL MAN

While the "Natural Man" has a **human** parentage, the "Spiritual Man" has a **DIVINE** parentage. All life must come from **"pre-existing life."** There is no such thing as **"Spontaneous Generation"** of life. No life can come without parentage. There must be a father and a mother. In the "Spiritual World" the Holy Spirit is the **FATHER**, and the "Human Heart" is the **WOMB** (Mother) into which the **"SEED"** of the "Word of God" is dropped. 1 Pet. 1:23. If seed in the Natural World is lifeless no plant will spring from it, and if the **"Seed of the Word"** is not **VITALIZED** by the "Holy Spirit" when it falls into the human heart there will be no **"New Life."** This explains how men and women can read and study the Scriptures and not be converted.

This "New Birth" imparts a **"NEW NATURE."** This Nature is **SPIRITUAL**. "That which is born of the **Spirit** (Holy Spirit) is **SPIRIT."** John 3:6. This New Nature **CANNOT SIN**. "Whosoever is born of God doth not commit sin; for His Seed (Life) remaineth in him; and he **cannot sin,** because he is **BORN OF GOD."** 1 John 3:9. This new "Spiritual Nature" is called **"CHRIST IN YOU"** (Col. 1:27), and imparts **ETERNAL LIFE**. "He that hath the **Son** (Christ in you) hath **LIFE."** 1 John 5:11-12. This "Life" is HID **WITH CHRIST IN GOD**. Therefore we cannot lose it, and **"when Christ who is OUR LIFE** shall appear, then shall we also **appear with Him IN GLORY."** Col. 3:3-4. The **"Fruit"** of the "Spiritual Life" is—"love, joy, peace, long-suffering, gentleness, goodness, faith, meekness and temperance." Gal. 5:22-23. The Spiritual Man is **SPIRITUALLY ENLIGHTENED**. "Eye hath not seen, nor ear heard, neither have entered into the heart of man (the natural man) the things which God hath prepared for them that love Him. But God hath **revealed them unto us** (the Spiritual Man) by His **SPIRIT** (Holy Spirit): for the **SPIRIT** searcheth all things, yea, the deep things of God." 1 Cor. 2:9-10.

We see from this description of the "Spiritual Man" that he is not an **Evolution** or **Development** of the "Natural Man," but a **"New Creature"** or **"CREATION."** 2 Cor. 5:17. When the profligate Augustine sat under a Numidian Fig-tree thinking over his past life, there flashed into his memory, vitalized by the Holy Spirit, the words of Rom. 13:12-14, "The night is far spent, the day is at hand: let us therefore **cast off** the works of darkness, and let us **put** on the armor of light. Let us walk honestly, as in the day; not in rioting and drunkenness, not in chambering and wantonness, not in strife and envying. But **PUT YE ON THE LORD JESUS CHRIST, AND MAKE NOT PROVISION FOR THE FLESH, TO FULFIL THE LUSTS THEREOF,"** and at once the "Seed of the Word" thus dropped into the **"Womb of His Heart,"** created a "new life," and the profligate arose from the ground a **"New Creature"** known thereafter as Saint Augustine.

The Spiritual man then is a "New Creation," and entirely different from the Natural man, and **opposed** to him in character, temperament and disposition. So far all is clear, but here we are brought face to face with the **PARADOX,** that while there are **TWO SEPARATE MEN** spoken of in the Scriptures, the "Natural Man" and the "Spiritual Man," these two men make up in the Believer but one **PERSONALITY,** known as—

III. THE REGENERATED MAN

When the "New Man" is born in the heart of the Believer the "Old Man" does not die. He is still there and very much alive. There are now two natures, diametrically opposed, fighting for the possession of the same body, like two tenants fighting for the possession of the same dwelling house. Paul graphically describes it in Gal. 5:17. "For the **FLESH** (the Old Man) lusteth against the **SPIRIT,** and the **SPIRIT** (the New Man) against the **FLESH;** and these are **contrary** the one to

the other: so that ye **cannot do the things that ye would."**
See the Chart the "Two Natures." This explains the
"SPIRITUAL WARFARE" so vividly portrayed by the
Apostle Paul in Rom. 7:14-25. This was the Apostle's
own experience after his conversion and before he learned
how **THROUGH JESUS CHRIST** (verses 24-25) to
overcome the flesh, and let the Holy Spirit reign in his
life. Read Rom. 8:1-39.

It is not until we have been "Born Again" that we
awake to a knowledge of the depravity of our heart and
discover tendencies that we never knew we possessed,
and realize the power of sin over us. It is this awakening that startles and dumbfounds us, and makes us doubt
our conversion and salvation.

HOW IS THIS WARFARE BETWEEN THE TWO NATURES TO BE CONDUCTED?

1. We must remember that we cannot get rid of the
"Old Nature" until the death of our body of "Flesh."
Therefore the warfare must continue until death.

2. We must not try to improve or make a fair showing of the "Flesh." Gal. 6:12. We are to have **NO
CONFIDENCE** in it. Phil. 3:4.

3. We must **STARVE** the "Flesh," and make no
provision for it to fulfill the lusts thereof. Rom. 13:14.

4. We must **FEED** the "New Nature." The "New
Nature" at first is but a "babe," and must be fed with the
"Sincere Milk of the Word." 1 Pet. 2:2. It must also
be fed regularly. The best human literature ever written
will not feed and nourish the new nature of the Child of
God. We must remember that while we may starve the
Old Man, and he may become very feeble and cause little
trouble, and we may reckon him dead, he is **not dead,**
and if we begin to feed him again he will revive and
recover his strength and give us trouble. This accounts
for how some Christians who have lived for years a
consecrated spiritual life suddenly fall, having yielded
in an unguarded moment to some former habit of their
old nature. We must not forget that we cannot feed
both Natures at the **same time.** We cannot be studying
the Scriptures and listening to music, or a conversation

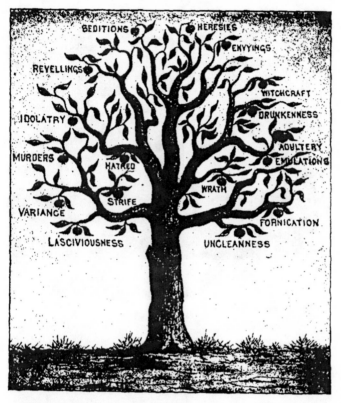

The Natural Man bringing Forth the "Works of the Flesh." GAL. 5: 20-21.

The "Spiritual Life" planted in the heart of the "New Born" man. But the "Old Nature" (the Trunk) is not dead.

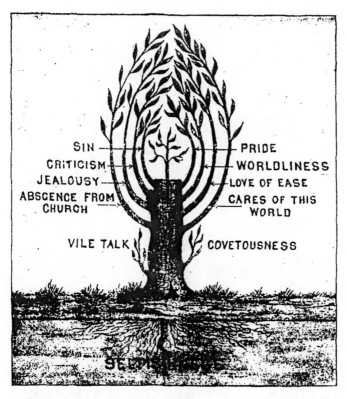

The result when the "Old Nature" is allowed to overshadow the "New Nature."

When the "New Nature" is finally given the right way, it will bring forth the "Fruit of the Spirit," (GAL. 5: 22-23) but the scars of worldliness and sin are seen on the Old Trunk.

that gratifies the Flesh, at the same time. Neither must we forget that what **feeds** one nature will **starve** the other. The "Spiritual Nature" will starve on novels, and the "Flesh Nature" on the Scriptures.

5. We must **"WALK IN THE SPIRIT."** "Walk in the Spirit, and ye shall not fulfil the lust of the Flesh." Gal. 5:16.

The Scriptures mention three ways in which the Believer can overcome the "Flesh."

1. BY AMPUTATION.

"If thy **hand** or thy **foot** offend thee, **cut them off.**" Matt. 18:8-9. Not literally, but if thy hand causes thee to **steal,** stop at once, don't taper off. If thy foot causeth thee to go to the **haunts of sin,** stop short as if you were footless. "If thine **eye** offend thee," causeth thee to look upon a woman to lust after her, it were better if you were suddenly to lose the power of sight.

2. BY MORTIFICATION.

"Mortify therefore your members which are upon the earth; fornication, uncleanness," etc. Col. 3:5-10, Rom. 8:13. To mortify is to cause some part of a living body to die. There are some things we cannot amputate, they must be removed in some other way. So there are things in our lives that take time to overcome, as weak nerves, impatience, pride, etc., these we must destroy by mortification. This treatment is more "medical" than "surgical," and is **INTERNAL** rather than external. It is not by our own effort, but by letting **GOD "work in us."** Phil. 2:12-13.

3. BY LIMITATION.

"Lay aside every weight, and the sin which doth so easily beset us." Heb. 12:1.

There is a difference between **"Weights"** and **"Sins."** All **"weights"** are not **"sins,"** though all **"sins"** are **"weights."** It is not a sin to be a slave to your business, nor to be so absorbed in social service as to neglect other important duties, but these things are **"weights"** and prevent the proper cultivation of the Spiritual life and should be limited. On the other hand every **sin** is a **"weight"** for it loads us down and interferes with our running the Christian race.

XX

Standing and State

There are "Three Classes" of Professing Christians.

1. Those who **are saved** and **KNOW IT.**
2. Those who **are saved** and are **NOT SURE OF IT.**
3. Those who are **not saved** but **THINK THEY ARE.**

When asked if they are saved, some Christians say, "I **hope** so," others say, "I **trust** so," while many think it **presumptuous** to be positive and say we cannot know until we die. The reason why so many Christians are not sure that they are saved is because they do not distinguish between their **"STANDING,"** their **"STATE,"** and their **"EXPERIENCE."**

I. THE CHRISTIAN'S STANDING

The only place we can find out as to this is in the Word of God. What does the Bible say about it? It says that the Christian's "Standing" is that of a **SON.** "As many as **received** Him, to them gave He power to become the **SONS OF GOD."** John 1:12-13. We become a "Son of God" by **receiving** Christ as our personal Saviour. And we are a "Son" **NOW.** "Beloved **NOW** are we the Sons of God." 1 John 3:2. And this "Sonship" makes us **HEIRS.** "And if 'Children,' then **HEIRS; heirs of God, and joint heirs with Christ."** Rom. 8:17. And this "HEIRSHIP" guarantees our **PRESERVATION,** for we are kept by the **"POWER OF GOD,"** unto an inheritance incorruptible, and undefiled, and that fadeth not away, **"RESERVED IN HEAVEN"** for us. 1 Pet. 1:4-5. And no man shall be able to **pluck us out of our FATHER'S HAND** (John 10:27-29), for we are **"SEALED"** unto the Day of Redemption (Eph. 4:30), and our "life" (Spiritual Life) is **HID WITH CHRIST IN GOD.** Col. 3:3. If my "life" is **"hid in Christ"** by God for safe keeping I have it not and therefore **cannot lose it.** But I think I hear some one say, "How about the

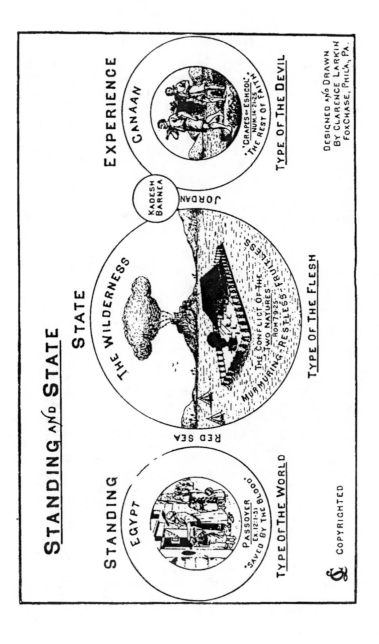

STANDING and STATE

STANDING

EGYPT

"PASSOVER"
Ex. 12:1-31
"SAVED BY THE BLOOD"

TYPE OF THE WORLD

STATE

THE WILDERNESS

RED SEA

The Conflict of the
"TWO NATURES"
Rom. 7:9-25
"MURMURING" "RESTLESS" "FRUITLESS"

TYPE OF THE FLESH

KADESH BARNEA

JORDAN

EXPERIENCE

CANAAN

"GRAPES OF ESHCOL"
NUM. 14:21-25
"THE REST OF FAITH"

TYPE OF THE DEVIL

DESIGNED AND DRAWN
BY CLARENCE LARKIN
FOXCHASE, PHILA., PA.

COPYRIGHTED

words 'fall way' " (Heb. 6:4-6), and if we sin wilfully after that we have received the knowledge of the truth? Heb. 10:26. Are you a **JEW**? Then those words are intended for you, but if a Gentile, then not. Those words were spoken to apostate Jewish professors of Christianity and are not intended for Gentile believers. The moment the Children of Israel put the **blood** of the Passover Lamb on the doorposts of their dwellings the inmates were **safe,** and the promise of God that "when **HE** (not them) **saw the BLOOD,**" He would "**pass over them,**" (Ex. 12:13), made them sure. So the "Blood of Christ" makes us **SAFE,** and the "**WORD OF GOD**" makes us **SURE.** See the Chart "Standing and State." Page 218.

II. THE CHRISTIAN'S STATE

While the Christian's "Standing" is **SETTLED** and **SURE** his "State" is **VARIABLE.** This is owing to the fact that after our "New Birth" we have "**TWO NATURES**" where before we had but one. We do not lose the "Old Adam" or "**FLESH Nature**" when we receive the "New Adam" or "**SPIRITUAL Nature,**" for that which was born of the "Flesh" is still **FLESH,** and only that which is born of the "**HOLY SPIRIT**" is **SPIRIT.** John 3:6. This explains the "**SPIRITUAL WARFARE**" so vividly portrayed by the Apostle Paul in Rom. 7:14-25. This was the Apostle's own experience after his conversion and reveals the fact that the Believer has a **DUAL NATURE,** and he is **sinless** or **sinful** according to which nature is uppermost, for that which is "**born of God**" in him, his "Spiritual Nature," **CANNOT SIN.** 1 John 3:9. But as long as we permit our "**FLESH Nature**" to control us, we cannot say "**we have no sin,**" if we do we "**deceive ourselves,**" and the "**truth is not in us.**" 1 John 1:8-10. Here we must distinguish between "**SIN**" and "**SINS.**" "**SIN**" is that disposition to do wrong that we inherit from Adam called "Original Sin" or "Natural Depravity." "**SINS**" are the specific acts of sin that we commit due to the disposition to sin in us. Jesus died on the Cross to remove the disposition to sin from us, and by accepting Him as our personal Saviour we get a **NEW NATURE** in which there is no disposition to sin. It is that Nature therefore that cannot sin. See the Chapter on "The Two Natures."

But you say does not the Apostle Paul say that we are "dead to sin," and ought not to live any longer therein? Rom. 6:1-2. Yes. But what he means is that we are **JUDICIALLY DEAD.** That is, we are in our "New Nature" dead to the "**LAW OF SIN,**" that "Law" has no further power over us, therefore, the Apostle adds, we should "**RECKON OURSELVES DEAD**" (Rom. 6:11), that is, we should consider ourselves **dead to sin** and live and act like a man who had died to his old manner of life. How is it to be done? "**Walk in the SPIRIT, and ye SHALL NOT FULFIL THE LUST OF THE FLESH.**" Gal. 5:16. We are told not to let sin "REIGN" in our mortal body, and the promise is—"sin shall not have **DOMINION over you.**" Rom. 6:12-14.

We see from all this that while a "Believer's Standing" is "Settled" and "Sure," his "State" is **VARIABLE** and will be **sinful** or **sinless** according to whether the "Old" or "New Nature" is in control.

III. THE CHRISTIAN'S EXPERIENCE

As to "Experience" the Believer may be in any one of three places. (1) He may be in **EGYPT,** the "Type of the WORLD.**" (2) He may be in the **WILDERNESS,** the "Type of the FLESH.**" Or (3) he may be fighting for the possession of **CANAAN,** the "Type of the DEVIL.**"

The "Children of Israel" were **safe** in Egypt the moment they sprinkled the "Blood" of the "Passover Lamb" on the doorposts of their dwellings. So the Believer is **Saved** the moment he applies the "**BLOOD OF CHRIST**" by faith to his soul though he may in experience be still living in the world of which Egypt is a **type,** though he should not be content to dwell there. Some Believers have left Egypt behind, but as to experience they are still wandering in the Wilderness, sometimes on the Egyptian side of the Wilderness longing for the leeks, onions, and garlic of their old Egyptian life, at other times on the Canaan side longing for the new corn and wine and figs and pomegranates of the Promised

Land, but mostly wandering in the centre of the Wilderness, in a state of murmuring, restlessness and unfruitfulness.

Some have visited Kadesh Barnea and taken a journey over into Canaan and tasted of the "Grapes of Eshcol" but have been frightened by the "Giants" and "Walled Cities" and refusing to go in and "possess the land" they have been compelled to wander for many years in the Wilderness to the great loss of themselves and their loved ones, due to their lack of faith. Num. 13:1-33.

Other Believers have left the Wilderness and entered Canaan and are now under the leadership of their Joshua (Christ), endeavoring to drive out the Canaanites, Hittites, Hivites, Perizzites, Girgashites, Amorites, and Jebusites of their soul that they may get posession of the land, for they have the promise that they shall get "possession" by "dispossession," and control every portion of territory over which their feet shall tread. Joshua 1:1-3. While Canaan is a type, not of Heaven, for there is no conflict in Heaven, but of the "Rest of Faith" or the "Victorious Life," it is also a **"Type of the Devil,"** for the Devil is satisfied to have the Believer remain in Egypt (the World), or in the Wilderness overcome by the "Flesh," but when the Believer gets over into Canaan the Devil is going to contest every foot of the way, and prevent if possible a **"Life of Victory."**

From what has been said we see that our **"Fellowship"** with God can be broken, but our **RELATIONSHIP** never. The Prodigal Son severed his "Fellowship" with his father by going off into a "far country," but he did not lose his **"SONSHIP"** for as a **SON** he was welcomed back. Luke 15:24. "Who then shall **SEPARATE** us from the 'Love of Christ'." Rom. 8:35-39.

XXI

Regeneration and Baptism

There is more or less confusion as to the relation of Baptism to Regeneration. Some teach that Baptism is a saving ordinance, and that in the administration of the rite the candidate is regenerated or "born again," and for this reason it is called a "Sacrament." Because of this belief many parents hasten to have their infants baptized for fear that they will be eternally lost. For a proper understanding of the subject it is necessary that we ascertain the Scriptural meaning of the words "Regeneration" and "Baptism," and we shall find that one is an "Inner Experience," and the other is an "Outward Act."

I. REGENERATION

In the third chapter of John's Gospel we find two "**Divine Necessities.**" First, "Ye must be **BORN AGAIN**," (John 3:3, 5), second, "The Son of Man must be **LIFTED UP.**" To whom did Jesus utter these words? Not to a gambler, a drunkard, a thief, a libertine, a heathen, a non-church goer, but to a Church Member. To Nicodemus, a Ruler of the Jews, a Pharisee, a Rabbi, a member of the Great Sanhedrin, learned in the "Law" and "Holy Scriptures," one of the Religious Leaders of his day and a "Master in Israel." As a Jew he was entitled to all the "Birthright Privileges" of a son of Abraham, and to be told by Christ that all his boasted "Birthright Privileges" did not entitle him to a place in the "Kingdom of God" was **startling.** "How," said Nicodemus, "can a man be born when he is old? Can he enter the second time into his mother's womb, and be born?" Surely not! And if he could there would nothing be gained by a second **NATURAL** birth more than by the first. If a natural man could re-enter 10,000 times into his mother's womb and be born he would be naught but a **NATURAL** man after all, for "That which is born of flesh is FLESH."

Why must men be born again? Because—"That which is born of flesh is **FLESH**, and that which is born

Can the Ethiopian change his skin, or the Leopard his spots?

of the 'Spirit' (Holy Spirit) is **SPIRIT.**" John 3:6. Men are not by nature the "Sons of God," they are the "Children of the Devil," (1 John 3:10), and Jesus so informed the Jews. John 8:37-44. There is a restricted "Fatherhood of God" and "Brotherhood of Man." It is only those who receive Christ as their personal Saviour that can become the "Sons of God." John 1:12. There is much being said in these days about "Building Character," which is only another phrase for the "Moral Evolution" of human nature, and by selection, or the intermarriage of the "Physically, Morally and Intellectually Fit," to produce a race of Supermen and Women. But this is impossible, being contrary to the history of the race and to Scripture.

The "New Birth" is not a change of the "Old Nature" into a "New Nature" by either a gradual or sudden transformation, called development or reformation. Religious reformation may very much **improve the flesh**, but after all it is only **religious FLESH.** To use a Scriptural illustration, if we were to take a "nettle" from the roadside and bring it into a garden or hothouse, and watch over it, dress and water and warm it, we might be able to produce beautiful and different varieties of "nettles," but they would only be **"NETTLES,"** we could never get **"FIGS"** from them. "Do men gather **grapes** of **thorns,** or 'FIGS' of 'THISTLES'?" Matt. 7:16. "Can the Ethiopian change his skin, or the leopard his spots?" Jer. 13:23.

What then is the "New Birth?" "It is the **COMMUNICATION OF A NEW LIFE,** the **IMPLANTATION OF A NEW NATURE** by the 'SPIRIT OF GOD.'"

There is no such thing as **"Spontaneous Generation of Life."** All life must come from **PRE-EXISTING LIFE.** We speak of the "Inorganic" and "Organic" Kingdoms. The Kingdoms of "No-Life" and of "Life." A dead stone cannot pass of itself from the "Inorganic" into the "Organic" Kingdom. There is a door between the two Kingdoms, but it opens on the Organic Kingdom side. While the stone cannot open that door the plant can, and by thrusting its rootlets into the soil can disintegrate the stone and take of its chemical constituents and give them of its own life. Likewise there is a door between the "Vegetable Kingdom" and the "Animal Kingdom," but it opens on the "Animal Kingdom" side. The plant cannot turn itself into flesh, but the animal by eating the plant can change it from "vegetable life" to "animal life." So there is a door between the "Natural" and "Spiritual" worlds, but it cannot be opened from the "Natural" side. Therefore a man to have "Spiritual Life" must be born from above. A sculptor may take a piece of marble and carve from it a lifelike figure, but it is still **MARBLE** and **LIFELESS**.

In the "Human Kingdom" there can be no life without parentage. There must be a father and a mother. The same is true of the "Spiritual Kingdom." In the "Spiritual Kingdom" the Holy Spirit is the **FATHER,** and the "Human Heart" is the **WOMB** (Mother) into which the "**SEED**" of the "Word of God" is dropped. "Being **born again**, not of corruptible seed, but of incorruptible, by the **WORD OF GOD**." 1 Pet. 1:23. If seed in the Natural World, either of plant, animal, or man, is **lifeless**, there will be no new life, and if the "Seed of the Word of God" is not **VITALIZED** by the Holy Spirit when it falls into the human heart there will be no "**New Birth**." This explains how men and women can read and study the Scriptures and not be converted. To illustrate, a man may have heard or read a thousand times the words—"Ye will not come to me, that ye might have life." John 5:40. But one day on the street he is handed a card on which those words are printed in large letters. Angered by the publicity of the act, and offended at the intimation that he needs to be saved, he tears the card into pieces and throwing it into the gutter with an oath he passes on. But he cannot dismiss the incident from his memory. Do what he will it persists in returning. He finds himself unfitted for business. The evening is spent in a place of amusement, but the words on the card haunt him, and he leaves the theatre to go home and spend a sleepless night. What is the matter? Why that "text" was no longer "lifeless," it had been "**vitalized**" by the Holy Spirit, it had fallen into the womb of the man's heart and was in the process of generating a "New Life" in the man. Leave it alone and it will do its office work and the man will become a "New Creature" in Christ Jesus. If in our experience we can remember or recall the verse of Scripture that was the means of our conversion then we can point to it as the Holy Spirit vitalized seed of the Word that caused the generation of the "New Life" in our heart.

HOW TO BE BORN AGAIN

If I must be "born again," I may be born again, for God never commands an impossible thing. We have considered the manner and the means of the communication of the New Birth, it now remains to show how it may be secured. In the night interview of Nicodemus and Jesus, Jesus used three illustrations. (1) That of a **BIRTH.** (2) That of the **"BRAZEN SERPENT."** (3) That of the **WIND.** We have explained the first, let us now consider the second. **"AS** Moses lifted up the 'Serpent' in the Wilderness, even **SO** must the 'Son of Man' be lifted up." Nicodemus being a "Master" in Israel knew well the incident of the "Brazen Serpent." Num. 21:4-9. He knew how that when the Children of Israel essayed to compass the land of Edom and became discouraged, that they murmured against Moses, and the Lord sent "Fiery Serpents," and they bit the people and many died, and Moses was commanded to make a "Brazen Serpent" and put it on a pole, that whosoever looked upon it should be healed of the poisonous bite. The "Fiery Serpents" were a type of the Devil, and the "Brazen Serpent" was a type of Jesus lifted up upon the Cross to counteract and destroy the work of the Devil. From this we see that it is not Jesus as an example, but Jesus **"lifted up"** and **CRUCIFIED** that saves. The "Brazen Serpent" was "lifted up" that all Israel might see it, and Jesus was "lifted up" that all men might see HIM. "And I, if I be lifted up from the earth, will draw all men unto me. This He said, signifying what death he should die." John 12:32-33. How forcibly that night interview must have been recalled to Nicodemus' memory as he and Joseph of Arimathea bent over the body of

Jesus preparing it for burial. I think I can hear Nicodemus say to Joseph, "Joseph, He told me it would be
this way that night I visited Him at John's house in
Jerusalem and He explained to me how I might be born
again. He said as Moses lifted up the 'Brazen Serpent'
in the Wilderness so He must be lifted up, and now He
has been 'lifted up.' Handle Him tenderly Joseph, for
He is our Lord and Saviour."

Let us study that Wilderness scene, for if we can
grasp its lessons we will know the steps we must take to
be saved.

1. **The first thing necessary for an Israelite to know
was that he was BITTEN.**

Not until he felt the sting of the serpent's bite would
an Israelite feel concerned about his health. So the
sinner has no concern about his spiritual health until he
realizes that the "poison of sin" will destroy his soul.

2. **The second thing for an Israelite to know was that
there was a GOD-PROVIDED REMEDY.**

Now an Israelite might have been bitten and not have
known about the "Brazen Serpent" and have perished
for want of knowledge. So there are many who know
that sin is destroying their lives but do not know of the
way of deliverance. It is necessary that they learn in
some way of God's "provided remedy" for sin—JESUS.

3. **The third thing for an Israelite to know was that
the God-provided remedy was of no account UNTIL
APPLIED.**

If a bitten Israelite, knowing of the "Brazen Serpent,"
refused to look at it he died. So the sinner, who, conscious of his sinful state, refuses to accept Christ as his
Saviour will die in his sins.

We can imagine a bitten Israelite when asked to look
at the "Brazen Serpent," saying—"Oh! I have got no
faith in that piece of brass. I will just try a **poultice** or
drink this medicine that I have in the house." So men
and women today instead of looking to Christ, resort **to**
man-made remedies to soothe the pangs of conscience,
such as good works, penances, music, worldly entertain-
ments, and religious fads.

We can imagine another bitten Israelite saying—"I will not have anything to do with the 'Brazen Serpent' until I know how it cures. I want to know the philosophy of the thing. If God had told us to rub the bitten place with a piece of brass in the form of a serpent, or to take a piece of brass and boil it with some herbs and make a medicine that we were to take, then I could understand the philosophy of the thing, but to simply look at a 'Brazen Serpent' on a pole that is all foolishness and I will perish before I do it." So men and women argue today. They say, "I cannot understand the philosophy of the Atonement, and I will not accept the work of the Cross until you make it plain to my reason."

Again we can imagine a bitten Israelite saying—"I will wait until tomorrow to see if I am not better, and if I am no better then I will go and have a look at the 'Brazen Serpent' to see whether there is anything in it." So men and women today live in the hope that tomorrow there will be an improvement in their spiritual condition, and if not, they say they will have a "try" at religion.

Another bitten Israelite comparing his wound with that of his neighbor may have said, "My wound is not half as bad as my neighbor's, so I will not do anything as long as he lives." So men and women compare their spiritual condition with that of their neighbors and say, 'I am not as bad as they are and if they are saved I will be." But comparing ourselves with others, or looking at the wound will not do, we must look to the REMEDY. It was not the "Brazen Serpent" that healed, it was the "LOOK OF FAITH." It was because the bitten Israelites believed the "Promise of God" that a "LOOK" would save them, that they were saved. So it is not necessary for us to understand the philosophy of the "Plan of Salvation," but simply believe what God has said that if we accept the "Crucified Christ" as our Saviour we shall be saved. Let us then take our eyes off of our neighbor, off of ourself, off of the Church, off of the ordinances, off of the Priest, and fix them on the "Cross of Calvary," and accept the finished work of Christ.

The Israelites were shut up to the "Brazen Serpent," so we are shut up to Christ. He is God's only remedy for sin. There is no salvation in any other. Acts 4:12. As every bitten Israelite who refused to look at the "Brazen Serpent" died, so all who refuse to look to Christ for salvation—"shall be punished with everlasting destruction from the Presence of the Lord, and from the Glory of His Power." 2 Thess. 1:7-10.

HOW MAY I KNOW I HAVE BEEN BORN AGAIN?

This leads us to the consideration of Jesus' third illustration, that of the **WIND**. "The wind bloweth where it listeth, and thou hearest the sound thereof, but canst not tell whence it cometh, and whither it goeth: so is every one that is born of the Spirit." John 3:8. You cannot **see** the wind, it is in itself **invisible**. The only way you can tell that it is in motion is by its **effects**, as seen in the swaying trees and the clouds of dust. So it is with the Holy Spirit, He is invisible and the only way you can tell that He is at work is by His influence on the hearts of men. When we see a vile and wicked sinner changed into a new creature in Christ Jesus, then we know that the Holy Spirit has been at work. Here are some of the **"BIRTH-MARKS"** of the "New Born" child of God.

1. He that is "Born of God" hath the witness **IN HIMSELF.** 1 John 5:10. Rom. 8:16.

2. He that is "Born of God" **ABIDETH IN HIM.** 1 John 3:24.

3. He that is "Born of God" **LOVETH THE BRETHREN.** 1 John 3:14.

4. He that is "Born of God" **OVERCOMETH THE WORLD.** 1 John 5:4.

5. He that is "Born of God" is **LED BY THE HOLY SPIRIT.** Rom. 8:14.

He that is "Born of God" will have a new nature and disposition. He will have a **"New Tongue."** He will speak the language of Canaan and love to talk about Heavenly things. He will feed on **"New Food."** It will no longer be the novel and light literature, but the Word of God. He will have a **"New Song."** No longer operatic airs and minstrel melodies, but sacred music. He will seek "New Society." Old companionships will be broken off and he will seek the society of God's people.

II. BAPTISM

Having seen the meaning of Regeneration and that it is an "Inner Experience," let us now examine the meaning and purpose of Baptism that we may see that it is but an "Outward Act" that symbolizes the "New Birth," and is to be observed not as a means to our salvation, but because we have been saved. Right here someone may ask, "Did not Jesus say to Nicodemus— 'Verily, verily, I say unto thee, except a man be born of **WATER** and of the **SPIRIT,** he cannot enter into the Kingdom of God' (John 3:5), and does not **WATER** mean Baptism, and does it not therefore require both the 'New Birth' and 'Water Baptism' to save a soul?" No. The word "Water" does not mean "Water Baptism." Water stands in the Scriptures for the "Word of God." "Of His own will 'begat' He us with the **WORD OF TRUTH."** James 1:18. "Being 'born again,' not of corruptible seed, but of incorruptible, by the **WORD OF GOD."** 1 Pet. 1:23. It must not be forgotten that Baptism is only for **BELIEVERS.** Acts 8:36-37. Therefore a person must be saved, or "New Born," before they should be baptized. This forbids the Baptism of infants, but not of children who have reached the age of accountability and are old enough to believe and exercise saving faith.

What is the purpose of Baptism? First it is to symbolize the "Death" and "Resurrection" of Christ.

> "Know ye not, that so many of us as were baptized into Jesus Christ were baptized into His **DEATH?** Therefore we are **BURIED** with Him by Baptism into **DEATH;** that like as Christ was raised from the dead by the glory of the Father, even so we also should walk in newness of life. For if we have been planted together in the likeness of His **DEATH,** we shall be also in the likeness of His **RESURRECTION."** Rom. 6:3-5.

Believers' Baptism

Writing to the Corinthians Paul said—"I declare unto you the Gospel which I preached unto you . . . how that Christ **DIED** for our sins . . . that He was **BURIED**, and that He **ROSE AGAIN** the third day." 1 Cor. 15:1-4. Here we have the Gospel in a nutshell. It is the proclamation that Jesus **DIED**, was **BURIED**, and **ROSE AGAIN** for our sins according to the Scriptures. So we see that Baptism symbolizes the "Death," "Burial" and "Resurrection" of Christ, and that only one mode of Baptism can symbolize them, and that is complete

IMMERSION IN WATER.

In the second place Baptism is a public confession that the **"Believer"** has died to the "old life" and risen to a "New Life," and what can better symbolize this than the Believer being buried in the watery grave of the Baptistry and rising again from that liquid tomb to walk in resurrection life. And this symbolism can only be expressed by baptizing the candidate backward in the water but once. For we do not bury people **face downward**, nor **three times.**

In the third place Baptism symbolizes our death, burial, and resurrection **with** Christ. That is, it expresses our union with Him. See the Chapter on "The Reciprocal Indwelling of Christ and the Believer."

From what has been said we see that the "New Birth" and "Baptism" are not the same. That the "New Birth" is supernatural and can only be brought about by the Holy Spirit, while Baptism is an "Outward Act" performed for us by a properly qualified administrator, and that it simply symbolizes what has already taken effect in us by the "New Birth." Therefore there is no regenerating or saving power in Baptism. Why then should I be Baptized you ask? First, because your Saviour has commanded you to be. Mark 16:15-16. Secondly, because it is the mode prescribed for a public confession of your faith in Christ. Acts 8:36-37, 16:14-15, 27-33. Thirdly, because as a Believer you should connect yourself with some body of Believers, and the door to such a connection is Baptism. Acts 2:41-42.

XXII

Election and Free-will

There is no question but that the "Doctrine of Election" is taught in the Scriptures, and that it applies not only to "service," but to "salvation." It is equally true that the "Doctrine of the Freedom of the Will" under certain conditions is also taught. We may not be able to reconcile the "Sovereign Will of God," with the "Free-will of Man," but that is no proof that they are not reconcilable. They are the corresponding halves of the Doctrine of Salvation, "Election" is the Godward side, and "Free-will" the manward side. The perversion of the "Doctrine of Election" leads to the "Doctrine of Inability" or Fatalism, which denies the freedom of man's choice, and therefore his accountability or responsibility for his salvation. It was this Doctrine that the Rev. Charles G. Finney thundered against during all his evangelistic ministry.

Election does not mean that God has chosen some to be saved and others to be lost. The Scriptures clearly teach that all men are lost. "For there is no difference: for all have sinned and come short of the glory of God." Rom. 3: 22-23. Election simply means that God for some purpose best known to Him, and for which He can justify Himself, has chosen certain ones to be saved, but as we shall see He has not limited the number that shall be saved to those, for the door is left open for the "Whosoevers." The Election of God is seen all through the Scriptures. God chose Abel instead of Cain, Shem instead of Ham and Japheth, Abraham rather than Nahor, Jacob the crafty rather than Esau the generous-hearted, Ephraim the younger is preferred before Manasseh the elder, and so all down through the Old Testament we see the selecting hand of God, not only in the choice of individuals but of nations. As proof texts we have "For He saith to Moses, I will have mercy on whom I will have mercy, and I will have compassion on whom I will have compassion. So then it is not of him that willeth, nor of him that runneth, but of God that sheweth mercy." Rom. 9:15-16. "Therefore hath He mercy on whom He will have mercy, and whom He will He hardeneth." Rom. 9:18. "Hath not the potter power over the clay, of the same lump to make one vessel unto honor, and another unto dishonor?" Rom. 9:21. "Ye have not chosen me, but I have chosen you." John 15:16. "As many as were ordained to eternal life, believed," Acts 13:48. "According as He hath chosen us in Him before the foundation of the world . . . having predestinated us unto the adoption of children . . . according to the good pleasure of His will." Eph. 1:4-5. "God hath from the beginning chosen you to salvation through sanctification of the Spirit." 2 Thess. 2:13. "Who hath saved us, and called us with an holy calling, not according to our works, but according to His own purpose and grace, which was given us in Christ Jesus before the world was." 2 Tim. 1:9.

From these scriptures we see that God has "elected" some even before the foundation of the world. The passage in Acts 13:48, "As many as were ordained to eternal life, BELIEVED," is most striking. It shows (1) that "Believing" is the consequence, and not the cause of God's decree. (2) That only a limited number are ordained to eternal life. (3) That this ordination is to salvation and not service. (4) That among those hearers all who were ordained believed, no more, no less.

On the other hand we have the "Freedom of the Will" taught. "All that the Father giveth Me shall come to Me, and him that cometh to me I will in no wise cast out." John 6:37. "God so loved the world, that He gave His only begotten Son, that WHOSOEVER believeth in Him should not perish, but have everlasting life." John 3:16. "As many as received Him, to them gave He power to become the Sons of God, even to them that believe on His name." John 1:12. "Ye will not come to me, that ye might have life." John 5:40. The last call of the Bible is a general call. "And the Spirit (Holy Spirit) and the bride (the Church) say, Come. And let him that heareth say, Come. And let him that is athirst come. And **whosoever will**, let him take the water of life freely." Rev. 22:17.

How are we to reconcile these apparently contradictory statements of Scripture? The "key" is the use of the word—

"FOREKNOWLEDGE."

"Elect according to the **FOREKNOWLEDGE** of God." 1 Pet. 1:2. "For whom He did **FOREKNOW**, He also did **predestinate** to be conformed to the 'Image of His Son,' that He might be the first born among many brethren." And the Apostle goes on to add—"Moreover whom he did **predestinate**, them He also **CALLED**; and whom He called, them He also **JUSTIFIED**: and whom He justified, them He also **GLORIFIED**." Rom. 8:29-30. One important step seems to be here omitted, that of **SANCTIFIED**, which belongs between the last two, but it is implied in the phrase "to be conformed to the Image of His Son" of the preceding verse, and is supplied in the first reference from Peter—"Elect according to the foreknowledge of God the Father, **through sanctification of the Spirit.**"

In the Epistle to the Ephesians Paul uses three words: "Chosen," "Predestinated," "Foreordination" (before ordained). The word "Chosen" refers to our choice in the "Eternal Past" (Eph. 1:4), the word "Predestination" to our inheritance in the "Eternal Future" (Eph. 1:11), and the word "Foreordination" to our "good works" in the "Living Present" (Eph. 2:10), and links us with the first two, thus showing the co-ordination of "God's Will" and "Man's Will" in the actual process of salvation. All prophecy is based on God's Foreknowledge, but it does not predetermine human conduct or events. God's Foreknowledge of what men will do does not compel men to do those things. God foreknew that Adam would fall, and that Judas would betray Jesus, but His foreknowledge of what they would do did not compel them to do what they did. They did those things because they wanted to do those things, and God held them responsible for their choice.

From what has been said it is clear that God's choice or predestination of individuals is based on His foreknowledge or prescience of what they would do when the Gospel was offered to them. It is therefore no arbitrary or compulsory choice and does not conflict with the "Freedom of the Will." For illustration God foresaw in eternity past, before the creation of this earth, that on the 28th day of October, 1850, the Author of this book would be born, and that on a certain evening in May, 1869, in a Y. M. C. A. prayer meeting, he would accept Jesus Christ as his personal Saviour, and because of that foreknowledge He ordained him unto Eternal Life, and had his name recorded in the "Lamb's Book of Life." Phil. 4:3. Rev. 3:5. More, He foresaw that the Author would have certain temperamental and artistic gifts that would fit him to present Scriptural truth in chart form, and to that end He imparted to him, through the Holy Spirit, the needed wisdom to "Rightly Divide the Word," so that he might write and publish such books on the Holy Scriptures, as he has by the Grace of God been permitted to do.

Now the Author confesses that he would not have naturally done this, though he was born with a religious temperament, but that it was the outward or external influence of the Holy Spirit that led him to accept Christ. In that sense he admits that he was called or elected of God. On the other hand he disclaims that he was in any sense forced or coerced to take the stand, against his own will. The step was voluntary on his part and was in harmony with his desire. Therefore he holds that there is a harmonious relation between the "Sovereign Will" of God, and the "Free-will" of man.

This leads to some remarks on the "Human Will." The "Will" is the faculty of choice. The will does not originate. It is not the mind. It is simply the instrument that decides the course that is to be taken. The governing part of man is the heart. If a man's heart is bad, his will is bad and vice versa. In the natural man there is no good thing, the disposition of his heart is to do evil continually, therefore if his will is to act contrary to the natural tendencies of his heart it must come under the governing control of some power outside of himself. This power is that of the Holy Spirit. Therefore the unregenerate man cannot come to God until his will comes under the power of the Holy Spirit. When it does the man of his own free will will turn to God. In unfallen Adam the will was **free,** free to choose good or evil. Adam was created in a state of **innocence.** He was neither holy nor unholy. His will was in a condition of "Moral Equipoise." There was no bias toward good or evil. But it is not so with fallen man—he has a bias toward evil, his will is not in a state of "Moral Equipoise." His heart is "deceitful above all things and desperately wicked." Jer. **17:9.** The "will" of the "Last Adam" (Christ) was not like that of the First Adam, in a state of "Moral Equipoise," but it was the reverse of the will of the natural man, it had no bias toward evil, but only a bias toward "Holiness," therefore there was no possibility that the will of Christ would have permitted Him to sin.

Because the choice of the human will, governed by a bad heart, is toward evil, nothing can prevent the Natural man from going to the bad but the "Grace of God." And by badness is not necessarily meant wickedness, but a hardening of his heart against all good influences and a yielding to the carnal desires of the flesh. The nature that is under the **dominion of sin,** cannot of itself originate that which is holy. Jesus said—"No man can come to me except the Father which hath sent me draw him." John **6:44.** And Paul said—"No man can say that Jesus is the Lord, but by the Holy Ghost." 1 Cor. **12: 3.** From this we see the **impotency** of the natural man. But this does not excuse the natural man from seeking salvation. For the moment he realizes that if he is to be saved it must be by a power **outside** of himself, it is his duty to inquire where that power may be found. That is why we are commanded to preach the Gospel, for it is the **"POWER OF GOD UNTO SALVATION TO EVERY ONE THAT BELIEVETH."** Rom. **1: 16.** But as "Faith cometh by **hearing,** and hearing by the **WORD OF GOD"** (Rom. **10: 17),** a man cannot **believe** unless he knows what to believe. The instrument the Holy Spirit uses to convict a man of his need of salvation, and to produce a "New Nature" in him, is the "Word of God." John 3:5.

It is right here that a man may exert his "Free-will" by resisting the tender wooing of the Holy Spirit. Stephen's charge against his persecutors was—"Ye stiff-necked (stubborn) and uncircumcised in heart and ears, ye do always resist the **HOLY GHOST.**" Acts 7:51. Therefore it is true that a man in the exercise of his "will," governed by a proud and stubborn heart, may refuse the pleadings of the Holy Spirit to his own destruction. This refusal of some men to yield to the work of the Holy Spirit, shows that they cannot be saved against their will.

If the "forgiveness of sins" is preached through Christ to all men (Acts 13:38), and God now commands all men everywhere to repent (Acts 17:30), and we are to beseech men to be reconciled to God (2 Cor. 5:18-20), surely the work of Christ on the Cross was not limited to the elect only. God does not mock men. When an offer of salvation is made to **"whosoever will come"** it is a **"BONA-FIDE"** offer. It is not true that because God has chosen a certain person to salvation that he will be saved whether he believes or not. He must be saved through the God-ordained method of salvation. You cannot be elected unless you are a candidate. As it has been well put—"The elect are the **"whosoever wills,"** and the non-elect are the **"whosoever won'ts."**

WHAT ARE THE SIGNS OF ELECTION?

1. A Consciousness of the New Birth.
2. The Fruits of the Holy Spirit in the life.
3. A progressive Sanctification.
4. A consistent walk.
5. A perseverance in the faith.

XXIII

The Reciprocal Indwelling of Christ and the Believer

The thoughtful and observing reader of the New Testament will notice a number of paradoxical statements that clearly teach a "Reciprocal Indwelling." First of the Father and Jesus. "I am in the Father and the Father in Me." John 14:8-11. "The Father in Me, and I in Him." John 10:38. "That they all may be one; as Thou, Father, art in Me, and I in Thee." John 17:21. Secondly as to Christ and the Believer. "He that eateth My flesh, and drinketh My blood, dwelleth in Me, and I in him." John 6:56. In the Parable of "The Vine" we read—"Abide in Me, and I in you . . . He that abideth in Me, and I in him . . . If ye abide in Me, and My words abide in you." John 15:4, 5, 7. It is botanically true that the branches abide in the vine, and the vine in the branches. As the two grow they grow into each other. Any attempt to separate them will tear the fibres that interlock with each other and mutilate both. This "Reciprocal Indwelling" is beautifully illustrated in nature. Take the four elements, earth, air, water and fire. The plant is in the soil, and the soil is in the plant. The bird is in the air, and the air is in the bird. The fish is in the water, and the water is in the fish. The iron is in the fire, and the fire is in the iron. The mutual interrelation of the plant to the soil, the bird to the air, and the fish to the water, is necessary to their life. So the mutual indwelling of Christ and the Believer is necessary to the Spiritual life of the Believer. When Jesus was about to depart He said—"Because I live, ye shall live also. At that day ye shall know that I am in My Father, and ye in Me, and I in you." John 14:19-20. Let us look at these two "Cardinal Facts" of the mutual indwelling of Christ and the Believer.

I. IN CHRIST

This is the position of the soul that has accepted Christ as its personal Saviour, and has been regenerated by the Holy Spirit. This particular phrase with its equivalent "In Christ Jesus," or "In Him," or "In Whom," etc., occurs over 130 times in the New Testament, and means organic union with Christ, as the vine to the branches, and the head to the body. In the Diagram, page 240, this union is illustrated in concentric circles, but a better illustration would be that of a sphere. If you should draw a circle on the floor and step within it, it would surround you, but only on one plane, but if you were to take a position in the centre of a spherically shaped room you would be surrounded on all sides, and equally protected in every direction from all external foes and perils, and dependent upon the atmosphere of that spherical room for your life and safety. To illustrate, the unborn infant is encompassed within the mother, and is protected from all outside perils, and its life is sustained from the mother's life, as her life blood flows through it, and it can be said of it that it is in the mother and the mother in it.

This phrase, "In Christ," is the "Key" that the "Heavenly Interpreter" uses to unlock every separate book in the New Testament, from Matthew to Revelation. For illustration take the Epistles of Paul, counting the Epistles to the Corinthians as one, and the Epistles to the Thessalonians as one:

Romans—"In Christ **JUSTIFIED.**" Rom. 3:24.
Corinthians—"In Christ **SANCTIFIED.**" 1 Cor. 1:2.
Galatians—"In Christ **CRUCIFIED.**" Gal. 2:20.
Ephesians—"In Christ **ASCENDED.**" Eph. 1:3.
Philippians—"In Christ **SATISFIED.**" Phil. 1:11.
Colossians—"In Christ **COMPLETE.**" Col. 2:10.
Thessalonians—"In Christ **GLORIFIED.**" 2 Thess. 1:10-12.

The Believer's **POSITION** "in Christ" is the same as that of Christ Himself. Believers "In Christ" are—

1. **CRUCIFIED** together "with Him." Rom. 6:6.
2. **BURIED** together "with Him." Col. 2:12.

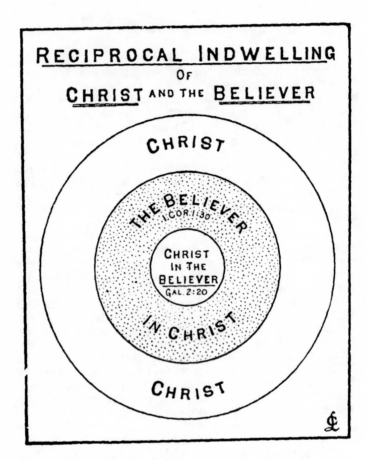

3. **QUICKENED** together "with Him." Eph. 2:5.
4. **RISEN** together "with Him." Col. 3:1-3.
5. **HEIRS** together "with Him." Rom. 8:17.
6. **SUFFERERS** together "with Him." Rom. 8:17.
7. **GLORIFIED** together "with Him." Rom. 8:17.

This does not mean that when Christ was crucified, like one of the thieves, I was crucified on a separate cross with Him, or that when He rose from the grave I also arose from a nearby grave, but it means that when He was crucified and arose I was so identified as a Believer in His Crucifixion and Resurrection as to be said to be crucified, etc., with Him. When Adam sinned he died to God, and as I am by nature the child of Adam, I died **"in Adam"** to God. But the very moment I accept Christ as my personal Saviour I am born into the family of the Second Adam (Christ), and thus become a partaker of the Christ life, and it follows that whatever was done by Christ was done in and for me, so that when He **died on the Cross** I died with Him, when He was **buried I was** buried with Him, when He **arose** from the grave I arose with Him, when He **ascended** I ascended with Him, when He was **glorified** I was glorified with Him, and when He shall **come again** I will come with Him.

When a child is born into a family the **law of heredity** entitles that child to all the past history, tendencies (good or bad), social and political rights and privileges of the family as far back as the lineage can be traced. And there is another law, the **law of inheritance** that guarantees to that child the future possession of the family inheritance. So the person who is born by the Holy Spirit into the family of God, and thus becomes a "partaker of the Divine Nature," is not only entitled to the future inheritance of a Child of God, but to all the past experiences of Christ.

Christian experience is the making real in our life of what is true as to our standing in Christ, and means that we are to make actual in practice that which we in the Scriptures are declared to be. That is, we are to act in accordance with our standing. A king will act like a king, a millionaire like a millionaire, a beggar like a beggar, and a child of God like a child of God. When our Lord arose and came out of the tomb He had no further use for grave-clothes and so He left them behind. They would have been unbecoming and hindering to the risen body of Christ. But He went not forth naked, He was clothed upon with garments befitting His Resurrection state. Have you been crucified, buried and risen with Christ? Then leave in the grave the garments of the "Old Man." "PUT OFF all these, anger, wrath, malice, blasphemy, filthy communication out of your mouth. Lie not one to another, seeing ye have **PUT OFF THE OLD MAN WITH HIS DEEDS** . . . and **PUT ON** therefore, as the elect of God, holy and beloved, bowels of mercies, kindness, humbleness of mind, meekness, longsuffering, forbearing one another, and forgiving one another, . . . and above all these things **PUT ON CHARITY** (love) which is the bond of perfectness." Col. 3:8-14.

How am I to get into this "Sphere of Life" in Christ Jesus? By regeneration. But it is not enough to get into this sphere, I must have capacity to live and breathe in its atmosphere. Every form of life has its sphere for which it is adapted, as the bird to the air, the fish to the water. To live in these spheres there must be conformity to their laws. To pass from one to the other needs a new creation. So if I am to pass from the Natural to the Spiritual I must be recreated. "Therefore if any man be 'in Christ' he is a **NEW CREATURE**." 2 Cor. 5:17. It is a great privilege to be "Insphered in Christ"—to have the security that position insures to the Believer, and to be sure of the glorious inheritance that awaits us in Christ, and to know that "when Christ, who is our life, shall appear, then shall we also appear with Him IN GLORY." Col. 3:4.

II. CHRIST IN YOU

While the "New Life" is conditioned on our being "In Christ," the manifestation of that "Life" is dependent on "Christ being in us." The only way we can manifest life is by activity or fruitfulness. The test of true Discipleship is **FRUITBEARING**. "By their 'FRUITS' ye shall know them." Matt. 7:16, 20. To illustrate this Jesus spake His last and Master Parable of "The Vine." John 15:1-8. As much as to say—"What that vine is in the 'Vegetable World,' I am in the **SPIRITUAL WORLD."** The first thing that the vine suggests is **UNITY,** not mechanical unity but organic unity. From the lowest root to the tip of the highest branch, the root, the trunk, the branches, the leaves, the blossoms, and the fruit are **ONE.** Jesus said—"I am **THE VINE, YE** are **THE BRANCHES . . . WITHOUT ME** (apart from me) ye can do **NOTHING."** The mission of the vine is to bring forth fruit. The mission of the child of God is the same. Here we must distinguish between **"Works"** and **"Fruit."** "Works" are external, such as Christian service of various kinds. "Fruit" is internal and is the work of the Holy Spirit in the Believer. "The 'Fruit of the Spirit' is **love, joy, peace, long-suffering, gentleness, goodness, faith, meekness, temperance."** Gal. 5:22-23. Here we have nine kinds of "fruit" that the "Child of God" is expected to bear. To some of God's dear children the effort to be good and fruitful is a continuous strain, but they have not learned the secret; it is not trying to be good, but it is to let the Holy Spirit have His way with us. It is His business to bring forth fruit in our lives if we will let Him. The branch is not responsible for fruitbearing, that is the work of the Vine. It is the "sap" that produces fruit. All the branch has to do is to let the "sap" flow through it and do its office work and fruit will of necessity follow. But if something prevents the proper flow of the sap then there is little or no fruit. So the obstruction of worldliness, pride, covetousness or other things may prevent a child of God from bearing much fruit. This leads to the use of the "Pruning Knife." "Every branch that beareth fruit, He **PURGETH** (pruneth) **IT,** that it may bring forth **more fruit."** Vs. 2. Here we have the secret of chastisement. Notice that the pruning is not because the branch bears no fruit, but that it may bear **MORE** fruit.

There are two things peculiar to the vine. (1) It has the largest capacity for producing **SAP,** and (2) the

largest capacity for producing **WOOD**. If you would have fruit, then you must prevent the sap from producing wood, and compel it to produce fruit. This is done by pruning. That is, pinching off the end of the stem back to the bud. So the "Divine Husbandman" when He would produce "More Fruit" in our lives, pinches off by chastisement the excess of woody growth of riches, undue love of worldly things, etc. This is a very precious thought, that while our fruitfulness depends on our **abiding in the vine**, the **AMOUNT** of our fruitfulness is largely due to the careful pruning of the "Divine Husbandman."

But not only is our "Fruit-bearing" dependent on "Christ being in us," but also our "Prayer Life." "If **ye abide in Me, and my words abide in you**, ye shall ask what ye will, and it shall be done unto you." John 15:7. Here are two conditions of prayer and one promise. The conditions are—"**If ye abide in me**," and "**My words abide in you.**" The Promise is—"**Ye shall ask what ye will and it shall be** done unto you." Here is the "Magna Charta" of prayer. The first condition then of answered prayer is that we be **IN CHRIST**—"If ye abide in Me." The second is that "**CHRIST BE IN US**"—"My words abide in you." The Apostle John tells us—"That if we ask anything **ACCORDING TO HIS WILL** He heareth us.** 1 John 5:14. Now how can we know the "**Will of God**" or the "**Mind of Christ**," or the "**Mind of the Spirit**" unless we know the "Word of God," the Holy Scriptures. We cannot pray for a certainty unless we know what God has promised to give. Jesus promised His Disciples that after His Ascension He would send the "Holy Spirit" to them and that He would bring all things to their **remembrance**. That is He would recall to their memory all the sayings and promises of Christ. Then they would be able to pray with certainty and whatsoever they should ask the Father in "**Christ's Name**" at that Day (the Day of Pentecost), He would give unto them. John 16:23-26. So we not only have the Scriptures to tell us what we may ask for with certainty, but we have the "Spirit of Christ" (the Holy Spirit) to make intercession for us. In Rom. 8:26-27

(R. V.), we read—"The Spirit (Holy Spirit) also helpeth our infirmity; for we know not how to pray as we ought, but the Spirit Himself **maketh intercession for us** with groanings which cannot be uttered; and He that searcheth the hearts knoweth the '**MIND OF THE SPIRIT**,' because He maketh intercession for the saints according to the '**WILL OF GOD**.'" "Now we know that if we **ask** anything according to **HIS** (God's) **WILL, HE HEARETH US,** and if we know that He hears us, whatsoever we ask, we know **THAT WE HAVE** the petitions that we desired of Him." 1 John 5:14-15. To pray the "Prayer of Faith" then it is necessary that not only shall we be **IN CHRIST,** but that **CHRIST SHALL BE IN US.**

There is a promise that all Christians love to quote for their assurance in prayer—"If **TWO** of you shall **AGREE ON EARTH** as touching anything that they shall ask, it shall be done for them of my Father which is in heaven." Matt. 18:19. The common opinion of this promise is, that when two or three persons mutually agree to pray for a certain person or object, that their prayer will be answered. But that is not the idea at all. The word here translated "**AGREE**" is a very suggestive one. It is the Greek word from which our word "**SYMPHONY**" comes. The thought is, if two shall "**ACCORD**" or "Symphonize" in what they ask they have the promise. Ananias and Sapphira "agreed together" to tempt the Spirit of the Lord. Acts 5:9. There was mutual accord, but guilty **DISCORD** with the Holy Spirit, for as in tuning a musical instrument all the notes must be keyed to the standard pitch, else harmony were impossible, so in prayer, it is not enough that two persons **agree with each other,** they must accord with a **third— THE LORD,** and the Holy Spirit the "Divine Tuner" must put them in accord. The "key" to the promise is found in the next verse—"For where two or three are gathered together **IN MY NAME,** there am I in the **MIDST OF THEM.**" Matt. 18:20. That is to say, if there are two persons present and praying, there is also a **third,** if there are three persons present, there is a **fourth.** But this fourth person is invisible and is no other than the Lord Jesus in the person of the Holy Spirit, who causes the supplicants **without previous agreement** to symphonize and thus **accord** with the "Divine Will" and the condition of "My Words abide in you" being fulfilled the prayer is answered.

When Jesus said—"Verily, verily, I say unto you, Whatsoever ye shall ask the Father 'IN MY NAME,' He will give it you" (John 16:23), and the expression "IN MY NAME" is six times repeated, it was a **new teaching.** No one in Old Testament times asked in "JESUS' NAME," neither had the Disciples up to that time, because the **unity** of Jesus with His Disciples had not yet been revealed, and it was not until Jesus spake the "Parable of the Vine" that the Disciples understood their union with Him. When I ask anything in another's name, not I, but they are the **Asker.** It follows then that when I ask in **"Jesus' Name"** He is the supplicant and not I. But Jesus is not supposed to ask anything that is not according to the "Will of God," therefore to have my prayers answered when I ask in "Jesus' Name" I must not only be "In Christ," but He must be **"In Me,"** or our wills will not be in accord. To illustrate, if I am to paint like Raphael, it is not enough for me to copy his paintings and try to imitate him, I must have him **in me** and it must be he who uses my brains and hands. And if I am to pray as Christ would pray I must have Christ in me to enlighten me how to pray as He would pray, otherwise my prayer in "His Name" will be of no avail.

XXIV

The Threefold Work of Christ

The "Office Work" of Christ is "Threefold," that of "PROPHET," "PRIEST" and "KING." But He does not hold these offices conjointly but successively. His "Prophetic Work" extended from Creation to His Ascension; His "Priestly Work" extends from His Ascension to the Rapture of the Church; and His "Kingly Work" from His Revelation at the close of the Tribulation Period, until He surrenders the Kingdom to the Father, that "God may be All and in All." I Cor. 15:28

I. HIS PROPHETIC WORK

While Christ as a Prophet foretold many things before His Incarnation, it was not until after His Incarnation that He entered fully on His Prophetic Office. He was the Prophet foretold by Moses. "The LORD thy God will raise up unto thee a Prophet from the midst of thee, of thy brethren, like unto me; unto Him ye shall hearken." Deu. 18:15: And Peter in his sermon in the Temple declared that Christ was that Prophet. Acts 3:19-26. As a Prophet Christ foretold His Death and Resurrection. His Parabolic Teaching was full of prophetic statements, and in His "Olivet Discourse" (Matt. 24:1-25:46) He outlined events that should come to pass from the time of His Ascension until His Return. But His crowning work as a Prophet was His Revelation to the Apostle John, on the Isle of Patmos, of the history of the Christian Church, as outlined in the "Messages to the Seven Churches," the awful character of the "Tribulation Period," the Battle of Armageddon, the binding of Satan, the "Great White Throne Judgment," the "Renovation of the earth by Fire," and the "New Heaven," "New Earth" and "New City."

II. HIS PRIESTLY WORK

Christ's present work is that of a High Priest. He is now "TARRYING WITHIN THE VEIL." As the High Priest entered through the "veil" into the "Most

Holy Place" once a year on the "Day of Atonement," to present the blood of the sacrifice and make intercession for the SINS of the people, so Jesus entered into the "Holy of Holies" of the Heavenly Tabernacle when He ascended and passed through the "Veil of the Cloud" and disappeared from earthly view. Acts 1:9. Heb. 4: 14. "For Christ is not entered into the Holy Places made with hands (such as the Tabernacle or Temple) which are the figures of the true; but INTO HEAVEN IT-SELF, now to appear in the presence of God for us." Heb. 9:24. Heaven not earth, is the sphere of Christ's PRIESTLY Ministry. He never appeared as a Priest in the Temple of Jerusalem. He went there to teach but never to offer sacrifices or burn incense.

The sacrifices and ceremonies of the Tabernacle and Temple services did not make the offerers perfect, or they would not have ceased to be offered. They were but SHADOWS or Types of things to come. Heb. 10: 1-3. Among them was the "Day of Atonement." On that day the High Priest entered alone into the Holy Place, and having divested himself of his garments of "Glory and Beauty," he washed himself, and arrayed himself in linen clothes with a linen Mitre upon his head. He then filled a Censer with burning coals from off the Incense Altar and entered through the "Veil" into the "Most Holy Place," and putting incense upon the coals of the Censer, so that the smoke would cover the "Mercy Seat" on the "Ark of the Covenant" and hide it from view lest he die, he withdrew from the "Most Holy Place" and passed out into the Court of the Tabernacle, where he slew a bullock for a "Sin Offering" for himself and his house, and taking of its blood he re-entered the Tabernacle and passing through the "Veil" he sprinkled with his finger of the blood seven times eastward before the "Mercy Seat," thus making Atonement for himself and his household. He then returned to the Court of the Tabernacle and slew the goat that had been selected by lot for the "Sin Offer-ing," and took of its blood and re-entered for the third time the "Most Holy Place," and did with its blood as he had done with the blood of his bullock, thus making Atonement for the sins of the Congregation. He then

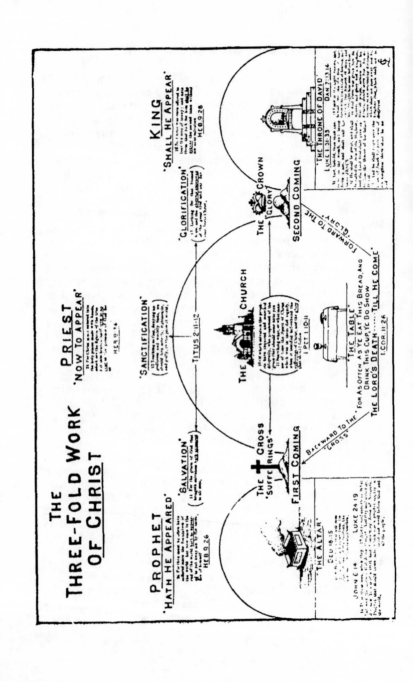

THE
THREE-FOLD WORK
OF CHRIST

returned to the Court, and going to the "Brazen Altar" he made Atonement for it by sprinkling of the mixed blood of the bullock and goat upon it with his finger seven times, after he had first anointed the Horns of the Altar with the blood.

He then took the live goat, called the "Scapegoat," and laying both of his hands upon its head, he confessed the sins of the Children of Israel, thus placing them upon the head of the "Scapegoat," and then he sent it by a "fit man" into the wilderness, into a land uninhabited, where it was left, thus carrying away the iniquities of the people.

Aaron then returned to the Holy Place of the Tabernacle and took off his linen garments, washed himself, and robed himself again in his garments of "Glory and Beauty," and then returned to the Court of the Tabernacle. Until he thus appeared the people were in doubt as to whether God had accepted the "Sin Offering" or not. If his stay was unduly prolonged they would fear that the offering had been rejected and the High Priest smitten with death. They listened then for the tinkling of the bells upon the bottom of the High Priest's robe, and when they heard them they were assured that the sacrifice had been accepted.

When the High Priest came out in his garments of "Glory and Beauty" he went to the "Brazen Altar" and offered a "Burnt Offering" for himself, and one for the people, as a token of their revived consecration to God.

Let us take the work of the High Priest on the "Day of Atonement" and apply it to our High Priest, Jesus Christ. When Jesus "emptied Himself" of His Heavenly Glory (Phil. 2: 5-8), He laid aside His garments of "Glory and Beauty," and put on the "Linen Garment" of humanity in which to minister. He had no occasion to offer incense in the "Most Holy Place," or to offer a bullock as a "Sin Offering" for Himself, for He was sinless, but He had to offer a Sin Offering for the world. It is here that we see that no single offering could typify the work of Christ, for Christ's work is twofold. First He died as a "Sin Offering" for SIN, and then rose from the dead and ascended through the "Veil of the Cloud" into the "Holy of Holies" of the "Heavenly Tabernacle" and offered **HIS OWN BLOOD** as an Atonement for the sin of the world. This could only be foreshadowed by the use of **two** goats. The first was made a "Sin Offering" and as such had to die, the second was called the "Scapegoat" and bore away the sins of the people into the wilderness. Lev. 16: 8-10, 20-22.

The High Priest entered into the "Most Holy Place" once a year with the blood of others, but Jesus Christ our High Priest entered **once for all** with His **OWN BLOOD** into the "Holy of Holies" of the "Heavenly Tabernacle," otherwise He must have suffered yearly since the foundation of the world (Ages), "but now once in the **END OF THE AGE** (the Old Testament Age) hath He appeared to put away sin by the sacrifice of Himself." Heb. 9: 24-26.

Having, as our High Priest, taken His own blood within the "Veil," Jesus still tarries engaged in His High Priestly work, and will continue to tarry throughout this

"GREAT DAY OF ATONEMENT,"

and at its close he will lay aside His High Priestly robes and come forth in His Kingly dress of "Glory and Beauty" to rule and reign in Kingly splendor.

There was no provision made for sitting down in the Tabernacle or Temple, for there was no time for sitting down, as sacrifices were continuously being offered; but Jesus our High Priest offered the sacrifice of Himself **"ONCE FOR ALL,"** and then **"SAT DOWN"** at the right hand of God, on God's Throne (Heb. 12:2), which is in this Dispensation the "Throne of Grace." Heb. 4: 16. In Acts 7: 55-56, we read that Stephen saw Jesus **STANDING** at the right hand of God. This may mean either of two things. Either Jesus rose to receive Stephen or that He had not yet sat down, for we must not forget that Jesus really did not begin His High Priestly work until after His final rejection by the Jews, that culminated in the stoning of Stephen, who charged them with being "stiff necked" and resisting the Holy Ghost. Acts 7: 51.

Christ's present work is twofold.

1. MEDIATOR.

Paul writing to Timothy said that the will of God was that all men might be saved, and that he had appointed to that end a "MEDIATOR" between God and man, the **MAN CHRIST JESUS.** 1 Tim. 2:3-6. He is a "Mediator" for both believers and unbelievers, but He had to become a **MAN** to "Mediate" between God and man. A man can mediate between two men, but he cannot mediate between a man and a horse, because he has not the nature of both a man and a horse. So the Son of God could not mediate between God and man until He became the "Divine **MAN,**" that is, had the nature of both God and man. It was necessary then for the Son of God to become a **MAN** that He might mediate between God and man, and when He ascended He took up His **MANHOOD** with Him, and He is now in Heaven the **MAN CHRIST JESUS.** 1 Tim. 2:5.

2. ADVOCATE.

In 1 John 2:1 we read—"My little children, these things write I unto you, that ye sin not. And if any man sin, we have an **ADVOCATE** with the Father, Jesus Christ the righteous." From this we see that Jesus is the Advocate of the righteous only, for the Epistle is addressed to "My Little Children," and to those who were entitled to call God **FATHER.** The sinner does not need an Advocate he needs a **SAVIOUR.** What is the use of an Advocate when the trial is over, the jury has rendered its decision, the Judge pronounced sentence and the day of execution set? What a condemned man needs then is not an Advocate but a **PARDON.** The Bible distinctly states that, "he that believeth not **IS CONDEMNED ALREADY,**" and, "that the **WRATH OF GOD ABIDETH ON HIM.**" John 3:18, 36. What the sinner needs to do is not to ask Jesus to intercede for him, but to accept the **FINISHED WORK** of Christ on the Cross in his behalf.

If Jesus is our Advocate then what is He our Advocate for? Not for **SIN,** for that was Atoned for on the Cross. He is our Advocate for the "sins" we commit since we became a Christian. "My Little Children, these things write I unto you, that ye **SIN NOT.** And if any man **SIN,** we have an Advocate." 1 John 2:1. Our Advocate then is to intercede for us because we **SIN,** that is His business, that is why He remains constantly beside the Father. If a man breaks the law, or is accused of breaking it, the first thing he needs is a lawyer, or advocate, one who will plead his cause and see that he gets justice. So the believer when he sins needs an Advocate.

There is a vast difference between a **"SINNER'S SINS"** and a **"BELIEVER'S SINS."** Not that God does not hate both alike, the Believer it may be the most because he sins with greater light, but the difference is not in the sin, but in the **WAY GOD TREATS IT.** Here is a father who sends his son and his hired servant to do a piece of work. They are lazy and inefficient, and do not do the work. He bears with them, and tries them again, but it is no use. His son and his servant are good for nothing, his son perhaps the worse of the two. Now what does he do? He discharges the servant. He puts him out of the house. He will have nothing more to do with him. But does he discharge his son? Does he send him away from the house? Does he disinherit him? Nothing of the kind. He may rebuke him, cut off his allowance, punish him worse than he punished the servant, but he will not send him away because he is his son. We see then that **"Sonship"** is a **REAL THING.** Is "Sonship" then a shield from the punishment of sin? Does my "Sonship" make it **safer** for me to sin? Oh, no! It simply gives me the blessed privilege of having an Advocate, and since it is inevitable that I will sin, it is better to sin as a **SON** than as an unbeliever.

III. HIS KINGLY WORK

Christ's future work is that of **KING.** When Christ has finished His High Priestly work He will leave His Father's Throne and descend into the atmosphere of this earth to meet His espoused Bride—**THE CHURCH.** 1 Thess. 4:15-18. He will then accompany His Bride back to Heaven, and taking His place upon the "Judgment Seat of Christ" (Rom. 14:10) will judge the saints and reward them according to the works, after which He will present the Church to Himself, "a glorious Church, not having spot, or wrinkle, or any such thing." Eph. 5:27. Then follows the Marriage of the Lamb. Rev. 19:6-9. Then, having received the Kingdom from the Father, Christ, accompanied by the armies of Heaven, will descend to the earth, and the Battle of Armageddon will be fought (Rev. 19:11-21), following which He will sit upon the "Throne of His Glory" and judge the nations (Matt. 25:31-46), after which the Millennial Kingdom will be set up. At its close Satan will be loosed from the Bottomless Pit, there will be a great Apostasy, and fire will descend from heaven and destroy the wicked. The heaven and the earth will then be renovated by Fire, and the New Heaven and Earth will appear, upon which shall be placed righteous nations taken from the old earth, over which Christ shall reign as King of Kings and Lord of Lords, until such a time as He shall see fit to surrender the Kingdom to the Father, that **GOD MAY BE ALL IN ALL.** 1 Cor. 15:28.

MESSIAH THE PRINCE

It is clear from the Scriptures that it is the purpose of God to set up a Kingdom on this earth over which a son of King David is to reign **FOREVER.** The promise was given to King David through Nathan the Prophet. "Thine **House** and Thy **Kingdom** shall be established **FOREVER** before thee; thy **Throne** shall be established **FOREVER.**" 2 Sam. 7:16. This promise God afterward confirmed with an oath, saying—"I have made a Covenant with my chosen, I have sworn unto David my servant, thy **seed** will I establish **FOREVER,** and build up thy **Throne** to all generations......Once have I sworn in My Holiness that I will not lie unto David. His **seed** shall endure **FOREVER,** and his **Throne** as the sun **BEFORE ME.**" Psa. 89:3, 4, 35-37. This Covenant was unconditional and was reaffirmed to Israel through Jeremiah the prophet (Jer. 33:17-26), in which God promised that David should never want a **man** (son), to sit upon his Throne **FOREVER.** That this promise did not mean that there should be an "unbroken line" of successors on

David's Throne, is clear from the fact that, after Solomon, the kingdom was divided, and in B. C. 587 the last king of Judah was carried captive to Babylon. The promise then must refer to some "future" king of David's seed that is to be raised up to sit on the "Throne of David." To this king Jeremiah refers in Jer. 23:5-6. "Behold, the days come, saith the Lord, that I will raise unto David a righteous 'Branch,' and a 'King shall reign and prosper, and shall execute judgment and justice in the earth. In His days Judah shall be saved, and Israel shall dwell safely, and this is His name whereby He shall be called—"THE LORD OUR RIGHTEOUSNESS." When we compare this prophecy with Isa. 11:1-2, "There shall come forth a rod out of the stem of Jesse (David) and a 'Branch' shall grow out of his 'roots;' and the 'Spirit of the Lord' shall rest upon Him, the spirit of wisdom and understanding, the spirit of counsel and might, the spirit of knowledge and of the fear of the Lord," and note the word "BRANCH" that is common to both, and then note the last words of Isaiah's prophecy— "the 'Spirit of the Lord' shall rest upon him," etc, and recall Luke's description of the Child Jesus—"And the Child grew, and waxed strong in Spirit, filled with wisdom; and the Grace of God was upon Him" (Luke 2:40), we have no difficulty in identifying whom the Prophet meant.

But the Messiah was not only to be of the lineage of David, He was also to be of Divine Parentage. How this could be was a riddle until the Prophet Isaiah solved it by saying—"Behold a VIRGIN shall conceive and bear a son, and shall call his name IMMANUEL." Isa. 7:14. Later Isaiah says, as if he were present when the Virgin gave birth to the Child, "For unto us a Child is born, unto us a Son is given; and the Government shall be upon His shoulder; and His name shall be called 'Wonderful,' 'Counsellor,' the 'Mighty God,' the 'Everlasting Father,' the 'Prince of Peace.' Of the increase of His Government and Peace there shall be no end, upon the 'Throne of David,' and upon His Kingdom, to order it, and to establish it with judgment and with justice from henceforth, even FOREVER." Isa. 9:6-7. Where is the "key" that unlocks this passage? Listen.   "In the sixth month the angel Gabriel was sent from God unto a city of Galilee, named Nazareth, to a **VIRGIN** espoused to a man whose name was Joseph, of the 'HOUSE OF DAVID,' and the Virgin's name was Mary. And the angel said unto her—Fear not, Mary, for thou hast found favor with God. And, behold, thou shalt conceive in thy womb, and bring forth a **son**, and shalt call His name **JESUS.** He shall be great and shall be called the '**Son of the Highest**' and the Lord God shall give unto Him the **THRONE OF HIS FATHER DAVID**; and He shall reign over the **HOUSE OF JACOB** (Israel) **FOREVER**; and of His Kingdom there shall be **NO END.**" Luke 1 : 26-33. Some have maintained that the Prophet Isaiah referred to some maiden (virgin) of his own time, but this is refuted by Matthew, who says—"Now all this was done that it might be **fulfilled** which was spoken of **the Lord** by the prophet, saying—Behold, a **virgin** shall be with child and shall bring forth a **son**, and they shall call His name **EMMANUEL,** which being interpreted is **GOD WITH US.**" Matt. 1 : 23. For an account of the "Virgin Birth" see the Chapter on "The Mystery of Godliness." It is clear then that Jesus was the son promised to David who was to sit upon his Throne and reign over the House of Israel **FOREVER.**

As further and conclusive evidence that Jesus was the Messiah, the Old Testament not only mentions the **fact** and the **place** of His birth, but gives the **TIME.** In Dan. 9 : 24-25, we read that it was to be 69 Weeks from the going forth of the Commandment to restore and to build Jerusalem unto the "**MESSIAH THE PRINCE.**" Now here is a definite period of time mentioned—"**69 Weeks,**" and these weeks were to date from a certain edict—the commandment to **Restore and Rebuild Jerusalem.** See the Chart of Daniel's "Seventy Weeks," page 70.

The date of the "commandment" is given in Nehemiah 2 : 1 as the month "Nisan" in the twentieth year of Artaxerxes the king, which was the 14th day of March, B. C. 445. The day when Jesus rode in Triumphal Entry into Jerusalem as "**Messiah the Prince,**" was Palm Sunday, April 2, A. D. 30. Luke 19 : 37-40. But the time between March 14, B. C. 445, and April 2, A. D. 30, is more than 69 literal "weeks." It is 445+30=475 years. What explanation can we give for this? It is clear to every careful student of the Word of God that there is a "Time Element" in the Scriptures. We come across such divisions of time as "hours;" days;" "weeks;" "months;" "years;" "times;" "time and the dividing of time." To be intelligible and avoid confusion they must all be interpreted on the same scale. What is that scale? It is given in Num. 14:34. "After the number of the days in which ye searched the land, even forty days—Each Day FOR A YEAR, shall ye bear your iniquities, even forty years." See also Ezek. 4:6. The "Lord's Scale" then is—"A Day Stands for a year."

Let us apply this scale to the "Seventy Weeks." We found that the time between the "commandment" to restore and build Jerusalem, and "Messiah the Prince," was to be 69 weeks, or 69×7=483 days, or if a "day" stands for a year, 483 years. But we found that from B. C. 445 to A. D. 30 was 475 years, a difference of 8 years. How can we account for the difference? We must not forget that there are years of different lengths. The Lunar year has 354 days. The Calendar year has 360 days. The Solar year has 365 days. The Julian, or Astronomical year, has 365¼ days, and it is necessary to add one day every 4 years to the calendar. Now which of these years shall we use in our calculation? We find the "Key" in the Word of God. In Gen. 7:11-24; 8:3,4, in the account of the Flood, we find that the 5 months from the 17th day of the 2d month, until the 17th day of the 7th month, are reckoned as 150 days, or 30 days to a month, or 360 days to a year. So we see that we are to use in "Prophetical Chronology" a "Calendar" year of 360 days.

According to ordinary chronology, the 475 years from B. C. 445 to A. D. 30 are "Solar" years of 365 days each. Now counting the years from B. C. 445 to A. D. 30, inclusively, we have 476 solar years. Multiplying these 476 years by 365 (the number of days in a Solar year), we have 173,740 days, to which add 119 days for leap years, and we have 173,859 days. Add to these 20 days inclusive from March 14 to April 2, and we have 173,879 days. Divide 173,879 by 360 (the number of days in a "Prophetical Year"), and we have 483 years all to one day, the exact number of days (483) in 69 weeks, each day standing for a year. Could there be anything more conclusive to prove that Daniel's **69 weeks** ran out on **April 2, A. D. 30,** the day that Jesus rode in triumph into the City of Jerusalem.

We see from this that if the "Students of Prophecy" of Christ's day had been on the alert, and had understood Daniel's prophecy of the "Seventy Weeks," they would have been looking for Him, and would have known to a certainty whether He was the Messiah or not.

But the very passage from Daniel which gives us the "time" of the coming of "Messiah the Prince," also tells us that almost immediately **"He Shall Be Cut Off But Not for Himself."** Dan. 9:26. How then could be fulfilled the prophecy that declared that He was to be given the "Throne of David," and that He should reign over the "House of Jacob **forever,** and of His Kingdom there shall be **NO END?"** There is but one answer. His coming was to be in **Two Stages.** He was to come first as a **"Suffering Saviour,"** and then as a **"King."** Here is where the Jews of Jesus' day misread the Scriptures. They did not distinguish between the **Sufferings of the Messiah** and His **Glory.** 1 Peter 1:11. They could not understand how the Messiah was to be a mighty King and also be "cut off" for the sins and iniquities of His people. There was but one possible answer and that was by **Resurrection.** They accepted Psa. 16 as Messianic, and yet did not see that it prophesied the **"Resurrection of Jesus"** in the words—

> "Thou wilt not leave my soul in hell (Hades); neither wilt thou suffer thine 'Holy One' to see **corruption."** Psa. 16:10.

This passage Peter in his sermon on the Day of Pentecost quoted, saying that David, being a prophet, here speaks of the **Resurrection of Christ,** and added—"This **JESUS** hath God raised up, whereof we all are witnesses." Acts 2:25-32.

There can be no question but that "Jesus of Nazareth" was the promised "Son of David," who is to reign upon the "Throne of David." But being rejected and crucified, and risen from the dead, He now sits on His Father's Throne until the time comes for Him to take the Kingdom. The "Throne of David" was on the earth, and can never be anywhere else. To say that Christ now reigns on the "Throne of David," and that His Kingdom is "spiritual," is to subvert the meaning of the Old Testament prophecies. The "Throne of David" is now vacant, and has been for 2500 years, but when the "Times of the Gentiles" have run their course, and the time has come to set up again the "Tabernacle (House) of David" which has fallen down (Acts 15: 13-18), the "Throne of David" will be re-established and given to Christ.

XXV

Christic Our Passover

Wherever the Bible has gone the story of the night when the Passover was first observed in Egypt has been told. Wherever a Jew exists on the face of the earth that night is remembered, celebrated and pointed to as the greatest event in their national history. Of its historical truthfulness there can be no question. It is the most remarkable instance of Divine intervention recorded in the Scriptures. The Children of Israel from being the honored guests of Pharaoh became his slaves. As slaves they desired freedom, but their struggles for freedom only increased their bondage (Ex. 1:13-14), and in their despair they called upon God (Ex. 2:23-25), and God sent a "Deliverer"—**MOSES**, and through him said to Pharaoh—"Let '**MY PEOPLE**' go that they may serve Me." Ex. 8:1. The Children of Israel were not made for Egypt, nor Egypt for them, they were made for Canaan. God intended that they should drink of the water of Jordan and not of the water of the Nile. While they were **born in bondage** they were made for **LIBERTY**. God had told Abraham that his seed should be a **stranger** in a land that was not theirs, where they should be afflicted for 400 years, and afterwards should come out with great substance. Gen. 15:13-14. When the time for their deliverance and return to Canaan had come, God found it necessary to wean them from Egypt by making their lot in Egypt unendurable. To this end He stirred up the heart of Pharaoh to increase their burdens.

The deliverance of the Children of Israel from Egypt is a type of the deliverance of the sinner from the bondage of sin and is well worth our study. Egypt is a type of this present "**EVIL WORLD**." In Moses' day it presented the best specimen of worldly glory and magnificence that the world has ever seen. In it were gathered the world's wealth, art, and commerce. As seen in its ruins there was nothing lacking in that which would gratify the "Lust of the Flesh," the "Lust of the Eye," and the "Pride of Life." The food of Egypt was not only plentiful, but gross and stimulating. It was composed of cucumbers, melons, leeks, onions and garlic. Egypt was also famous for its fish. Num. 11:4-5. But Egypt was not to be compared with Canaan for beauty or food, for Canaan was a land of figs and pomegranates, of olive oil and honey, of new corn and wine. Deu. 8: 8-9.

Pharaoh was a type of "Satan." Egypt was full of idolatry, the very stronghold of Satan, and a "hotbed" of every species of sin. Having Israel in his power Pharaoh tried to make it permanent. That is what Satan tries to do with the sinner. It is Satan's "Taskmasters" who make the sinner sweat in hard bondage.

Moses was a type of Christ. Notice that God is always "BEFOREHAND" with His salvation. Salvation is no "AFTER-THOUGHT" of God's. God was preparing Moses in the Wilderness for the work he was to do in delivering Israel. The quickest way to get relief is "via" the Throne of God. Israel phoned to God, God phoned to Moses. God always knows where the man needed for the occasion is. In fact, owing to His foreknowledge, He has him ready. When Moses appeared in Egypt and made his mission known there was trouble. He was looked upon as a "labor agitator," and Pharaoh increased the burdens of the Children of Israel. So Satan makes the way rough for the sinner who desires to get away from him.

When Pharaoh refused to let the Children of Israel go then God took a hand, and proceeded to bring judgments, in the form of "Plagues," upon Egypt. The purpose of the "Plagues" was to make Pharaoh and the Egyptians see that the God of Israel was stronger than the "gods" of Egypt. The "Plagues" were 10 in number and distributed over about a year. With the exception of the first and the last they were "Natural Phenomena" common to Egypt, the miraculous thing being that they came and went at the command of God and were of great severity. The "Ten Plagues" were judgments against the "gods" of Egypt. (1) "Water into blood," against the Nile, the "Idol River." (2) **"Frogs,"** against the worship of frogs. (3) **"Lice,"** against the earth god "Seb" and the priests, who could not officiate when vermin was upon them. (4) **"Flies,"** against the atmosphere "Shu," son of "Ra," the SUN-GOD. (5) **"Murrain,"** against the "Sacred Bull"—APIS. (6) **"Boils,"** against "Sutech" or "Typhon," to whom victims were offered, their ashes being flung to the winds. (7) **"Locusts,"** against the "Sacred Beetle." (8) **"Hail,"** against "Shu." (9) **"Darkness,"** against the "Sun-God" —RA, of whom Pharaoh was believed to be the child. (10) **"Death of the First-Born,"** against the nation guilty of **wholesale infanticide** in ordering that all male Hebrew children should be cast into the river Nile. Ex. 1:22.

The first 9 Plagues may be divided into 3 groups of 3 Plagues each. In the first two of each group Pharaoh was warned; in the last no warning was given. The first group only affected the comfort of the people, and were universal upon Egyptians and Israelites alike. The second group affected only the Egyptians, the Children of Israel's cattle were spared for sacrifice. Here property suffered. The third group fell mainly upon the Egyptians, there being no hail in the land of Goshen, and the Children of Israel had light in their dwellings.

EGYPTIAN COMPROMISES

When Moses and Aaron appeared before Pharaoh they said—"Thus saith the Lord God of Israel, Let my people go, that they may hold a Feast unto me in the Wilderness." And Pharaoh said—"Who is the Lord that I should obey His voice to let Israel go? I know not the Lord, neither will I let Israel go." Ex. 5:1-2. Then Moses and Aaron demanded that Pharaoh let Israel go a three days' journey into the Wilderness. Pharaoh again refused, and practically said, the service of God is a **WASTE OF TIME.** He then increased the Children of Israel's burdens. But when after the first 3 Plagues there came the "Plague of Flies" upon the Egyptians only, Pharaoh thought it was time to **"compromise,"** so he sent for Moses and said—"Go ye, sacrifice to your **God in the land."** Ex. 8:25.

FIRST COMPROMISE

Pharaoh would not object to an occasional sacrifice **IN THE LAND** if that would make the Children of Israel satisfied to remain in Egypt where he could retain his power over them. So Satan does not object to an occasional "spasm" of religious endeavor as long as we still remain in the world. If Pharaoh's advice had been followed the Children of Israel would never have left Egypt. To it Moses replied—"It is not meet so to do; for we shall sacrifice the 'Abomination of the Egyptians' to the Lord our God . . . and they will **STONE US**." Ex. 8:26. As we have seen the "Sacred Bull"—**APIS**, was one of the gods of Egypt, and if the Children of Israel offered sacrifices of "bullocks" to Jehovah "in the land," that would be an "abomination" to the Egyptians, and they would **STONE THEM** for sacrificing the "**Gods of Egypt**." This compromise means that a man cannot be a Christian and worship God "in the land" without offending the world. Let him at the next meeting of his club get up and insist on offering a prayer, or engage in some religious exercise, and the members will "**stone him**" with ridicule. Moses refused to accede to Pharaoh's proposal, and said, "We will go **THREE DAYS' JOURNEY** into the Wilderness, and sacrifice to the Lord our God, as He shall command us" (Ex. 8:27), and, because the "Plague of Flies" was unendurable, Pharaoh proposed a

SECOND COMPROMISE.

"I will let you go, that ye may sacrifice to the Lord your God in the Wilderness; only ye shall not go **VERY FAR AWAY**." Ex. 8:28. The lesson is, Stand your ground, do not give in, and Satan will begin to compromise. This second proposition or compromise is more dangerous than the first, for Pharaoh knew it would be easy to get Israel back if they did not go **very far away**. So Satan says—"Yes, become a professing Christian, join the Church, but do not go **very far away**, observe Lent and other religious seasons, but the rest of the year be back in Egypt (the World) enjoying its pleasures." How could the Children of Israel reach Canaan by going only three days' journey into the Wilderness? **"Not very far away"** is incompatible with a happy Christian life for it means a vacillating life. The Israelites in the Wilderness did not like the manna God gave them. Their taste had been spoiled by eating cucumbers, garlic and onions, and they longed for the old Egyptian diet. When professing Christians no longer take delight in spiritual food it is plain that they long for their old worldly fare, if they have not already been down to Egypt and had a square meal of onions and garlic. Of all the distasteful dishes that can be imagined a mixture of **"Manna and Onions"** is the worst. An Egyptian dog would turn away from it. When you hear Christians ask—**"Is it right or wrong to do this?"** you may know that they have been caught in the **"NOT VERY FAR AWAY"** Compromise.

THIRD COMPROMISE

Between the Second and Third Compromise there were the Plagues of Murrain, Boils and Hail. Then Pharaoh's servants said unto him—"How long shall this man Moses be a snare unto us? . . . knowest thou not yet that Egypt is destroyed?" Ex. 10:7. Then Pharaoh sent for Moses and Aaron and said unto them—"Go, serve the Lord your God, but **WHO** are they that shall go?" And Moses said—"We will go with our **YOUNG,** and with our **OLD,** with our **SONS** and with our **DAUGHTERS,** with our **FLOCKS** and with our **HERDS** will we go; for we must hold a **FEAST UNTO THE LORD.**" Ex. 10:9. They needed their flocks and herds for sacrifices. But Pharaoh said—"Not so; go now ye that are **MEN.**" Pharaoh knew that if the men left their loved ones in Egypt it would not be long before they would be back. This Compromise means let the older people become Christians if they want to, but do not force religion on the young. Be a Christian if you want to, but do not force religion on your wife and children, for it is a personal matter. Let them enjoy their "Egyptian Pleasures" and you show no concern as to their salvation. With the offer of this Compromise Pharaoh drove Moses and Aaron away. Then followed the Plagues of the Locusts and the Darkness. These Plagues were too much for Pharaoh, so he sent again for Moses and offered a

FOURTH COMPROMISE.

"Go ye, serve the Lord; only let your **FLOCKS** and **HERDS** be stayed (remain in Egypt); let your **little ones** also go with you." Ex. 10:24. Moses, seeing that Pharaoh was weakening, now demands to be paid for going—"Thou must give us also 'SACRIFICES' and 'BURNT-OFFERINGS,' that we may sacrifice unto the Lord our God. **OUR** cattle also shall go with us; there shall not an 'HOOF' be left behind; for thereof must we take to **serve the Lord our God**; and we know not with what we must serve the Lord until we come thither." Ex. 10:25-26. They knew not what sacrifices would be required, for the "Law of the Sacrifices" was not given until they reached Sinai. This Compromise means be a Christian, give your soul to God, but keep your possessions for yourself. If you have paying investments in the world leave them there. Do not sell your "Brewery Stock" or part with those investments that pay large dividends even though it be at the expense of the poor. Many are caught right here. They fail to recognize their **STEWARDSHIP.** They invest their money for the purpose of increasing their wealth, while churches and chapels are burdened with debt, and missionary treasuries are empty, while their "flocks" and "herds" **FATTEN IN EGYPT.** Let them follow Moses' noble example and say—"Not a 'HOOF' **SHALL BE LEFT BEHIND."**

With the rejection of the Fourth Compromise by Moses he was driven out from the presence of Pharaoh, who forbade him to see his face again under penalty of death. That closed the "Day of Grace" for Pharaoh. Then followed the Tenth and Last Plague, the **"DEATH OF THE FIRST BORN."** From what has preceded we see the "Compromises" that the sinner must refuse if he is to escape from the world. Let us now see how he is to be saved from the power of Satan and redeemed by **BLOOD.**

THE PASSOVER

God's standard of "Power" in the Old Testament is the **EXODUS**, but before He could deliver Israel by His "Power," they must be redeemed by **BLOOD**. "The Passover" is a beautiful illustration of the "Plan of Salvation" through Christ. "For even Christ our 'PASS-OVER' is sacrificed for us." 1 Cor. 5:7. As the blood of the "Passover Lamb" saved Israel, so the **BLOOD** of the **"Lamb of God"** saves us. "Ye were not redeemed with corruptible things, as silver and gold, . . . but with the **precious BLOOD OF CHRIST, as** of a lamb without **blemish** and **without spot."** 1 Pet. 1:18-19.

As the Children of Israel dwelt in the "Land of Goshen," and it was a part of Egypt, they came under the "Doom of Egypt," which was that all the "First Born" should die. To offset this the Children of Israel were commanded to take a lamb, **without blemish,** of the first **year,** and **kill it,** and take of the blood and sprinkle it on the two side posts and lintel of the door of their dwelling, and when the Lord saw the blood He would pass over that house on that fateful night, and not destroy the "First Born" sheltered behind that blood-marked door. Ex. 12:1-28.

The Passover was to be to Israel the **"BEGINNING OF MONTHS."** Ex. 12:2. It was to be the First month of the year to them. A man does not begin to live until he is saved by the **"BLOOD OF CHRIST."** Until then he is spiritually dead in trespasses and sins. Eph. 2:1-3. The time spent in the **"brick-kilns"** of sin, and amid the **"flesh-pots"** of pleasure, do not count, and must be omitted from the life of the Believer. The Passover as a means of salvation was a plan of God's own devising. No man had a hand in it, except to do as God commanded. It was all of **GRACE.** Redemption is no **"AFTER-THOUGHT"** of God. It was not something to which He had to resort from force of circumstances. God is always **"FORE-HANDED"** with His salvation. Jesus was foreordained before the **foundation of** the **world** to be the Saviour of men. 1 Pet. 1:18-20. The Passover consisted of two parts. The "Sacrifice" and the "Feast."

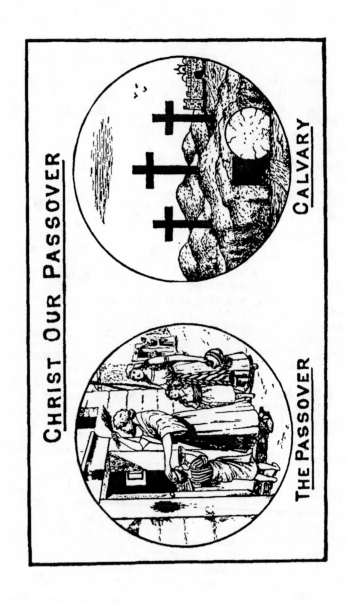

CHRIST OUR PASSOVER

CALVARY

THE PASSOVER

1. THE SACRIFICE.

The "Sacrifice" was to be a **LAMB.** Ex. 12:5. An **emblem** of meekness and purity, such was Jesus. "He **was** led as a **lamb** to the slaughter." Isa. 53:7. The lamb **was** to be young, a **male** of the first year. It was to be without **blemish.** If a spot had been found upon it, it would have been unfit for sacrifice. Jesus was without blemish. He was absolutely sinless. 2 Cor. 5:21, 1 John 3:5. He was perfect as a babe at Bethlehem, as **a boy** at Nazareth, as the "Son of Man." The words of the Father at His Baptism—"This is my beloved Son, in whom I am well pleased" (Matt. 3:17), had reference to Jesus' life from a boy. Pilate said of Jesus—"I find in Him no fault at all." John 18:38. And Judas said— "I have betrayed the innocent blood." Matt. 27:4. The lamb was to be **KILLED.** Ex. 12:6. It was not enough to take a lamb into the house and **fondle** it, to make a **pet** of it, to let God see how much they **loved** the lamb. It was not enough to **tie** the lamb to the door, where it might be seen by the "Death Angel," it had to be **KILLED.** We are not saved by the **life** of Christ, but by **HIS DEATH.** If Jesus had not **DIED** upon the Cross there would have been no **"RENT VEIL,"** no **"SHED BLOOD,"** no **"OPEN TOMB,"** no **"INTER-CEDING HIGH PRIEST."** It is by His **"STRIPES"** we are healed, not by His example. "His own self bare our sins in His own body on **THE TREE."** 1 Pet. 2: **24.** He did not bear them anywhere else. He did not **bear** them in the **manger,** or at the Jordan, or in the **Wilderness,** or in the Garden of Gethsemane, but on the **CROSS.**

But the lamb was not simply to be **killed,** something had to be done with the **BLOOD,** and with the **FLESH.** They **were** to take the **BLOOD** and **sprinkle** it on the **two** side posts and on the upper door post (lintel) of their dwellings, and they were to **EAT** the flesh. Ex. **12:7.** The "First Born" was not safe when the blood **was** simply shed, or even when caught in the basin. It **was** not enough to "analyze" the blood, the blood had to be **used,** and they were not left in doubt **as to how** it was to be used, it was to be sprinkled on the door of their dwelling with a bunch of "Hyssop." Hyssop is a common plant, and grew everywhere in Egypt. It was not a rare plant that they had to send to some foreign country to get. Hyssop stands for "Faith." Faith is the commonest thing in the world, without it there could be no commercial, social, or domestic relations. None of the blood was to be put on the "threshold" or sprinkled on the floor of the dwelling. It was too costly and too sacred to be trodden under foot. Yet unbelievers, and religious teachers who make light of the "Blood of Christ," are treading under foot the Son of God, and counting His **BLOOD** as worthless. Heb. 10:29. It is worthy of note that a "Priest" had no part in procuring redemption for the Children of Israel. The Passover was not a "Priestly Sacrifice." It was the **"HEAD OF THE HOUSE"** who killed the lamb and sprinkled its blood on the door.

The blood was a **"TOKEN."** "When I see the **BLOOD**, I will pass over you." Ex. 12:13. It is not a question of "personal worthiness," nor of "good works," nor of "morality," but of the **BLOOD**. "It is the **BLOOD** that maketh an atonement for the soul." Lev. 17:11. The Israelites were not merely in a **salvable** state, they were **SAVED**, not partly but completely. If a hair of one of the "First Born" sheltered behind the blood had been touched, it would have proved Jehovah's word **void**, and the blood of the lamb **valueless**. It is not necessary for us to see the blood. We may have no assurance as to our salvation, but have we applied the "Blood of Christ" to our soul, are we trusting to it, and it alone, for our salvation? If so, all that is necessary is, that **GOD sees it**.

Having applied the blood, what next: Go in the house and stay there. Ex. 12:22. No "First Born" child of Israel was safe outside the house that night until after the "Death Angel" had passed, even though the blood was on the door. Doubtless many made light of the Passover method of salvation, but no one laughed in the morning. Men may mock at the Gospel plan of Salvation, and ignore the **BLOOD**, but **they will not laugh** at the Judgment.

2. THE FEAST.

"Ye shall eat of the **FLESH** in that night, **roast with fire,** and **unleavened bread;** and with **bitter herbs** ye shall eat it." Ex. 12:8-10. They were **SAVED** by the **blood**, but it was not enough to kill the lamb and use its blood, they were to **FEED ON THE LAMB.** Some Christians stop short at being saved by the Blood, and fail to **FEED ON THE LAMB.** That is why they are not nourished and sustained in their Christian Life. There can be no true fellowship only as we eat of the Lamb. The lamb was not to be eaten raw, or sodden with water (boiled), but roast with fire. To roast it they had to use a "**SPIT.**" That is, they had to support it over the fire by a rod run lengthwise through it, and another rod at right angles through the shoulders to turn it by, thus symbolizing the **CROSS.** It was on the **CROSS** that Jesus' body was subject to the "Fire of God's Righteous Wrath" against sin, and we are now to feed by faith on His body by the observance of the Lord's Supper (Matt. 26:26-30. 1 Cor. 11:23-26), and the study of the Word. The trouble today is, that the world is not feeding on the "**CRUCI-FIED**" Lamb, but on the "**LIVING**" Lamb. They are trying to follow Christ as an **example** and not as a **SAVIOUR.** They are living on the other side of the Cross and not on this side. What we are to do is not to go back to the living Christ, but to look forward to the "Coming" of the **CRUCIFIED** and **GLORIFIED** Christ.

The Passover Lamb was to be eaten with **UN-LEAVENED** bread. Ex. 12:8. Leaven is a symbol of evil and therefore could not be used at such a Feast as that of the Passover, and the Apostle Paul calls on us to purge out the old leaven of malice and wickedness. 1 Cor. 5:7-8.

They were also to eat the Feast with "**Bitter Herbs,**" symbolical of their previous bondage, and they were to let nothing remain until the morning. They were to forsake sleep to feed on the lamb, and if any were left over they were to burn it lest it fall into unfit hands or be left behind in their hasty departure. What a beautiful picture we have here. While a terrible hurricane of Divine Judgment was sweeping at midnight over Egypt, destroying the "First Born" in every home unsheltered by the blood, the Children of Israel were **FEASTING PEACEFULLY AND JOYFULLY ON ROASTED LAMB.**

They were to eat the Feast with their loins girded, their shoes on their feet, and their staff in their hand. Ex. 12:11. They were to eat it as a people prepared to leave Egypt where death, darkness, and judgment reigned. Their girded loins and sandaled feet declared them a **"PILGRIM PEOPLE"** ready to set out and walk with God, even though their pilgrimage should lead them through the Red Sea and the Wilderness, for they knew that though the way be tedious and long their destination as a redeemed and separated people was **CANAAN**, a land flowing with milk and honey. The journey of the Children of Israel from Egypt to Canaan has been called the "Pilgrim's Progress" of the Old Testament, and beautifully portrays the Pilgrimage of a Christian as outlined in the New Testament. Everything depends on what we do with the **BLOOD.**

XXVI

Heaven and Hell

The Scriptures speak of two places, "Heaven" and "Hell," where the "righteous" and "wicked" respectively are to spend eternity. The one demands the other. There can be no Heaven without its counterpart Hell. If there is no Hell there is no Heaven, for the same Book speaks of both.

I. HEAVEN

Heaven is a "PLACE," it is not a state or condition. The New Jerusalem is not Heaven, though it is a city of Heaven. The Apostle John tells us that he saw it "coming down from God OUT OF HEAVEN." Rev. 21:2.

It is the "PLACE" that Jesus told His Disciples He was going away to prepare for them. John 14:2. It did not exist at the time Jesus was on earth. It was built between the time Jesus ascended in A. D. 30, and the time when John saw it in vision descend from Heaven in A. D. 96, or if not yet built, it will be built before the Rapture of the Church, for it is to be the Residence of the Bride, the Lamb's Wife. Rev. 21:9-10. Of Abraham we read—"He looked for a City which hath foundations, whose 'builder' and 'maker' is GOD." Heb. 11:10. The New Jerusalem is that City. The Apostle says—"Here we have no continuing city (permanent abiding place), but we seek one to come." Heb. 13:14.

The Scriptures speak of three Heavens. (1) The Heaven of the earth's atmosphere. "God gave you rain from heaven." Acts. 14:17. (2) The Heaven of the Stars. The "High Places" where the "Principalities and Powers" of evil have their abode. Eph. 6:12. (3) The Heaven where God dwells. It was to this "Third Heaven" that the Apostle Paul was caught up, when at Lystra he was stoned and his spirit apparently left his body. Acts 14:19-20. Paul calls it both the "Third Heaven" and "Paradise." 2 Cor. 12:1-4. The two then must be identical, or "Paradise" be a part of the "Third Heaven." It is to this "Paradise Section" of Heaven that the "Soul"

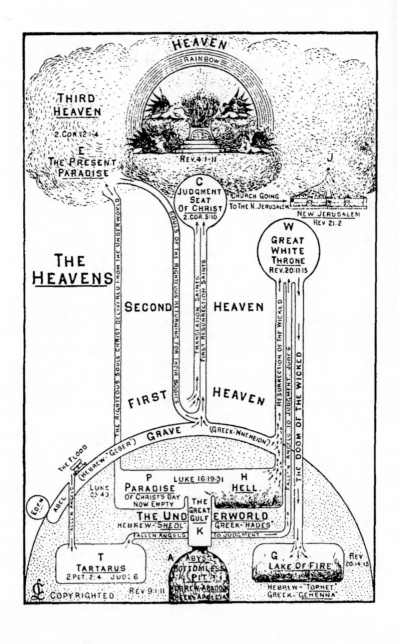

and "Spirit" of the Righteous go since the Resurrection of Christ. See the Chapter on "The Spirit World," page 88. The word "Paradise" means a "garden" or "enclosed place." It must therefore be a most beautiful place of trees and flowers and fruits. There the "Spirits" of the Righteous in their "Soulish" bodies, conscious and happy, and in fellowship with loved ones and the saints of all Ages, await the First Resurrection, when, having received their glorified bodies, and been judged at the Judgment Seat of Christ, and married to the Lamb (Christ), they go to dwell in the New Jerusalem, the home of the Bride. See Chart, page 274. From this we see that we must distinguish between Heaven proper, and its suburb Paradise, and the New Jerusalem.

But we must not forget, that while Paradise, the place where the Saints of God now dwell, is a glorious place, and the Saints are there in the enjoyment of Heavenly things, that they are under certain limitations. They have not as yet received their resurrection body with all its glorious powers, nor been judged so as to receive their reward, or crown, if they are entitled to any. The description of Heaven and the New Jerusalem as given in the Book of Revelation from the third chapter to the end of the Book, is still **future,** and the things there described will not come to pass until after the Rapture of the Church, so what is said of the New Jerusalem and its occupants does not apply until after the Judgment of Believers. See my book on Revelation. While the Saints were removed from the Paradise section of "The Underworld" when Christ rose from the dead, and taken to the Paradise of the "Third Heaven" to be near Christ, so that now to depart and be with Christ (Phil. 1:23) is most blessed, it does not follow that their state there is any more blissful than it was in The Underworld. It is well that we get this Scriptural view of the place and condition of the Saints between death and the resurrection of the body clearly in our mind, for there is so much unscriptural teaching as to the state of the dead between death and the resurrection.

While the state of the Righteous dead is incomplete, it is most blissful and happy, but more a state of rest and waiting than a state of activity or service. Rev. 14:13, 6:9-11. The Saints in Paradise will be free from sin and temptation, from sorrow, sickness and death. Their environment will be conducive to holy living, and the atmosphere of the place will be that of love. They will enjoy the society of holy men of old, as Abraham, Joseph, Moses, Joshua, David, Isaiah, Daniel, Peter, John and Paul. They shall meet and know their loved ones, and the mysteries of this life will all be solved. They will have a "New Song," and delight in ascribing their salvation to the Lamb. But after they get their resurrection body, and are rewarded for their works, they will be assigned to tasks for which they are best qualified, and for which their earth life fitted them. For instance David will be a King or Prince, Daniel a Statesman, Moses a Lawgiver, Paul a Missionary, for during the Millennial Reign of Christ the saints will be coworkers with Him. Moses and Elijah came back to earth as God's witnesses, and why shall not we? The angels work and the redeemed shall work. But with all our service we shall never grow old, nor tired, nor weary, and we shall pass the whole of eternity with our Lord as "joint heir" with Him of an inheritance incorruptible and undefiled, and that shall not fade away, reserved in Heaven for us. 1 Pet. 1:3-5. Heaven then is our "Father's House," it is a HOME, and a place of "many Mansions." John 14:2. It will be delightful to go there. Some people live in fear of death (Heb. 2:15), and cannot bear to think of it, but those of us who know that Heaven is to be our Eternal Home ought not to fear "Death," for it is "Death" that opens the door for our "Exodus" from earth to glory.

FIRST EXPERIENCES AFTER DEATH

Did you ever stop to think of what happens to the Righteous Soul during the first five minutes after death? Before the funeral has been held, and the body laid away in the cemetery, nay, before the undertaker has been sent for, or the neighbors and relatives notified, or the shades drawn, or the silent watchers at the bedside have realized that you are dead you have been **FIVE MINUTES** out of the body and reached Paradise and know where you are to spend eternity. Now what will be our experiences in those first five minutes? (1) Our first experience will be that death was so easy. That it was like falling asleep and awaking in a beautiful world. That there was no "Valley of Death," with its hobgoblins, satyrs, and demons, to traverse, no "dark river" to cross, but that "Ministering Angels" were waiting to convoy us to Paradise as they carried Lazarus. Luke 16:22. Heb. 1:13-14. What a delight it will be to meet our "Guardian Angel," who has watched over us in our "earth life," and who will not desert us in that supreme moment when we shall need a guide to conduct us to our Heavenly Home. (2) Our second experience will be the consciousness that we have left behind our earthly body with all its weaknesses, sufferings, and limitations, and have a body that is absolutely well and fitted in every way for the spiritual realm in which it is to dwell. (3) Our third experience will be that we are being transported swiftly upward through the ethereal space toward a beautiful country whose radiance is brighter than the sun, and as we approach it see coming out to meet us and escort us home, groups of angels who sing—"Blessed are they that do His Commandments, that they may have right to the Tree of Life, and may enter in through the gates of the city." Rev. 22:14. (4) Our fourth experience will be that we are in a new environment whose atmosphere is **LOVE**. That there is no discord, or lack of harmony in our new home, and that its chief characteristic is **HOLINESS**. (5) Our fifth experience will be the feeling that we are near Jesus. If we do not actually see Him, we shall have the consciousness of His nearness. (6) Our sixth experience will be that of meeting our loved ones. While the writer does not believe that our loved ones have any direct knowledge of what is going on on this earth, yet he believes that our "Guardian Angel" may communicate with our loved ones and inform them of our coming, and that they will be waiting to receive us. (7) Our seventh experience will be the meeting with the saints who have preceded us to glory, such as the patriarchs, prophets, apostles and Christian leaders of our own day. The experiences named may not all happen in the first five minutes after death, but they doubtless will happen before our funeral service is over and our body laid to rest in the tomb.

II. HELL

To have a correct view of the other world, and of "Hell," it is necessary that we have a Scriptural understanding of—

THE UNDERWORLD.

The Hebrew word "SHEOL" is found 65 times in the Old Testament. It is translated 31 times, "HELL;" 31 times, "GRAVE;" 3 times, "THE PIT." The corresponding word in the Greek of the New Testament is "HADES." It is translated 10 times "HELL." "Sheol" and "Hades" mean "The Unseen State," or the place to which the "Soul" and "Spirit" of the dead go between the death and the resurrection of the body. The "bodies" of the dead go into the "Grave," the word for which in the Hebrew is "GEBER," and in the Greek "MNE-MEION." Neither "Sheol" nor "Hades" denote the "Hell" of final punishment of the wicked. That is called in the Hebrew of the Old Testament "TOPHET," and in the Greek of the New Testament "GEHENNA." Neither do they denote "THE BOTTOMLESS PIT" (Rev. 20:1-3), that is "ABUSSOS," nor the "prison house" of the "Fallen Angels" (2 Pet. 2:4, Jude 6), that is "TARTARUS." Their general meaning is—"THE UNDERWORLD."

That we may the better understand the relation of the places mentioned above to each other let us turn to the Chart, "The Heavens," page 274. The word "Sheol" means a "hollow subterranean place," therefore "Hades" must mean the same. It has "gates," for Jesus said that the "Gates of Hell" (Hades), should not prevail against the Church. Matt. 16:18. And Jesus after His return from "The Underworld," said—"I am He that liveth, and was dead; and, behold, I am alive for evermore, Amen; and have the 'KEYS' (of the Gates) of hell (Hades) and of death (the Grave)." Rev. 1:18. To get these "Keys"

Jesus had to descend into the "lower parts of the earth."
Eph. 4:9. The Apostolic Creed says that Jesus descended into "Hell" (Hades). Therefore Hades, or "The
Underworld," must be in the "heart of the earth," and is
so pictured on the Chart. Jesus said to the penitent
Thief "TODAY shalt thou be with me in 'Paradise.'"
Luke 23:43. And as Jesus "that day" descended into
"The Underworld" or "Hades," "Paradise" must have
been in Christ's day in "Hades." But as it had been
prophesied of Jesus that His "SOUL" (for His body was
in Joseph's Tomb on the surface of the earth) should
not remain in "Hell" (Hades), (Psa. 16:10, Acts 2:27),
therefore, before His body could see corruption, Jesus
came back from "Hades." But He did not come back
alone. He seized the "Keys of Hades," unlocked the
Gates of the Paradise Section (P) in which He was confined, and emptied it of its captives, and when He
ascended on high He took them to the Paradise section
of the "Third Heaven" (E), where they now are, and
since then the Paradise Section of "The Underworld"
has been empty. Eph. 4:8-10.

In the account of the experience of the "Rich Man"
and "Lazarus" in the other world (Luke 16:19-31), Jesus
gives us a description of "The Underworld" as it was in
His day. According to the narrative, for it is not a
parable, for parables do not give proper names as Abraham and Lazarus, both the "Rich Man" and Lazarus
had died and their bodies had been buried, and what happened to them in the "Underworld," was descriptive of
what happened to them in their "disembodied state."
In that state they were conscious, could see, hear, speak,
and recognized each other. The difference was that
Lazarus was in the "Paradise" section of the "Underworld" (P), typified by Abraham's "bosom," while the
"Rich Man" was in the "Hell" section (H), not the final
Hell, which is "Gehenna" (Lake of Fire), but in the section of the "Underworld" where the "souls" of the
"Wicked" dead go, and remain until the resurrection of
the "Wicked" dead. Between the "Paradise" (P) section, and the "Hell" (H) section of the "Underworld"
there is an "Impassable Gulf" (K), (Luke 16:26), which

reveals the fact that there is no possibility of the "Wicked" dead ever getting out of "Hell" into "Paradise."

On the Chart this "Impassable Gulf" is represented as the entrance to the "Bottomless Pit," or "ABYSS" (A), the "prison house" of the "Demons" (Rev. 9:1-21), and where Satan is to be bound for 1000 years. Rev. 20: 1-3, 7-8. The Old Testament speaks of a place in "The Underworld" called in the Hebrew "ABADDON," and in the Greek "APOLEIA." The word is translated in the Old Testament, "DESTRUCTION" (Prov. 27:20. Job 26:6, 28:22, 31:12. Psa. 88:11. Prov. 15:11), and the same in the New Testament (Matt. 7:13. Rom. 9: 22. Phil. 3:19. 2 Pet. 2:1, 3:16). In Prov. 27:20 it says—"Hell (Hades) and 'Destruction' (Abaddon) are never full," thus connecting "Abaddon" with "Hades" (Sheol). The inference is that "Abaddon" is a part of "The Underworld," and when we turn to Rev. 9:1-3, 11, this inference becomes a certainty, for there we read that the "King" of the "Bottomless Pit" is called in the Hebrew tongue "ABADDON," but in the Greek tongue his name is "APOLLYON," that is, the King of the "Bottomless Pit" is named after the Hebrew and Greek words that are translated—"DESTRUCTION." Now the word translated "Bottomless Pit" is "ABUSSOS," or "ABYSS." Nine times do we read of this "Abyss" in the New Testament. Rom. 10:7. Rev. 9:1-2, 9:11, 11: 7, 17:8, 20:1-3. It is the place into which the Demons besought Christ not to send them. Luke 8:31. The "Bottomless Pit" or "Abyss" (A) then is a deeper compartment in "The Underworld" than "Paradise" (P), or "Hell" (H), and is the place where the "Demons" and baser spirits are temporarily confined until they are finally consigned to the "Lake of Fire" to spend eternity with their Master, Satan.

To the left of the "Bottomless Pit" is "TARTARUS" (T), the "prison house" of the "Fallen Angels." 2 Pet. 2:4. Jude 6. These "Angels" are not Satan's angels, for they are at liberty. These "Fallen Angels" confined in "Tartarus" are the "Sons of God" who married the "Daughters of Men," and whose abnormal sin caused the

Flood. See Chapter two, pages 21 and 22. They are to remain in their "prison house" until the "Great White Throne" Judgment, when they with the "Wicked Dead" are to be judged. Jude 6.

To the right of the "Bottomless Pit" is **"GEHENNA"** (G). This is the "Final Hell" or **"LAKE OF FIRE"** prepared for the Devil and his angels, into which the "Wicked," after the "Great White Throne" Judgment, will be cast to spend eternity. Matt. 25:41. Rev. 20: 12-15. It is called **"TOPHET"** in the Old Testament Hebrew (2 Kings 23:10. Isa. 30:33. Jer. 7:31-32, 19: 6, 11-14), and in the New Testament Greek it is twelve times called **"GEHENNA"** (Matt. 5:22, 29-30. 10:28. 18:9. 23:15, 33. Mark 9:43, 45-47. Luke 12:5. James 3:6), and five times the **"LAKE OF FIRE."** It is as yet unoccupied. The first persons to get into it are the **"Beast"** and the **"False Prophet"** (Rev. 19:20), then **"SATAN"** and his Angels a 1000 years later (Rev. 20: 10), and then after the "Great White Throne" Judgment the "Fallen Angels," now confined in Tartarus, and all the wicked whose names are not found written in the "Book of Life." Rev. 20:12-15. On the south side of Jerusalem was the "Valley of Hinnom." At a high place in this valley called "Tophet," in the times of Isaiah and Jeremiah, parents made their children to pass through the fire to Moloch. 2 Kings 23:10. This fire was kindled with brimstone. Isa. 30:33. The locality afterward became a place for the burning of garbage from the City of Jerusalem. The fires were kept up perpetually, and the decaying matter as yet unconsumed bred worms. Jesus took this valley called "Ge-Hinnom," corrupted into **"GEHENNA,"** and made it a type of "Hell" or the "Lake of Fire," where "their **worm dieth not,** and the **fire is not quenched."** Mark 9:43-48.

At the upper part of the Chart "Heaven" is shown. It includes the present "Paradise" (E), and the "New Jerusalem" (J). And also gives the relative location of the "Judgment Seat of Christ" (C), and the "Great White Throne" (W). The "Arrow" marked lines give the course and destiny of the "Righteous" and "Wicked" dead.

There are those who claim that "Sheol" (Hades) and the "Grave" are identical, and as there is no "knowledge" in the grave (Ecc. 9:5, 10), therefore the soul **"sleeps"** until the resurrection of the body. But as it is only the "body" that goes into the "grave," it is only the "body" that "sleeps" or has no knowledge. The "Soul" and "Spirit" of a man goes to **"Sheol,"** not to the **"Grave."** In Gen. 37:35 we read—"And all his (Jacob's) sons and all his daughters rose up to comfort him; but he refused to be comforted; and he said, 'For I will go down into the **GRAVE** unto my son mourning.'" The Revised Version substitutes for "Grave" the word **"SHEOL,"** and the American Revision has in the margin—**"Sheol, abode of the dead,"** and the American Baptist Publication Society edition, "The Underworld." So we see that Jacob did not mean that he would go "unto my son" in the **"GRAVE,"** for he did not believe that his son Joseph was in the "grave," but that he had been eaten by a "wild beast" (Gen. 37:33). What Jacob meant was that he would **"go down"** into **SHEOL,** "The Underworld," and there he would meet Joseph, for it would be no comfort to go to a place (the grave) where he would know no one.

In Gen. 25:8 we read—"Then Abraham gave up the ghost, and died in a good old age, an old man, and full of years, and was **'GATHERED TO HIS PEOPLE.'"** The expression "Gathered to his people" has no reference to the "Grave" or "Family Burial Place," for that was over in Chaldea, but it means that Abraham went to "The Underworld" where the souls of his ancestors had gone, and where he would be reunited to them. The same statement is made of Isaac (Gen. 35:29) with the additional statement, "and his sons **BURIED HIM,"** thus showing that while his "soul" was "gathered to his people" in "The Underworld," his "body" was buried in the "grave."

Among those who teach that the "Soul" at death goes to "The Underworld," are those who claim that the "souls" of those who are not as yet fully fit for Heaven go to a place called

PURGATORY.

The word "Purgatory" is not found in the Bible. The word means a **"PLACE OF PURIFICATION."** The "Doctrine of Purgatory" was not known in the first century, and was not promulgated as a doctrine until 600 years after Christ. It had its origin in the belief that the souls of men when they die are not fit to go immediately to Heaven, and so an "Intermediate Place" was invented where they might wait for a while and be purged of their sin. The instrument of purification is physical suffering. The Doctrine further teaches that the soul in Purgatory can do nothing towards its own deliverance, and is dependent upon **"prayers"** and **"masses"** said by the living. The purpose of the Doctrine was to secure revenue for the Church by so working on the sympathy of loved ones, that they would pay for "Masses" to deliver the souls of their relatives and friends from the torments of Purgatory.

The "Doctrine of Purgatory" is unscriptural. There is no **"INTERMEDIATE PLACE"** to be seen on the Chart between "Paradise" and "Hell," and the **"Impass-able Gulf"** declares that there is no possibility of the occupants of "Hell" ever passing over into "Paradise." This nullifies the "Doctrine of Purgatory," and also the

RESTORATION THEORY.

The "Restoration Theory" is that after the "Wicked" have suffered in Hell for a time, and been sufficiently punished for their sins, that they will be restored and transferred to Heaven. The "Theory" includes Satan and his angels and all the "Evil Powers" of the Universe, and the final wiping out of Hell. The Scripture the advocates of this "Theory" use is—

"Whom (Christ) the Heaven must receive until the 'Times of Restitution of **ALL THINGS,** which God hath spoken by the mouth of all His Holy Prophets since the world began." Acts 3:21.

The claim is that the **"ALL THINGS"** embrace everything in the Universe, and that therefore at the

"Times of Restitution" (Restoration), **"All Things"** will be restored to their original glory and place. But there is a qualifying clause in the text which limits the "All Things" to what **"God hath spoken by the mouth of all His Holy Prophets since the world began."** Now we must not forget that these words were spoken on the "Day of Pentecost" to the JEWS, and were to show the Jews that Christ would not return until they repented and were converted (Acts 3:19), and then He would restore to them the things that the Prophets had foretold He would.

What were those things? (1) Their restoration to the land of Palestine. Amos 9:14-15. (2) The restoration of the Fertility of the Land. Joel 2:24-26. (3) The restoration of the Kingdom. Dan. 7:13-14. (4) The restoration of Edenic harmony in the brute creation. Isa. 11:6-9. (5) The restoration of Patriarchal years. Zech. 8:4. (6) The restoration of the earth to its Original condition before the Fall. Rev. 21:1. Nowhere in the Bible through the Prophets does God promise the restoration of the "Wicked," or the "Evil Powers" of the Universe, but clearly and distinctly states that they are to be punished **FOREVER AND FOREVER,** or unto the "Ages of the Ages." Rev. 20:10. Matt. 25:46.

The "Restoration Theory" is based on the Doctrine of a **"SECOND CHANCE."** That is, that the "Wicked" in the "Hell Section" of the "Underworld" shall be given another opportunity to accept Salvation. But how is this second offer to be made? Some claim that when Jesus descended into "Hades" He preached to the "Lost Spirits" confined there, and they base their argument on the words of Peter.

"For Christ also hath once suffered for sins, the just for the unjust, that He might bring us to God, being put to death in the flesh, but quickened by the Spirit (Holy Spirit); by which also He went and **PREACHED TO THE 'SPIRITS IN PRISON'**; which sometime were disobedient, when once the longsuffering of God waited

(120 years) in the days of Noah, while the Ark was a preparing, wherein few, that is, eight souls were saved by water." 1 Pet. 3:18-20.

But Jesus when He descended into the "Underworld" did not go into the "Hell Section," but into the "Paradise Section," therefore He did not preach to the "Wicked Dead." Again the Scripture quoted above says He preached to the "Spirits in Prison." Now the "Spirits in Prison," as we have seen, are not the "Wicked Dead," but the Angels who lost their first estate by cohabiting with the Daughters of Men at the time of the Flood, and they are confined in "Tartarus," and Jesus did not visit "Tartarus" when He descended into the "Underworld." And Jesus did not preach to them Himself, He preached to them by the Holy Spirit, who through Noah preached for 120 years to those "Fallen Angels" while they were still on the earth, and before they were banished to "Tartarus."

If the Wicked are to have a "Second Chance" in the next world who is to proclaim it? If the things that are used by God in this life to lead men to Himself, such as providence, the Bible, the preaching of the Gospel, the striving of the Holy Spirit have no avail here, what is to lead men to God in Hell where those things are absent and their environment wholly evil? Character determines destiny. When character becomes fixed, condition is settled beyond change. "He that is unjust, let him be unjust still; and he which is filthy, let him be filthy still: and he that is righteous, let him be righteous still." Rev. 22:11. These words of revelation declare the "FIXEDNESS OF CHARACTER" at death.

But you say the sufferings of the Wicked, and the memories of the lost opportunities of this life will lead to repentance. It is doubtless true that they will be sorry for their sin, but it will not be "godly sorrow," for there will be no Holy Spirit there to lead them to "godly repentance," and without Him they cannot be saved. If punishment will turn men to God, then the Gospel is superfluous, and it would be better to punish men than to preach the Gospel to them. The fact is that punishment hardens criminals. The "Rich Man" in Hell (Luke 16: 23-28) showed no repentance, he did not beg for mercy, nor express a desire to be out of his place of torment and be where Lazarus was. He simply wanted relief for his parched tongue. The whole teaching of the Scripture is that punishment hardens the wicked. In the Book of Revelation we read how those who suffered under the Plagues of the Book instead of repenting and calling on God, called on the **rocks** and **mountains** to fall on them and hide them from the face of Him that sitteth upon the Throne. Rev. 6: 16-17. They also blasphemed God on account of the "Plague of Hail" (Rev. 16:21), and even Satan after a 1000 years of banishment in the "Bottomless Pit" comes out as bad as ever. Rev. 20:7-8. If men deliberately choose evil rather than righteousness in this world, they cannot keep Hell out of themselves, or themselves out of Hell. Men cannot sink so low in the moral scale but what they can sink lower, and the sad fact is that death will not retard their sinful development but will accelerate it, until it is beyond human conception to what depth the wicked will descend in Hell.

But I think I hear someone say, Is it not possible for God to devise some way to save the Wicked in the next world? Does not the Bible say that God "Will have all men to be saved" (1 Tim. 2:4); that he has "No pleasure in the death of the Wicked" (Ez. 33:11); and that Christ "Tasted death for **every man.**" Heb. 2:9? Yes it says all this and much more. But it also says—"Behold, **NOW** is the accepted time . . . **NOW** is the **Day of Salvation.**" 2 Cor. 6:2. I say it reverently, when God devised the "Plan of Salvation" through the death of His Son on the Cross, He went to the limit. If there had been any other way He would have provided it, rather than the Lord Jesus should suffer.

But you ask does it not say in Phil. 2: 10-11, "That at the name of Jesus **every knee should bow,** of things in 'Heaven,' and things in 'Earth,' and things '**UNDER THE EARTH**' (in The Underworld); and that **every tongue should confess that Jesus Christ is Lord?**" And does not John in the Book of Revelation describe that day when he says—"And **every creature** which is in

'Heaven,' and on the 'Earth,' and 'UNDER THE EARTH,' and such as are 'in the sea,' and ALL that are in them, heard I saying, blessing, and honor, and glory, and power, be unto Him that sitteth upon the Throne, and unto the Lamb forever and ever?" Rev. 5: 13. Yes, the Bible says all this, but confession is not REPENT- ANCE. A conquered foe will admit the supremacy of the conqueror by virtue of necessity, but that does not imply a changed heart. Satan and his angels and all the "Powers of Evil," in Heaven, Earth, and Hell, will con- fess that Jesus Christ is not only Lord, but King of Kings and Lord of Lords, but that will not restore them to Heavenly Glory. We must not forget that the issues of Eternity are settled in Time. Men and women are to be judged for what they do "IN THE BODY" (2 Cor. 5: 10), that is on this side of the grave, and not for what they do on the other side. Jesus said—"I go my way, and ye shall seek me, and shall die in your sins: whither I go YE CANNOT COME." John 8: 21. This shows that if men die impenitent they can never go where Jesus is.

The "Doctrine of Purgatory" is the result of

A DEFECTIVE VIEW OF THE WORK OF CHRIST ON THE CROSS.

It implies that the "Death of Christ" was not suffi- cient, for if it was sufficient then those who die in the faith have no need to spend any time in a "Purgatory," but should go at once to "Paradise." The fact that "MASSES" are offered for the dead shows a misconcep- tion of the purpose of the "Lord's Supper." The "Lord's Supper" is not a "Sacrament." There is nothing saving in it. It is simply a "MEMORIAL" that looks back to the "Cross," and forward to the "Coming." 1 Cor. 11: 26. Between the "Fall in Eden" and "Calvary" there is the "ALTAR," between "Calvary" and the "Second Coming" there is the "TABLE," and between the "Sec- ond Coming" and the "New Heaven and Earth" there is the "THRONE." See the Chart on the "Threefold Work of Christ," Page 250. What right then has any one to set up between "Calvary" and the "Second Coming" an "ALTAR," where Christ has placed a "TABLE?" To call the "Table" an "ALTAR" is to make that which is offered upon it a "SACRIFICE," and if the "Bread" and "Wine" represent the **REAL BODY AND BLOOD** of Christ, as those who teach the Doctrine of "TRANSUBSTANTIATION" claim, then every time a "MASS" is offered Christ is "SACRIFICED," and the partaker of the "Mass" is a "GOD-EATER," and also a "CANNIBAL" for feasting on the **FLESH AND BLOOD** of a human being.

We must not forget the circumstances under which the "Lord's Supper" was instituted. It was after the "Passover Supper." Jesus was about to shed His blood on the Cross as the "Lamb of God," which the Passover typified, and as the Disciples had just eaten of the "Passover Lamb," whose blood had been previously shed, Jesus wished to show them that they must feed upon Him by faith as the "Lamb of God." So He took the "Bread" and said—"This is (represents) my Body which was broken for you, this do in **remembrance of me.**" 1 Cor. 11:24. "After the same manner also He took the 'Cup,' when He had supped, saying, 'This "Cup" (the Fruit of the Vine in it) is the New Testament (Covenant) in My Blood: this do ye, as oft as ye drink it, in **remembrance of me.**'" 1 Cor. 11:25. When Jesus offered His Disciples the "Cup" saying of its contents this is "MY BLOOD," did He open a vein and let His life blood flow into the Cup? Did the Disciples that night actually eat the **FLESH** and drink the **BLOOD** of Jesus? To ask the question is to answer it. What Jesus meant was that the "Bread" symbolized His Body about to be broken on the Cross, and the "Cup" symbolized His Blood about to be shed. What He desired to set before His Disciples was the fact that His death on the Cross would fulfil what the "Passover Lamb" typified, and that they would be reminded every time they partook of the Lord's Supper that all animal sacrifices had been done away with, and that the offering of Himself was "once for all," and that there is to be "no more offering for sin." Heb. 10:12-18.

ANNIHILATIONISM

Annihilationism is the Doctrine that the wicked are to be destroyed at death, or later after Judgment. The Doctrine is based on a false view of Death, and a wrong interpretation of the word "Destruction." If the wicked are destroyed at death then there is no such thing as the resurrection of the wicked dead and their judgment after resurrection, both of which the Scriptures clearly teach. John 5:28-29. Rev. 20:12-15. We know from Luke 16:19-31, that the wicked "Rich Man" was alive in Hell, though as to his body he had died, and it had been buried on the earth. Judas died as to his body, but his soul went to its own place. Acts 1:25. Again we are told that "endless punishment" awaits the wicked, but "Annihilation" would not be "endless punishment" or any punishment at all. The "Fallen Angels" were not annihilated, they are now in "Tartarus," and are yet to be judged. Jude 6. There is no such thing as "Annihilation" in nature. Things pass into another form or condition, but are not destroyed. The word "Destruction" as used in the Bible never means annihilation or the blotting out of existence. It simply denotes "loss" or "ruin," and that the thing "destroyed" is no longer fit for the purpose for which it was made or intended, and that the "form of its existence" is changed. To illustrate, the servants of Pharaoh said to him—"Knowest thou not yet that Egypt is destroyed." Ex. 10:7. But Egypt exists today. And Jesus said—"Destroy this temple, and in three days I will raise it up." John 2:18-22. He meant the "Temple of His Body," and though they destroyed it by "Crucifixion," He raised it up on the third day.

FUTURE PUNISHMENT ETERNAL

In Matt. 25:46 we read—"And these (the Wicked) shall go away into 'EVERLASTING PUNISHMENT;' but the Righteous into LIFE ETERNAL." Primarily these words are spoken of "The Nations" (Matt. 25:31-32), but they apply to individuals. The words in this passage "Everlasting," and "Eternal," are both the same Greek word "AIONIOS," and should both be translated

"ETERNAL." The word "Aionios" comes from the Greek word "aion," which is the same as the English word "aeon," or AGE. It has been said that the word means "Age-long," that is, a "definite period" with a beginning and an ending, and not necessarily eternal in duration. The word "Eternal" is from the Latin word "aetas," or "Age." Now a year is a definite time. It has a beginning and ending. If we know its beginning we know that in exactly 365 days it will end. But an "Age" is an indefinite time. Of past "Ages" we know of their beginning and ending, though we may not be able to tell how long they were, for instance the "Creative Age." But of Future Ages we do not know when they will begin or end. So the word "Age" is the only word we have to express "indefinite time," and the phrase "Ages of the Ages" is the only way we have of expressing "Endless Duration," or "ETERNITY."

The lifetime of the "Lord God Almighty" is said to be "For Ever and Ever." Rev. 4:9-10, 5:14, 10:6, 15:7. And means for the "Ages of the Ages." And that is the time given for the punishment of the "Satanic Trinity" (Rev. 20:10), and the reign of the "Righteous." Rev. 22:5. And as the "Wicked" are to exist as long as the "Righteous" they are to exist for the "Ages of the Ages" or for all "ETERNITY." So we see if "Hell" is to be blotted out, "Heaven" will be blotted out, the Universe will become extinct, Eternity will end, and God be no more, a thought which is inconceivable.

THE SECOND DEATH

It is said of the "Righteous Dead" that after their resurrection they can "DIE NO MORE." Luke 20:36. But it is said of the "Wicked Dead" after their resurrection and Judgment that they shall "DIE AGAIN." Rev. 20:12-15. What is this "SECOND DEATH?" What was their "First Death?" It was the separation of their "Soul" and "Spirit" from their "Body," so that their "Soul" and "Spirit" could exist in the flames of the "Hell Section" of "The Underworld" as did the "Soul" and "Spirit" of the "Rich Man." Luke 16:24. But as the Wicked after Judgment are consigned to the "LAKE

OF FIRE" where a physical body would be consumed, it is necessary that they "DIE AGAIN," that is, lose their resurrection body, and go only "Soul" and "Spirit" into the "Lake of Fire," for "Soul" and "Spirit" can exist in flames. This explanation permits the "Lake of Fire" to be a Lake of LITERAL FIRE, and is in harmony with Christ's teaching to that effect.

It is a noteworthy fact that the "Doctrine of Hell" was mainly taught by Jesus Himself. It was He who said that the wicked shall be cast into the "Lake of Fire," and that there should be wailing and gnashing of teeth. Matt. 13:49-50. Matt. 25:41. He also taught that the fire was quenchless, and their worm would never die. Mark 9:43-48. And as the Book of Revelation is the "Revelation of JESUS CHRIST" (Rev. 1:1), then whatever it teaches of the final doom of the Wicked, is the teaching of Jesus Christ.

The Ethical value of the "Doctrine of Hell" and of "Endless Punishment" is beyond computation. Preach the doctrine of a "Second Probation" after death, that men and women after a life of sin here can get out of Hell and into Heaven by repentance and accepting the Gospel Plan of Salvation, and they will throw the reins of self-control on the neck of passion and ride at break-neck speed to perdition. It is the spread of such pernicious teaching that is the cause of the increase of lawlessness in the world. If there were more preaching of Hell in the pulpit there would be less of hell in the world. But why do men want to go to Heaven via Hell when they can go to Heaven direct? God is love, but God is JUST. He must preserve the Righteous from the Wicked. This demands that they be separated for all eternity. Therefore, O reader! if you are not a child of God, I beseech you to fly from the Wrath to come by accepting God's overtures of mercy ere it be too late.

XXVII

Judaism and Christianity

We must make a sharp contrast between **"JUDA-ISM"** and **"CHRISTIANITY"** or there will be confusion in our Scriptural Thinking. There is an overlapping between them, and the debatable ground is in that "Transition Period" between "Pentecost," A. D. 30, and the "Destruction of Jerusalem," A. D. 70, when the **"JEWISH AGE"** really ended in the "Dispersion" of the Jews. See the Chart, page 294. In Heb. 9:26, we read—

> "For then must He often have suffered since the foundation of the world; but now once in the **'END OF THE WORLD'** (AGE) hath He appeared to put away sin by the sacrifice of Himself."

The **"Age,"** in the **"END"** of which Jesus came to put away sin, was the **"JEWISH AGE."** Jesus did not live in this "Christian Age." He was crucified, dead, buried and ascended before it began. It began with the coming of the Holy Spirit on the "Day of Pentecost." Jesus said—"Think not that I am come to **destroy** the 'Law,' or the 'Prophets;' I am not come to destroy, but to **FULFIL.**" Matt. 5:17. The "Law" that Jesus came to fulfil was not the "Moral Law" (the Ten Commandments), though He kept that in every particular, but the "Ceremonial Law." The "Ceremonial Law" typified what the Messiah was to do, or fulfil, when He came. He was to be the "Passover Lamb." As such He was offered up at the "Passover Season." In Him the "Sin Offering" was fulfilled. As the Goat of the "Sin Offering" He shed His blood at the Altar of the Cross, and as the "Scape Goat" He carried His own blood away, not into the Wilderness, but into the Holy Place of the Heavenly Tabernacle. Heb. 9:11-12. In His conversation with the two disciples on the road to Emmaus, on the afternoon of the day He arose, He said—"O fools, and slow of heart to believe all that the Prophets have spoken: ought not Christ to have suffered these things, and to enter into His Glory? And beginning at Moses and all the Prophets, He expounded unto them in all the Scriptures the things CONCERNING HIMSELF." Luke 24:25-27. The same evening in the city of Jerusalem Jesus appeared to the "Eleven" and them that were with them, and said—"These are the words which I spake unto you, while I was yet with you, that all things must be FULFILLED, which were written in the 'Law of Moses,' and in the 'Prophets,' and in the 'Psalms,' CONCERNING ME." Luke 24:44. So we see that "Christ is the 'END OF THE LAW' for Righteousness to every one that believeth." Rom. 10:4. That is, He fulfilled the Law, and we as Believers are no longer under Law but under GRACE. But while we are no longer under the "Ceremonial Law," that being fulfilled in Christ, we are under the "Moral Law," the "Ten Commandments," for while they are distinctly Jewish, yet their observance is required of every Christian Believer as laid down by the Apostles in their Epistles, with one exception, and that the observance of the Sabbath, or the Seventh Day of the Week. That is not obligatory upon the Christian. He is supposed to observe the First Day of the Week.

The Ten Commandments as reproduced in the New Testament are as follows: (1) **One God.** 1 Tim. 2:5. 1 Cor. 8:4-6. (2) **Idolatry.** 1 Cor. 10:7, 14. 1 John 5:21. (3) **Profanity.** Col. 3:8. Matt. 6:9. (4) **Sabbath.** They are warned against keeping it. Gal. 4:10-11. Col. 2:16-17. (5) **Honor Parents.** Eph. 6:2. (6) **Murder.** 1 John 3:14-15. (7) **Adultery.** Eph. 5:3-5. Gal. 5:19. (8) **Stealing.** Eph. 4:28. (9) **False Witness.** Eph. 4:25. 1 Cor. 13:5. (10) **Covetousness.** Eph. 5:3.

In the "Transition Period" from Egypt to Canaan of the Children of Israel, the Lord employed "Signs" (Miracles) to authenticate the Divine Mission of Moses. Ex. 4:1-9. The same method was employed in the "Transition Period" between "Judaism" and "Christianity" to authenticate the Messiahship of Jesus, and the Divine Mission of the Apostles. The length of the

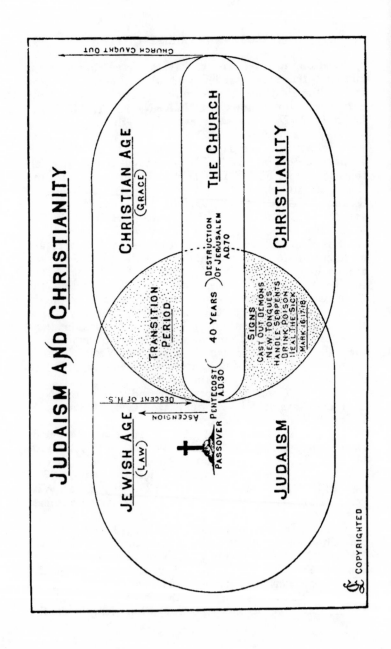

"Period" in both instances was the same, about 40 years. It was foretold of the "Messiah" that when He should come—"Then the **eyes of the blind shall be opened,** and the **ears of the deaf shall be unstopped.** Then shall the **lame man leap as an hart,** and the **tongue of the dumb sing.**" Isa. 35: 5-6. When John the Baptist, shut up in prison, had his doubts as to the Messiahship of Jesus, he sent two of his disciples to Jesus to ask him—"Art Thou He that should come, or do we look for another?" Jesus seemingly did not directly answer John's question, but after performing a number of miracles said to John's disciples—"Go and shew John again those things which ye do hear and see: the blind **receive their sight,** and the **lame walk,** the **lepers are cleansed,** and the **deaf hear,** the **dead are raised up,** and the **poor have the Gospel preached to them.**" Matt. 11: 1-5. Now the above reference from Isaiah, as the context shows, has reference to the Millennium, and therefore is a "Kingdom Sign," and as the Jews expected the Messiah when He came to set up the "Millennial Kingdom," the "Miracles of Healing" of Jesus were "Kingdom Signs" to prove His Messiahship.

In what is spoken of as "The Great Commission," we read—"Go ye into all the world, and preach the Gospel to every creature. He that believeth and is baptized shall be saved; but he that believeth not shall be damned. And these '**SIGNS**' shall follow them that believe; in my name shall they **cast out devils** (demons); they shall **speak with new tongues;** they shall **take up serpents;** and if they **drink any deadly thing, it shall not hurt them;** they shall **lay hands on the sick, and they shall recover.**" Mark 16: 15-18. While it is true that verses 9-20 of this chapter are not found in the two oldest Greek manuscripts, and that their authenticity is questioned, nevertheless the signs here promised, with the exception of "drinking deadly things," followed the preaching of the Gospel by the Apostles. It must not be overlooked that the command to go into all the world and preach the Gospel, was given to the "Eleven Apostles" and not the followers of Jesus in general. The difference between Matthew's account (Matt. 28: 16-20), and Mark's account (Mark 16:14-18) is striking. In Matthew's account no "Signs" are promised and it was to continue until the "end of the world," or this present "Age." While in Mark's account the promise seems limited to the days of the Apostles. Be sure it says— "And these 'Signs' shall follow them that **believe**," but that may mean only those who believed the Apostles, for such did "**speak with tongues.**" Acts 10:46; 19:6. As further evidence of the "time limit" of the promise we have the words of verse 20, "And they (the Eleven Apostles) went forth, and preached everywhere, the Lord working with them, and confirming, **the word with SIGNS FOLLOWING.**" To the "Eleven Apostles" we must add Paul who was chosen of the Lord to take Judas' place. Acts 9:15-19. Rom. 1:1. 1 Tim. 2:7. That these "Signs" were "Apostolic Signs," and were to confirm the claims of the Apostles, was the teaching of Paul. "Truly the **'SIGNS OF AN APOSTLE'** were wrought among you in all patience, in **'SIGNS,'** and **'WONDERS,'** and **'MIGHTY DEEDS.'**" 2 Cor. 12:12. These "Signs" were to convince the Gentiles (Rom. 15:16-19), and to confirm the "Great Salvation" promised through the Gospel (Heb. 2:3-4), and when their purpose was fulfilled they ceased. The reason they ceased was because they were no longer needed to confirm the Gospel or authenticate the mission of the preacher of the Word. While it is true that some of these "Signs" have attended the preaching of God's messengers where it was necessary to confirm their Divine authority, the fact that they have not generally attended the preaching of the Word since the days of the Apostles is an implication that they are not to be expected or looked for in these days. We do not need them to confirm the Scriptures. We have nearly nineteen centuries of Church History as evidence to the Divine origin of Christianity. We must not forget that in that "Transition Period" between "Judaism" and "Christianity" the Christian Church was largely Jewish, and it was hard for many to break away from the rites and ceremonies of the Jewish religion, but gradually they were weaned away until "Signs" were no longer necessary. We must not forget that there was no New Testament for the Apostles to appeal to in the first half of that "Transition Period." Therefore "Signs" and "Wonders" were necessary. The first New Testament book to be written was 1 Thessalonians, A. D. 52. The first Gospel was that of Mark, written between A. D. 57-63. The Acts was written about A. D. 65. Most of the New Testament was written between A. D. 60-70. All was written, except the writings of the Apostle John, before the Destruction of Jerusalem in A. D. 70. With the death of the Apostles and New Testament Prophets, the Apostolic and Prophetic Office ceased. Since then the Church of Christ has had no new revelation. Signs are not needed in these days because we have the more sure "Word of Prophecy."

As still further evidence that the "Signs," particularly that of healing, ceased before the close of that "Transition Period," we have the treatment of Paul of his fellow workers. In writing to Timothy (1 Tim. 5:23) he advised him to—"Drink no longer water, but use a little wine for thy stomach's sake and thine often infirmities." And of Trophimus he wrote—"But Trophimus have I left at Miletum sick." 2 Tim. 4:20. If "Divine Healing" was more than a "Sign," if it was part of the Gospel, and was conferred on the Believer because Christ's death on the Cross included physical healing along with the salvation of the soul, then why did the Apostle Paul advise Timothy as he did, and leave Trophimus at Miletum sick?

The writer is a firm believer in "Divine Healing," and that the "Prayer of Faith" will heal the sick. He has had too much evidence in his own family and congregation to that effect. But he does not believe that it is a lack of saving faith to be sick. Some go so far as to say that if a Christian has not faith to be healed, he has not the faith that saves. God does heal, and in many cases instantly, in answer to the "PRAYER OF FAITH." James 5:14-15. But that "Faith" must be implanted by God Himself. All "Divine Healing" is of "God's Sovereign Will." If prayer alone could heal there would be none of us sick. The fact that the majority of God's saints have not had their bodily infirmities removed in answer to prayer, implies that healing of the body is not a part of the atoning work of Christ, else they would have been healed the moment they took Christ as their Saviour. If the pulpit would teach the Scriptural method of Divine Healing, professing Christian people would not resort to the Satanic devised Healing Cults of the day for healing.

SPEAKING WITH TONGUES

Another "Sign" of the "Transition Period" between "Judaism" and "Christianity" was "Speaking With Tongues." In the last hundred years there has been an attempt to revive this Apostolic "Sign." In discussing this "Sign" it is necessary to know why it was given. John the Baptist pointed out Jesus as the one who would "Baptize His Disciples with the **HOLY GHOST** and **FIRE**." Matt. 3:11. And Jesus just before His Ascension commanded His Disciples to not depart from Jerusalem until they received the promised "Gift" of the Father of the "Baptism of the Holy Ghost." Acts 1: 4-5. This "Baptism" was for a twofold purpose. First to endue them with **POWER** (Luke 24:49), and secondly to incorporate them into the "**BODY OF CHRIST**"—the **CHURCH**. The "Church" did not exist until Pentecost. There could be no "Body" until there was a **HEAD**, and there was no **HEAD** until Jesus had died, risen, and ascended to the Father. In Eph. 1:22-23, we read—"And hath put all things under His feet, and gave Him (Jesus) to be the 'HEAD' over all things to the 'Church,' which is His **BODY**." The Church came into existence by the union of all "Believers" at that time into **ONE BODY**. This union was brought about by the "Baptism of the Holy Spirit" on the "Day of Pentecost." It is referred to in 1 Cor. 12:13, R. V. "For in one **SPIRIT** (Holy Spirit) were we all baptized into **ONE BODY**, whether Jews or Greeks, whether bond or free; and were all made to drink of one Spirit." This does not refer to "Water" baptism, but to **SPIRIT** baptism. The "Upper Room" being the "**BAPTISTRY**" in which the disciples of Jesus were immersed in the Holy Spirit.

The "Baptism of the Holy Spirit" was not for the purpose of regenerating the disciples of Jesus, they had already been regenerated. Jesus had said to them in the "Upper Room"—"Now ye are clean THROUGH THE WORD which I have spoken unto you." John 15:3. What does that mean? Let Peter answer—"Being BORN AGAIN, not of corruptible seed, but of incorruptible, by the 'WORD OF GOD.'" 1 Pet. 1:23. The disciples then had been "Born Again," yet they needed to be "Baptized with the Holy Spirit" for POWER. From this we see that the "Baptism of the Holy Spirit" is something separate and distinct from being "Born of the Holy Spirit." There can be no question but that Jesus was regenerated from His birth, and yet He needed the "Baptism of the Holy Spirit" before He could enter upon His public ministry. This He received at the Jordan when the Holy Spirit as a "Dove" descended on Him. John 1:32-33. The Holy Spirit took the form of a "Dove" when He baptized Jesus, the "Dove" being an emblem of purity, but when He baptized the disciples at Pentecost He took the form of "FIRE"—the emblem of purification. In regeneration the Holy Spirit imparts LIFE. In Holy Spirit Baptism He imparts POWER. These two may be simultaneously imparted, or there may be a "time space" between them, due to a lack of complete consecration, or a lack of scriptural knowledge.

The "Baptism of the Holy Spirit" on the Day of Pentecost was preceded by a "sound from Heaven as of a rushing mighty wind." There was no wind, only a sound of wind, and it was the sound, not a wind, that filled the house where they were sitting. There also appeared unto them "Cloven Tongues" like as of fire, it does not say it was literal fire, but the "Flaming Tongues" typified the purifying effect of literal fire, and they were all filled with the Holy Spirit. The result of this Baptism of the Holy Spirit was that all who were in the house began to speak with "other tongues" as the Holy Spirit gave them utterance. There was no confusion of Tongues, as at Babel, of which Pentecost was the reversal, but each one praised God in a foreign language. It was this fact, that was noised abroad, that caused outsiders to assemble, and they were amazed and marvelled at each man hearing in his mother tongue. The "Gift of Tongues" was given, not to evidence to the disciples that they had received the "Baptism of the Holy Spirit," they knew that from the power of the Holy Spirit in them, but it was given as a "Sign" to the assembled multitude.

Why was the "Gift of Tongues" given on the "Day of Pentecost?" Because it was a "Feast Day," and there were gathered in Jerusalem Jews from all parts of the world. Acts 2:8-11. Some probably had remained over from the Passover, and during those 50 days many startling and wonderful things had occurred at Jerusalem. Jesus had been crucified and buried, and it was reported that He had risen from the dead, and had appeared at different times to His Disciples, and that they were expecting some special "Gift" from Heaven. Opinion was divided as to the truthfulness of all these tales. Tomorrow, the Feast of Pentecost being over, these Jews were going to depart for their distant homes, and would carry with them the strange tales they had heard. It was necessary that they should know exactly what all these things meant. The report that the disciples of Jesus had been given the power to "Speak with Tongues" spread like "Wild-fire," and soon the street in front of the house where they were stopping was filled with a crowd of Jews of all nationalities anxious to hear in their own tongue what had happened. Notice that no Tongue was an **UNKNOWN** Tongue. They each heard in their **OWN TONGUE,** the Tongue of the nation in which they had been born.

The "Sign" of the "Gift of Tongues" was very appropriate. Every Jew would understand it. Like "Healing" it was a "Kingdom Sign." It furnished Peter with a "Text" for his sermon. His text was—"**This is THAT.**" This is that which was spoken by the Prophet Joel, that it shall come to pass in the "Last Days," saith God, "I will pour out my Spirit upon all flesh," etc. Joel 2:28-32. While Peter said "This is that," he did not say this is the fulfilment of the prophecy of Joel, for what happened that day was only a partial fulfilment, for there were no wonders in the heavens and on the earth, such as blood, and fire, and pillars of smoke, with the sun turned into darkness, and the moon into blood. The complete fulfilment of the prophecy of Joel awaits the future. The prophecy of Joel has nothing to do with the Church. It relates to Israel. It belongs to the "Day of the Lord," which is the Millennium. Joel 1: 15. A careful reading of the context shows that the "Gift of Tongues" is not to be given until after the Jews have been gathered back to their own land and been converted, then the Lord will pour out His Spirit upon them and they shall prophesy, etc. Again the prophecy shall not be fulfilled until after the "Latter Rain" has been restored to Palestine, which "Latter Rain" is not Spiritual but literal, as the context shows. Palestine today is suffering for water. It is a curse that came upon it because the Children of Israel turned aside to worship other gods. Deu. 11: 13-17. The "Former" and "Latter Rain" are to be restored (Joel 2: 23-27), and the land of Palestine shall again blossom as the rose, and be covered with vineyards and olive groves. Isa. 35: 1-2.

The outpouring of the Holy Spirit on the Day of Pentecost was but a "foretaste" of what is to happen after the Lord Jesus Christ comes back, and was used by Peter as an argument for the Jews to repent nationally at that time that their sins might be blotted out, that the "Times of Refreshing," the fulfilment of the Prophecy of Joel, might come. Acts 3: 19-21. From this we see that the "Gift of Tongues" is a "Kingdom Sign," that it has nothing to do with the Church, or this Age, and when the need for it in that "Transitional Period" passed it ceased, and is not to be restored until Christ comes to set up His Kingdom.

While it is true, as has been already stated, that there is a bestowal of the Holy Spirit separate and following the regenerating work of the Holy Spirit, which is given to impart power, there is no command or exhortation in any of the Epistles that we should pray for another Pentecostal outpouring of the Holy Spirit, with its accompanying gift of "Speaking with Tongues." We might as well look for another Calvary as for another Pentecost in this Age.

The second account of "Speaking with Tongues" is recorded in Acts 10:44-48. This occurred in the house of Cornelius at Caesarea, and was to convince Peter and the Jews that accompanied him, that the Gentiles also were included in the Church. Acts 11:15-18.

The third account is found in Acts 19:1-7. When Paul visited Ephesus he found some disciples of John the Baptist, who probably had been converted by the preaching of Apollos, but who were ignorant of the work of the Holy Spirit, whom, when they had been properly instructed and baptized Paul laid his hands on, and the Holy Spirit came on them and they "spake with Tongues" and prophesied. This "Sign" was to convince these 12 disciples that there was such a thing as the Holy Spirit. See verse 2. When Peter and John went to the Samaritans and laid their hands on them and they received the Holy Spirit, it was not evidenced by "Speaking with Tongues." Acts 8:14-17. So we see that the "Baptism of the Holy Spirit" may be received without the testimony of "Speaking with Tongues."

It was not the "Sign" of "Speaking with Tongues" that converted the Jews on the Day of Pentecost, it was Peter's sermon, and Peter did not speak with "Tongues," but in the ordinary language of the people, and his sermon was interpreted by the Disciples who received the "Gift of Tongues," to the foreign Jews who were present. This led to the conversion of many, and fitted them to carry the Gospel to their home land. They doubtless received the "Baptism of the Holy Spirit," for Peter told them that if they repented and were baptized (with water) they would receive the "Gift" of the Holy Spirit. Acts 2:38. But we are not told that with the "Gift" of the Holy Spirit they received the power to "Speak with Tongues." Those who spoke with "Tongues" on the Day of Pentecost only needed the "Gift" for that special occasion, and we are nowhere told that they exercised it afterward.

The only Epistle where the "Gift of Tongues" is mentioned is the First Epistle to the Corinthians. the twelfth to the fourteenth chapters inclusive, and there it is looked upon with disfavor. The "Gifts of the Spirit" are enumerated in chapter 12, verses 4-11. They are nine in number, and the "Gift of Tongues" is next to the last, showing that it is of minor importance. It must not be forgotten, that, while there are "Nine Gifts" of the Holy Spirit, it does not follow that these "Gifts" are dispensed regularly and in equal proportions, and that each individual may possess all of them, for we are told in verse 11, that the Holy Spirit divides to every man severally as He will, and the inference is that some "Gifts" are limited to certain periods or stages of the world's history, as for instance the "Gift of Tongues" to the Apostolic Period, and in the future to Israel in the commencement of the Millennial Age.

Again we must not forget the condition of the Church at Corinth to whom the Epistle to the Corinthians was written. The walk of the members was carnal, they tolerated all kinds of sinful practices, and were filled with sectarianism and vainglory. 1 Cor. 3:1-4; 5:1-2. It is no wonder then that some of them for the purpose of display sought the "Gift of Tongues." For this Paul reproved them, and said—"Let all things be done decently and in order," for God is not the author of **CONFUSION.** 1 Cor. 14:33, 40. It also appears from 1 Cor. 14:34-35, that the women of the Church were prominent in the "Speaking with Tongues Movement," and for this cause Paul commanded that they keep **"silent"** in the churches, and if they wanted to know anything to ask at home of their husbands.

From this it would appear that the "Speaking with Tongues" in the early church was for a "Sign," that it was not for edification, nor was it the practice of the Apostles. The Apostles emphasized the "Filling" of the Spirit, but not the "Baptism," and nowhere in their Epistles do they affirm that "Speaking with Tongues" is an evidence that one has been Baptized with the Holy Spirit, and is necessary for such evidence. Paul says—"Wherefore 'Tongues' are for a **'SIGN,'** not to them that believe, but to them that **BELIEVE NOT."** 1 Cor. 14:22. Therefore the "Believer" is not to seek the "Gift of Tongues" for any witness to himself. It is also strongly hinted that "Speaking with Tongues" is peculiarly open to **SPURIOUS IMITATION.** Satan is always on the watch to take advantage of any opportunity to "ape" the "Gifts" of the Holy Spirit, and when those who claim to have the "Gift" of "Speaking with Tongues" speak in an inarticulate and unintelligible manner, and behave unseemly, it is an evidence of the work of the Devil, for the Holy Spirit is always dignified, quiet, and edifying in His manifestations.

As has been already said the Church is the **BODY OF CHRIST.** Now a body is made up of different members and organs, each of which has its own peculiar function, and limitation. If one is diseased or improperly functions the whole body suffers. Even the muscles and joints have their functions, and the Apostle says that the Church, as the "Body of Christ," is to be— **"FITLY JOINED TOGETHER** and compacted by that which every **JOINT** supplieth, according to the effectual working in the measure of **EVERY PART."** Eph. 4: 11-16. That is, every individual member of the Church, even though he be but an insignificant **JOINT,** must function properly, or there will be schism. Any undue emphasizing, or dislocation of any Scriptural truth, only tends to disturbance in the "Body of Christ," the Church.

As a negative argument it is well to note the **OMISSIONS** of the "Gift of Tongues" in the Apostolic Church. There is no record that the 3000 converts of the Day of Pentecost, or the 5000 converts of a short time afterward, nor the converts at Samaria who received the Baptism of the Spirit by the laying on of hands (Acts 8:14-17), received the "Gift of Tongues." With the exception of the Church at Corinth, where the "Gift" was of no practical value, the Churches do not appear to have possessed the "Gift." The Apostles did not consider it of sufficient importance to mention it in their Epistles to the Churches, and the fact that it has never been a doctrine of the Church, is evidence that it does not belong to the Church, but was simply a Judaistic **SIGN.**

It is not proper to use the word "Pentecostal" in connection with the work of the Holy Spirit in the Church. Pentecost was a Jewish Feast, and was associated with the Jewish calendar, and has no meaning outside of that fact. The "Baptism" of the Holy Spirit on the Day of Pentecost was not a "Pentecostal Blessing," it had nothing to do with the day. The Feast Day was utilized simply because, as has been stated, it was a suitable occasion to reach those Jews of all lands who had come up to the Feast and were soon to depart for their homes.

We must not forget that other "Gifts," beside those mentioned, that were bestowed upon the Church in that "Transition Period," passed away with the Period. The Apostles were a "Gift" to the Church (1 Cor. 12:28; Eph. 4:11-12), but they passed away. The New Testament Prophet was a "Gift," but as soon as the Canon of Scripture was closed his office ceased. This was anticipated by Paul when he said—"Whether there be prophecies, they shall fail (cease)." 1 Cor. 13:8. During that "Transition Period" the dead were raised to life. Are they still raised? Prison doors miraculously opened and prisoners were set free. Handkerchiefs, and aprons and "Shadow Casting" (Acts 5:15) were used as instruments of healing—have they any such power today? It is not a question of what God can do, but what He has been doing in the Church for the past nineteen centuries. There is just as strong faith in the Church today as in Apostolic times. To demand and depend on physical signs is not of faith. The distinguishing difference between "Judaism" and "Christianity" is, that "Judaism" is a "Ceremonial Religion," largely dependent upon "Signs," while "Christianity" is a LIFE. Those "Transition Days" were days of "GRACE" to the Jews, and when they failed to profit by them, they were scattered over the earth and "Judaism" passed into a state of ECLIPSE.

XXVIII

The Circles of the Christian Life

A number of years ago at Northfield, Massachusetts, Robert E. Speer, D.D., gave an address on "The Inner Circle." Its purpose was to show the different concentric circles or spheres of the Christian Life in their relation to Christ. The outline of Dr. Speer's address has been put in diagram form by the writer, see Chart on "The Circles of the Christian Life," page 307. The description of the "Circles" is mainly that of the writer.

FIRST CIRCLE—"THE FIVE HUNDRED"

In 1 Cor. 15:6, we read—"After that, He was seen of above **FIVE HUNDRED BRETHREN** at once." The word "Brethren" denotes that the "Five Hundred" were "Believers," that they had **"FAITH,"** and were saved persons. This "Circle" then is the

"CIRCLE OF FAITH,"

and represents the large body of Christian Believers in the Church who have been saved by faith in Christ, but are not walking in nearness to Christ, but are following "afar off," and therefore are mere followers of Christ.

SECOND CIRCLE—"THE SEVENTY"

In Luke 10:1-11, we read—"After these things the Lord appointed other 'SEVENTY' also, and sent them two and two before His face into every city and place, whither He Himself would come." Jesus sent the "Seventy" forth "two by two" so that they would have company and could consult with each other. Probably they were of different gifts, as preacher and singer, and of different temperaments so as to harmonize their work. They were fully instructed as to their conduct, where they were to go, what they were to do, and what they were to say. When their mission was successfully

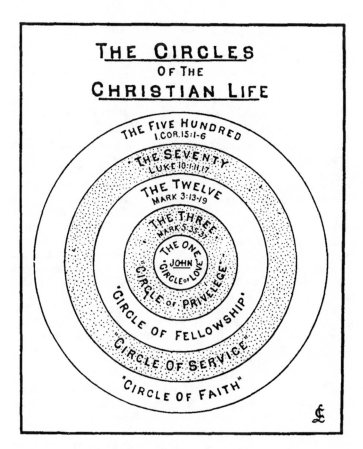

THE CIRCLES
OF THE
CHRISTIAN LIFE

THE FIVE HUNDRED
I.COR.15:1-6

THE SEVENTY
LUKE 10:1.II.17

THE TWELVE
MARK 3:13-19

THE THREE
MARK 5:35-37

THE ONE
JOHN
"CIRCLE OF LOVE"

"CIRCLE OF PRIVILEGE"

"CIRCLE OF FELLOWSHIP"

"CIRCLE OF SERVICE"

"CIRCLE OF FAITH"

finished they returned with joy, saying, "Lord, even the devils are subject unto us through Thy name." Luke 10:17.

The "Seventy" were picked out from the "Five Hundred" for SERVICE. This "Circle" then is the

"CIRCLE OF SERVICE."

In every Church there is only a small number, in proportion to the membership, who are fit for service. Shall we say that the proportion is only 70 in every Church of 500 members? How was it with Gideon when he went against the Midianites? He had an army of 32,000 men (Judges 7:1-8), but the Lord told him that they were too many, that if they were successful they would lay it to their number, so he told Gideon to test them to see how many were fit for service, and Gideon found there were but 300. In this we see the weakness of numbers. The "fearful" and "afraid" in every Church are a source of weakness. Only those of "faith" are fit for service. It is a great thing to be saved, to be in the "Outer Circle" of FAITH, but it is a greater thing to be fit for service and to be honored by a place in the "Circle of Service."

THIRD CIRCLE—"THE TWELVE"

The next inner circle is the "Circle of the Twelve." "And He goeth up into a mountain, and calleth unto Him whom He would; and they came unto Him. And He ordained TWELVE, that they should be with Him, and that He might send them forth to preach, and to have power to heal sicknesses, and to cast out devils (demons)." Mark 3:13-15. Jesus called the "Twelve" for a twofold purpose.

1. That they might be with Him.
2. That He might send them forth.

Jesus was a lonely man, as all men are who live above their fellows and have visions of the future. This was seen in His desire for fellowship, and His "Homesickness" was revealed in His prayer in the "Upper Room" in which He said—"And now, O Father, glorify Thou Me with Thine Own Self with the GLORY WHICH I

HAD WITH THEE BEFORE THE WORLD WAS."
John 17:5. To meet this "loneliness" and to overcome
this "homesickness," Jesus chose the "Twelve Apostles."
This "Circle" then is the

"CIRCLE OF FELLOWSHIP."

But Jesus was not selfish in His desire for "Fellowship." He wanted as companions men whom He could
use in His work, and whom He could send forth as He
had sent forth the "Seventy." The names of these men
are given in Matt. 10:2-4. These men were doubtless
chosen not from the "Five Hundred" but from the
"Seventy." While all the "Seventy" were fit for "Service" they were not all fit to be "APOSTLES." There
are therefore among the workers in every church some
who are especially fit for office in the church, such as
"Deacons." For the good of the Church, and the helpful-
ness of the Pastor, these officers should be men of his
own choosing, so that their fellowship may be mutually
helpful and pleasant. These Officers should be paired off
for service, so the Pastor can send them forth to minister
on the field.

FOURTH CIRCLE—"THE THREE"

Among the "Twelve Apostles" there were three men
that Jesus chose to go with Him on special occasions.
Those men were Peter, James and John. Why He always
chose the same three men we are not told, doubtless it
was because of their special fitness. We do know that
those three men, unknown to themselves, had special
work ahead of them. Peter was to be the leading
Apostle, James was to be the head of the Church in Jerusalem, and John was to be the "Apocalyptic Seer" of the
Church. It was necessary therefore that these three
men should never question the "DEITY" of Jesus. To
this end He took them to places where He manifested
His "Deity."

1. The Home of Jairus.

Jairus sought Jesus that he might ask Him to come
and heal his dying daughter. On the way Jesus was
delayed, and when they reached the home of Jairus his

daughter was dead. Mark 5:22-43. Jesus put out the curious crowd and taking only Peter, James and John, and the parents of the dead girl, entered the chamber where she lay dead, and raising her from the dead He restored her to her sorrowing parents. Why did Jesus take Peter, James and John to that "Chamber of Death"? He took them there that He might reveal to them His **"RESURRECTION POWER."** That they might see in that "Power" His **DEITY.**

2. The Mount of Transfiguration.

The second place to which Jesus took Peter, James and John was the "Mount of Transfiguration." Mark 9:1-10. His purpose was to reveal to them His **"GLORY."** To let them have a vision of the "Glory" He had with the Father before the world was (John 17:5), that they might see that He existed before His Incarnation, and that He was not a stranger to Moses and Elijah, but had known them and they Him before He became a man. It is noteworthy that Jesus forbade them to tell at that time what happened in the home of Jairus, or upon the Mount of Transfiguration because the announcement of His **DEITY** then would be premature and interfere with His work.

3. The Garden of Gethsemane.

The third place Jesus took Peter, James and John alone was to the recesses of the "Garden of Gethsemane." Mark 14:32-52. Doubtless all who were in the "Upper Room" and had partaken of the "Lord's Supper" accompanied Him to Gethsemane, but all but Peter, James and John, were forbidden to enter the recesses of the Garden. Even they were not permitted to witness the "Agony" of Gethsemane, that was too sacred, but they did see when He awakened them the marks of suffering on His face. Jesus took the "three" into the Garden that He might reveal to them His **"SORROW,"** and that they might get a vision of what the sufferings of the Cross cost Him. The sad thought is that they did not measure up to their opportunity, for they fell asleep. That night was a microcosm of present world conditions. 1. A praying Christ. 2. A sleeping Church. 3. An active Devil.

The "Circle of the Three" was the

"CIRCLE OF PRIVILEGE."

It was a great privilege for them to have been chosen by Jesus for special revelations of His "Power," "Glory" and "Sufferings." It is a great privilege for a chosen few of the Officers of a Church to be singled out by the Pastor, and have revealed to them things that are not best to give to the world, yet increase their faith in him. You may say "I am not fit to belong to the 'Circle of Privilege,' I am a vacillating, unreliable, and impulsive man." So was Peter, but he was chosen. And James and John were self-seeking men, who, through their mother, sought to sit on the right and left of Jesus in His Kingdom, yet Jesus chose these men. Why? Because He saw in them when they were "sifted as wheat" the golden grain of character that would make them leaders in the Church. How did they get in? Why, they "forsook all" to follow Him. Jesus knew that they were consecrated men and therefore He chose them.

FIFTH CIRCLE—"OF ONE"

Jesus said—"A new Commandment I give unto you. That ye **LOVE** one another; as I have **LOVED** you, that ye also **LOVE** one another. By this shall all men know that ye are my Disciples, if ye have **LOVE** one to another." John 13:34-35. If there ever was a Disciple of Jesus that fulfilled this Commandment it was **JOHN**. He never boasted that he loved Jesus, but with great humility spoke of himself as the Disciple whom **JESUS LOVED**. John 21:20. Love seemed to be the "Key-note" of his life, and he breathed it out in that wonderful fourth chapter of his First Epistle, in which he uses the word 26 times. The "Circle of One" then is the

"CIRCLE OF LOVE."

Love will brave any danger for those it loves. A mother's love will face the most malignant disease for the sake of her child. We read that at the time of the

Arrest in the Garden of Gethsemane all the Disciples of Jesus forsook Him and fled. Mark 14: 50. But there was an exception, and that exception was **JOHN**. He was the "another disciple" who went in with Jesus into the Palace of the High Priest to the trial. John 18: 15. The intimacy of love exceeds all other intimacy. A Pastor may respect the Officers of his Church, and take them to a large extent into his confidence, but he will not become intimate only with those he loves.

Now to which of these "Circles" do you belong? **Do you belong to the outermost Circle, the "Circle of Faith?"** Are you only one of the "Five Hundred," saved, but no good for service? Do you belong to the "Circle of Service," are you one of the "Seventy" busy about the Master's work? Or do you belong to the "Circle of Fellowship," having been called from among the "Seventy" to be one of the "Twelve" and hold some Office in the Church? If so, are you one of the "Inner Circle of Privilege" where you enjoy the special favor of your Pastor? Or can it be said of you that you are the "Beloved Disciple" whom Jesus loves? Your usefulness and service depends on which "Circle" you are in. May we all live the "Pillowed Life" of rest on the Bosom of Jesus.

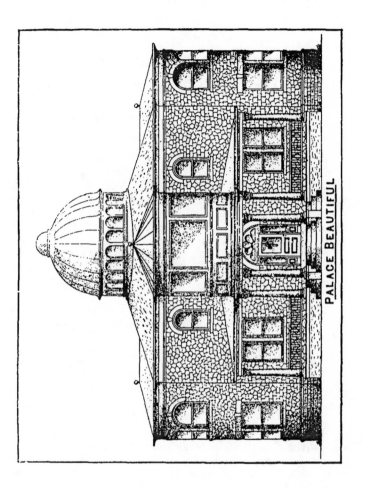

PALACE BEAUTIFUL

XXIX

Palace Beautiful, or the Christian Life Under the Similitude of a Palace

Bunyan in his "Pilgrim's Progress" describes "Palace Beautiful." He pictures Christian as approaching it at nightfall and asking for lodging, and being met at the door by a Damsel named Discretion, and afterwards welcomed by Prudence, Piety and Charity. That night Christian slept in a large upper-room or chamber, whose window opened towards the sunrising. In the morning after breakfast they showed him over the Palace, first taking him to the "Study." The next day they visited the "Armory." The third day, before they would let him depart, they took him to the top of the Palace and showed him in the distance the "Delectable Mountains," at the foot of which lay "Immanuel's Land." They then took him into the "Armory," and having armed him, sent him on his journey.

In Dr. F. B. Meyer's little book, "Steps Into the Blessed Life," in chapter three, he speaks of the "Chambers of the King," in which he compares the successive experiences of the Christian to the chambers of a Palace, such as the "Chamber of the New Birth," the "Chamber of Assurance," the "Chamber of the Surrendered Will," etc., these chambers opening one into the other.

Dr. George F. Pentecost in his little book on "Grace Abounding in the Forgiveness of Sins," takes up the thought of Bunyan and Meyers and enlarges on it. He says—"I have often conceived to myself God's Salvation being provided for us in a splendid mansion, set in the midst of a garden of delights and parks of loveliness, into which there is an always-open gate. Many people wander into the grounds and go from flowerbed to flowerbed, and stroll with delight about the grounds, casting now and again a passing glance at the splendid mansion, which is God's 'House of Mercy;' but, upon

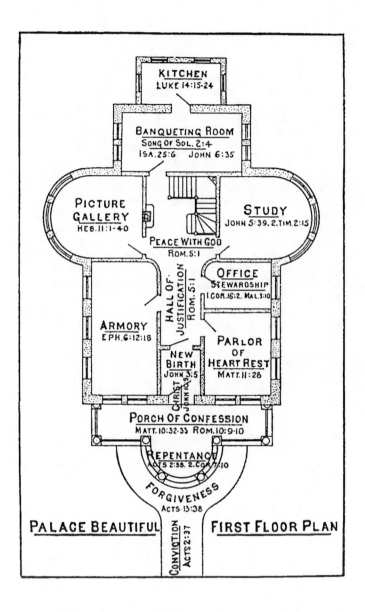

KITCHEN
LUKE 14:15-24

BANQUETING ROOM
SONG OF SOL. 2:4
ISA. 25:6   JOHN 6:35

PICTURE GALLERY
HEB. 11:1-40

STUDY
JOHN 5:39, 2 TIM. 2:15

PEACE WITH GOD
ROM. 5:1

HALL OF JUSTIFICATION
ROM. 5:1

OFFICE
STEWARDSHIP
1 COR. 16:2, MAL. 3:10

ARMORY
EPH. 6:12:18

NEW BIRTH
JOHN 3:5

CHRIST
JOHN 10:9

PARLOR
OF
HEART REST
MATT. 11:28

PORCH OF CONFESSION
MATT. 10:32-33   ROM. 10:9-10

REPENTANCE
ACTS 2:58, 2 COR. 7:10

FORGIVENESS
ACTS 13:38

CONVICTION
ACTS 2:37

PALACE BEAUTIFUL   FIRST FLOOR PLAN

the whole, are content to stay outside, satisfied with the free range of the grounds. Some are anxious to avail themselves of the privilege, which is freely published abroad, of entering the house and becoming guests of Him who dwells therein. These approach the door and mount the wide marble steps and are cheered by the inscription written over the doorway—'**Whosoever will, let Him Come,**' and '**Him That Cometh I Will in no Wise Cast Out.**' The splendid door of this great house is set wide open, and on either side there are servants of God who stand day and night publishing God's free invitation to sinners to enter. No price is demanded, no certificates of character are required, no questions are asked as to previous conduct or present condition, neither wealth nor social standing are inquired into; whether in the garb of prince or beggar, all alike are welcome. . . . In my fancy I have seen some come up to the threshold of the door and look in and sigh and turn back. Some linger for days and weeks longing to enter in, but not doing so because they say, they are not fit, or are too unworthy, or that they cannot believe, though the invitation remains written over the door of the mansion."

The thoughts of these three writers, Bunyan, Meyer and Pentecost have suggested to me the idea of drawing the plan of

"PALACE BEAUTIFUL,"

with all the halls, stairways, public rooms, and private chambers, with their spiritual significance, in the "Palace of Mansoul," and thus present in pictorial form the "Steps in the Christian Life."

The Pilgrim approaches "Palace Beautiful" by the broad paved pathway of

CONVICTION
(John 8:9. Acts 2:37)

that widens out into the circular pavement

FORGIVENESS
(Acts 13:38)

that stretches completely around the circular steps of

REPENTANCE
(Acts 2:38. 2 Cor. 7:10)

up which the Pilgrim must walk to the

PORCH OF CONFESSION
(Matt. 10:32-33. Rom. 10:9-10)

that runs completely across the front of the Palace, and that is railed in except where the steps lead up to it. The knowledge that God has forgiven men, and all that is needed is that they be reconciled to Him, is necessary to lead men to repentance. 2 Cor. 5:18-20. We are now ready to enter the Palace.

1. THE DOOR.

The "Door" is **CHRIST,** who said of Himself, "I am the **DOOR; by ME** if any man enter in he shall be saved, and shall go in and out, and find pasture." John 10:9. Paul puts the same truth thus—"For **THROUGH HIM** we both have access by one Spirit (Holy Spirit) to the Father." Eph. 2:18. The front door Christ leads into—

2. THE VESTIBULE

of the "NEW BIRTH," without passing through which experience no one can take possession of the Palace, for "Except a man be born of water (The Word) and the Spirit (Holy Spirit), he **CANNOT ENTER** into the Kingdom of God." John 3:5. The "Vestibule of the New Birth" opens into—

3. THE HALL OF JUSTIFICATION.

From this "Hall" access is had to the whole of the interior of the Palace by doors and stairways. It ends on the first floor in a larger Hall or room in which is the main stairway. This larger Hall is lighted from above, and is known as the Hall of

PEACE WITH GOD.

Over the open "Fireplace" in this larger Hall are painted the words—

"Therefore

BEING JUSTIFIED BY FAITH, WE HAVE PEACE WITH GOD

through our

LORD JESUS CHRIST."

Rom. 5:1.

The first room that we enter on the right from the "Hall of Justification," after passing through the "Vestibule of the New Birth," is—

4.   THE PARLOR OF HEART REST.

Over the door of entrance into the "Parlor" are the words—

"Come unto me, all ye that labor and are heavy laden and

I WILL GIVE YOU REST."

Matt. 11:28.

The "Parlor" is furnished with easy chairs and luxurious couches, and over the mantelpiece hangs an allegorical picture of the saying of the prophet—"And a man shall be as an hiding place from the wind, and a covert from the tempest; as rivers of water in a dry place, as the SHADOW OF A GREAT ROCK IN A WEARY LAND." Isa. 32:2.   At the rear end of the room is a picture of Elim, the resting place of Israel after their deliverance from Egypt, where they refreshed themselves under the three-score and ten palm trees, and beside the twelve wells of water.   Delightful music from the sweetest of instruments, accompanied by the most melodious of voices, floats through the air of the room, now near and loud, and then low and far away as evening chimes from some far-off belfry calling to worship and filling the soul with peace, and causing the hearer to forget all weariness and sorrow and imagine that he has entered unto "the rest that remaineth for the people of God." Heb. 4:9.

On the opposite side of the "Hall of Justification" is—

5. THE ARMORY.

Over the door of entrance are the words—

"FIGHT THE GOOD FIGHT OF FAITH."
1 Tim. 6:12.

In this room are preserved many of the instruments of warfare used by God's servants in ancient times. Here is to be seen "Moses' Rod;" the "Hammer and Nail" with which Jael slew Sisera; the "Pitchers, Trumpets and Lamps" with which Gideon put to flight the armies of Midian; the "Ox-Goad" wherewith Shamgar slew 600 men; the "Jawbone" with which Samson destroyed 1000 Philistines, and last, but not least, the "Sling and Stone" with which David slew Goliath of Gath. There are also many other relics as "Ram's-horns," "Handkerchiefs" to heal the sick, the "Cruse" in which the widow kept her oil, etc.

But the purpose of this room is principally to furnish weapons and armor for Christian soldiers, and in it are to be found in abundance helmets, swords, shields, breastplates, girdles and sandals, "For we wrestle not against flesh and blood, but against "Principalities," against 'Powers,' against the 'Rulers of the Darkness' of this Age, against 'SPIRITUAL WICKEDNESS' IN HIGH PLACES." Wherefore we are to put on the whole "Armor of God." Eph. 6:13-18.

Crossing again to the right of the Hall, in the rear of the Parlor we find a small room called—

6. THE OFFICE.

This is a room not sufficiently noticed in the Christian life because it is the room of "Christian Stewardship" from which come the funds to carry on all Christian work. It is neatly fitted up with desk, chairs, safe, and shelves to hold the annual reports of Missionary Societies and different organizations of Christian work. There are also boxes to hold envelopes for weekly and monthly offerings, on the back of which is printed "UPON THE FIRST DAY OF THE WEEK let every one of you lay by him in store, as God hath prospered him." 1 Cor. 16:2. And over the safe hangs the "Scripture Text"—

"Bring ye all the TITHES into the store-house, that there may be meat in my house, and prove me now herewith, saith the Lord of Hosts, if I will not open you the 'Windows of Heaven,' and pour you out a blessing, that there shall not be room enough to receive it." Malachi 3:10.

Passing out of the "Office" we enter into

7. THE STUDY.

This is a beautiful room with a circular bay window facing the sunrising, and splendidly adapted to the early morning study of the Scriptures. On the broad flat-top study table are to be found translations of the Scriptures, concordances, Bible textbooks and dictionaries, commentaries, etc., while the shelves that line the room are filled with biographical sketches of missionaries, martyrs, and the saints of all ages, church histories, expositions of Bible doctrines, volumes of sermons, and Christian evidences of all kinds. On the wall in front of the study table are the words—

"SEARCH THE SCRIPTURES, for in them ye think ye have 'Eternal Life;' and they are they which testify of me."
John 5:39.

Opposite the "Study," on the other side of the Hall is—

8. THE PICTURE GALLERY.

This room is as beautiful as the "Study," with a circular bay window, and as it faces the West the light is good to produce the best effect on the pictures that line its walls. These pictures are representations of Old and New Testament incidents that bring out in type the life and character of the Master. Among the great paintings in the "Gallery" are—"Abraham Offering Isaac," "The Blood upon the Doorposts," "Moses smiting the Rock," "The Serpent in the Wilderness," "The Scape Goat,"

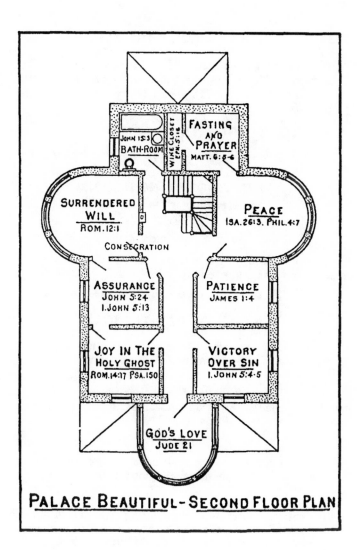

PALACE BEAUTIFUL – SECOND FLOOR PLAN

"Daniel in the Lion's Den," "The Transfiguration," "The Crucifixion," "The Resurrection" and "The Ascension."

Passing out of the "Picture Gallery" it is but a step to the left to

9.   THE BANQUETING ROOM.

Over the door of entrance is painted in large letters—

"He brought me to
'THE BANQUETING HOUSE'
and His Banner over me was
LOVE."
Song of Solomon 2:4.

In this room the tables are laden with the richest viands and the most costly wines, for

"The Lord of Hosts shall make unto all people a
'FEAST OF FAT THINGS,'

a Feast of wines on the lees, of fat things full of marrow, of wines on the lees well refined." Isa. 25:6.

The ceiling and walls of this "Banqueting Room" are richly frescoed in fruit and floral designs, and over the sideboard are the words—

"I AM THE BREAD OF LIFE:

he that cometh to me shall never hunger; and he that believeth on me shall never thirst."
John 6:35.

In the rear of the "Banqueting Room" is "THE KITCHEN," where the employes of the Palace prepare the Feasts that they serve in the "Banqueting Room."

Retracing our steps to the large Hall we leave the first floor and ascend the broad stairway, stopping on the first landing to admire the beautiful old Grandfather's Clock that stands there, but quicken our pace as we read on its dial the words—

"REDEEMING THE TIME,
because the days are evil."
Eph. 5:16.

The first room to the right at the head of the stairs is—

10. THE BATHROOM.

Here there is every convenience for the cleansing of the body and the application of cosmetics, but we will not stop here, for we are already supposed to be clean through the Word (John 15:3), and to have been saved "By the washing of REGENERATION" (Titus 3:5), which we have symbolized by "Baptism." Rom. 6:3-4.

We now enter the first chamber—

11. THE CHAMBER OF THE "SURRENDERED WILL."

The door to this Chamber is called "CONSECRATION," and over it are written the words—

"1 beseech you therefore, brethren, by the mercies of God, that ye present your bodies

'A LIVING SACRIFICE,'

holy, acceptable unto God, which is your reasonable service." Rom. 12:1.

The doorway is narrow and only those can enter who are willing to not only give up every known sin, but to lay aside every WEIGHT that interferes with their running the Christian race. Heb. 12:1.

This room is directly over the "Picture Gallery," and it has a bay window of glass, and as it faces the West, the setting sun floods it with glory, and fills the soul that is conscious of having yielded all to God with a heavenly light.

From this Chamber, through a communicating door, we pass into

12.   THE CHAMBER OF "ASSURANCE."

The door to this Chamber is not called **"Feeling,"** as some suppose, but **KNOWLEDGE**, and over it are the words—

> **"These things have I written unto you that believe on the name of the Son of God; that**
> ### YE MAY KNOW
> that ye
> ### HAVE ETERNAL LIFE,
> **and that ye may believe on the name of the Son of God."** ! John 5 : 13.

The walls of the "Chamber of Assurance" are covered with Scripture texts, such as—

> "He that **believeth on the Son HATH EVERLASTING LIFE."** John 3 : 36.
> "Verily, verily, I say unto you, He that heareth my word and believeth on Him that sent me, **HATH EVERLASTING LIFE,** and **shall** not come into condemnation: but **IS PASSED FROM DEATH UNTO LIFE."** John 5 : 24.
> "Beloved, **NOW ARE WE THE SONS OF GOD,** and it doth not yet appear what we shall be: but we know that, **when He shall appear,** we shall be **LIKE HIM;** for we shall see Him as He is." 1 John 3 : 2.

From the "Chamber of Assurance," through another communicating door, it is but a step into—

13.   THE CHAMBER OF "JOY IN THE HOLY GHOST."

On the glass of this communicating door are painted in letters of gold, shaded with red, the words—

> **"For the Kingdom of God is not meat and drink; but righteousness, and peace, and JOY IN THE HOLY GHOST."** Rom. 14 : 17.

This room is filled with Musical Instruments, Hymnals, and **Songs** of Praise, so that the glad heart may voice its joy in the inspired psalms, hymns, and songs of those who have been especially gifted of the Lord in this direction. On the wall hangs in illuminated text Psalm 150.

It is but a step or two across the hall to the door of—

14. THE CHAMBER OF "VICTORY OVER SIN."

But while we enter this room directly from the hall, it will be to no use unless we have first been in the Chamber of "The Surrendered Will." Over the door of the Chamber of "Victory over Sin" are inscribed the words—

> "WHOSOEVER ABIDETH IN HIM
> SINNETH NOT."
> 1 John 3:6.

The peculiarity of this room is the "Symbols of Death" to be seen everywhere about it. On the wall of one side is a picture of the "Crucifixion of Christ" under which are the words—

> "I AM CRUCIFIED WITH CHRIST."
> Gal. 2:20.

While on the opposite wall is a picture of the empty tomb of Joseph of Arimathea, under which are the words—

> "If ye then be RISEN WITH CHRIST,
> seek those things which are above, where Christ
> sitteth on the right hand of God." Col. 3:1.

The whole teaching of the room is—"RECKON ye also yourselves TO BE DEAD indeed unto sin, but alive unto God through Jesus Christ our Lord." Rom. 6:11.

Passing out of this Chamber and into the next on the same side we find ourselves in—

15. THE CHAMBER OF "PATIENCE."

over the door of which are the words—

> "LET PATIENCE HAVE HER PERFECT
> WORK." James 1:4.

This room is for the purpose of retirement when we are fretted by our work, or have had our patience sorely tried. Passing out into the hall again we step into the Chamber over the study—

16. THE CHAMBER OF "PEACE."

Over the door are the words—

"Thou wilt keep him in PERFECT PEACE whose mind is stayed on Thee." Isa. 26:3.

It was in this Chamber that the sisters laid Christian to sleep, and as it looked out toward the East, he awakened at the rising of the sun. It is the Chamber of the "PEACE OF GOD," and when the sleeper awakes in the morning he sees before him on the opposite wall—

"And the 'PEACE OF GOD,' which passeth all understanding, shall keep your hearts and minds through Christ Jesus." Phil. 4:7.

The furniture and decorations of this room are very soothing.

The Chamber of "Peace" communicates with a private Chamber—

17. THE CHAMBER OF "FASTING AND PRAYER."

Into this the occupant of the Chamber of "Peace" should go in the morning before he breaks his fast and commune with God. This anteroom has no side windows, so the occupant may not be disturbed from without. But it has a "Skylight," by which he can look into the heavens, upward to the "Throne of Grace." In this Chamber is a dark closet, the contents of which seem to reflect upon the character of the Palace and its inmates It is a "WINE CLOSET," into which, after or before prayer the occupant of the Chamber of "Peace" is directed or commanded to go and be filled. The command is written on the door of the Closet in large characters and reads—

"Be not drunk with wine, wherein is excess; but be

FILLED WITH THE SPIRIT."
Eph. 5:18.

It was from this "Upper Room" of "Fasting and Prayer," with its closet filled with the "New Wine" of the Holy Spirit that the "One Hundred and Twenty" emerged on the morning of the "Day of Pentecost," **GOD-INTOXICATED MEN.**

But there is one Chamber on this second floor that we have not yet visited—

18. THE CHAMBER OF "GOD'S LOVE."

It is located in the front of the house, over the porch, and is in the form of a circular "Bay Window," with a dome-shaped top, but strange to relate it is made all of glass, both sides and top, like a conservatory, and is for the purpose of taking a **"SUN BATH."** To sit in this room is the secret of "Spiritual Health," for the chemical rays from

"THE SUN OF RIGHTEOUSNESS"

fill the soul with spiritual vitality and vigor. The Motto over the door being—

"KEEP YOURSELF IN THE LOVE OF GOD."
Jude 21.

And last, but not least, is the

"OBSERVATORY."

It is located on the roof of the Palace and is reached by the main stairway. From it a view can be had of the country for miles around, but the most beautiful landscape lies to the South. There in the distance are to be seen vineyards and orchards, springs and fountains. There the sun shineth in its strength, and as it is within sight of the

"CELESTIAL CITY,"

the "Shining Ones" often walk there. It is called the

"LAND OF BEULAH,"

and from its hilltops on clear nights, the "Celestial City" can be easily seen.

All these things are clearly revealed to the "Eye of the Soul" from the "Observatory" of the Palace, for the Apostle tells us—

> "Eye hath not seen, nor ear heard, neither have entered into the heart of man, the things which God hath prepared for them that love Him. But God **HATH REVEALED THEM UNTO US BY HIS SPIRIT**: for the Spirit searcheth all things, yea, the **deep things of God**." 1 Cor. 2:9-10.

Dear Friends—Our "Similitude of a Palace" is not all a dream. Many of us have lived in the Palace and experienced its delights, and in the Paradise of God we shall dwell in it forever.

Printed in the United States
93977LV00004B/55/A